W9-DDJ-232

CLIMBING JACOB'S LADDER

We are climbing Jacob's Ladder,
every round goes higher, higher . . .
—Traditional spiritual

And he dreamed, and behold a ladder set up on
the earth, and the top of it reached to heaven:
and behold the angels of God ascending
and descending on it.
—Genesis, chapter 28

Verily I say unto you, inasmuch as ye have done it
unto one of the least of these my brethren,
ye have done it unto me.
—Matthew, chapter 25

CLIMBING JACOB'S LADDER

*A Trial Lawyer's Journey
on Behalf of 'the Least of These'*

JOCK M. SMITH

WITH PAUL HEMPHILL

NEWSOUTH BOOKS
Montgomery

NewSouth Books
P.O. Box 1588
Montgomery, AL 36102

ISBN 1-58838-078-5 (trade)
ISBN 1-58838-108-0 (special)

Printed in the United States of America

TO

My beloved and long-suffering mother, BETTELOU SMITH, who believed in me when no one else did; to my late and supportive grandmother, REBECCA A. BOWERS, who assisted my mother with the raising of my sister and me during our formative years; to my dear, supportive and ever-encouraging wife, YVETTE SMILEY-SMITH; to my wonderful daughter JANAY, the future of our family; and to my steadfast sister PAULA SMITH who, along with Yvette, set the examples that resulted in my being led to the Lord.

I also dedicate this book to every client who has ever given me an opportunity to represent them before the courts of Alabama and the courts of this nation. From each of their cases, I learned the lessons of life during my climb up Jacob's ladder. To each and every one of them, I am eternally indebted.

Contents

Photos begin on Page 129

FOREWORD

I.

By Johnnie L. Cochran, Jr., Esq.

Many years ago, I learned that in pursuing my journey to justice, it simply was not enough to despise injustice—I needed to love justice for its own sake. Although simply stated now, this concept was a very difficult lesson to absorb at the time as I was wracked with frustrations over the shortcomings of a justice system that harbors so much innate potential. In reflecting on my own personal struggles in learning to love justice for its own sake, I can fully appreciate that Jock Smith's climb up Jacob's Ladder in pursuit of higher aims and ideals has been a noble quest indeed.

First of all, what is Jacob's Ladder? To some, it is a metaphorical dream. To others, a tangible connection between human nature and divinity. To Jock Smith, perhaps it was the higher aims and morals set forth by his father, Jacob Smith. You, as the reader will ultimately have to decide.

When faced with a ladder, many of us will seek another way to the top. Not because of vertigo, but because ladders are not always secure and because, frankly, using them takes hard work and energy. One can only ascend a ladder by grappling for the next rung, meanwhile trusting all one's body weight to the rung that one is standing on. There is no guardrail, no room to go sideways. One has to go up or down. In addition, the ladder may not be placed on a perfectly flat surface. And there may be no one close by to hold the ladder steady at the base. Given these facts, most people would choose the elevator or escalator or even the stairs.

Jock Smith did not have that option when presented with Jacob's Ladder. Momentous events occurred early in Jock's life, forever shaping his path. It was almost as if the ladder he was on at the time was suspended in midair, reaching forever upwards with the bottom burned out from underneath him. When confronted with remaining stationary and becoming stagnant, or with pushing forward and persevering upwards, *there was no choice in the matter.* By the grace of God, Jock proceeded upwards. This determination and sense of commitment is one of the things I love about Jock and one of the reasons why I selected him as my national law partner. Indeed, his story is an universal lesson that perhaps we should not look for automated elevators or escalators to take us to heights that we can only reach through the exertion of our own sincere effort.

I caution the readers of Jock's account against focusing exclusively on the glorious end results. I wish for readers also to walk away with a meaningful appreciation of the growth process shared by this man within the following pages. As the great statesman Booker T. Washington indicated, "Success is to be measured not so much by the position that one has reached in life as by the obstacles which he has overcome." Reflecting on Jock Smith's life to date provides a humbling reminder as to how far some of us must climb to reach the levels that we attain.

Jock has remained steadfast in his climb up Jacob's Ladder, forever stretching out to the heavens in reach of his father Jacob and his ideals. In all of my associations with Jock, I have been thoroughly convinced that by learning to love justice for its own sake, that Jock was able to climb Jacob's Ladder at a faster rate than he would have in harboring the heavy feelings of hatred for injustice. As you will read, Jock Smith certainly has sustained his share of injustices, and he certainly has overcome all of them. May his continued climb inspire us as we eagerly watch as he goes higher and higher up Jacob's Ladder.

JOHNNIE L. COCHRAN, JR., is one of America's leading trial lawyers and the senior partner in Cochran, Cherry, Givens & Smith.

II.

BY JAN RICHARD SCHLICHTMANN, ESQ.

In the pages of this book is the poignant, moving, and inspiring story of one of the brightest stars in the firmament of American trial lawyers. It is Jock Smith's story, to be sure, but it is more. On one level, Climbing Jacob's Ladder is the captivating story of how one man overcame tragic loss in childhood to become one of this country's most successful and sought-after trial attorneys—a man with all the material rewards and indicia of success. It is the story of how a lawyer realized the dream of becoming "rich and famous doing good," in the yearning youthful words that Jonathan Harr ascribed to me as he chronicled my journey through the American justice system in *A Civil Action*. And for that, it is a good read. This book satisfies the need that many of us have to see through another's journey the key to our own.

But, dear reader, you are indeed fortunate, for this book, like the man himself, is much more than the cover story.

This was made clear to me when I first met Jock. The meeting had been arranged because I had recently joined with Fred Levin and Mike Papantonio's law firm which had partnered up with Jock and Johnnie Cochran's powerhouse to develop a national environmental and mass tort practice. This was an important business meeting, an opportunity for me to introduce myself to Jock and to establish a framework for our working together. Prior to this meeting, I had only known Jock by reputation and a brief exchange of pleasantries when we chanced to be on the same dais during an earlier lawyer conference. But what little I knew of the man intrigued me. Jock—a man Johnnie Cochran called "partner"—was famous for obtaining justice on behalf of the "least of us" in the form of verdicts and settlements in cases considered impossible to win. I found him to be a curiously soft-spoken man whose eyes shone with the fierce green fire of life, but I knew nothing of the why or wherefore of the man.

Our backgrounds seemingly had little in common beyond the fact that we were both plaintiff's trial attorneys and from the same generation. Jock had enjoyed extraordinary success as a criminal and personal injury lawyer representing folks who were victimized by institutional or corporate abuse. He was an African American, a devoutly Christian man, whose legal skills had been forged in the civil rights furnace of the Deep South. I was a Jewish boy from Boston's North Shore. My environmental practice sprouted from the ashes of the nine-year litigation war in which I represented eight Massachusetts families whose children had contracted cancer from contamination of the city's drinking water supply by two of the country's largest corporations. It was a case that made for a great book and a good movie but was a painful learning experience. Yet I sensed a resonance between our two disparate career experiences representing the disenfranchised and I hoped to know more.

It was supposed to be a "quick" business breakfast. From the outset, I was entranced by Jock's open and honest manner — a "do unto others as you would have others do unto you style" that is his disarming trademark. He has a way of embracing you as a friend, both in speech and body language, that is difficult to describe but palpable to experience. As we began our discussion of firm matters, I became very curious as to the source of this man's engaging presence. To a trial lawyer, a person who makes a living trying to convince judges and jurors as to what is the right thing to do about a courtroom-based conflict, such questions are of more than passing or personal interest. For the ambitious trial lawyer who dreams of succeeding in that multi-tracked venue thick with the cross-chatter of human emotion, there is a substantial practical necessity in understanding what makes people march to another's drum. Was there, I wondered, a particular experience or mindset responsible for this man's captivating aura? Was there a lesson for me in Jock's life experience that would help me to be a better, more effective lawyer? Did Jock know a secret I did not?

In the course of the conversation I learned to my surprise and delight that Jock had written a book about his life. I asked to see it, and he was happy to share it with me. The manuscript, of course, was a draft of the book you are reading.

I began reading the manuscript soon after our meeting ended and didn't put it down until I had finished some hours later. Emotion welled up as I learned of Jock's early childhood and the special and precious relationship he had with his father, Jacob Abraham Smith, a great man and pioneering lawyer whose life was cruelly cut down in the prime of its flowering. We come to realize that from the acorn of Jacob's moral teaching and with the strong and constant nurturing of a loving mother and extended family, a mighty oak of a man grew in the person of Jock Smith. But as Jock makes clear in *Climbing Jacob's Ladder*, the transformation took time and the process was not geometric. As Jock's story evidences, sometimes the shortest distance between two moral points of light is a lifetime of nonlinear growth. Jock, in an unusual and engagingly personal and honest way, allows us to bear witness to this growth.

Through Jock's retelling of his life's journey, I came to better understand the moral force that fuels this man and touches everyone who is honored to know him. It is a story that can help each one of us, caught as we are in that moment between promise and performance, where we are and where we can go, and what we are and what we can become. Jock's climb from the childhood in which his birthright was violently taken from him—a potentially enslaving experience—to the spiritual riches of redemption and renewal in the maturity of his manhood, is a quintessential American morality tale—a story of a people, told through the example of one person, coming of age. Jock's story is the American story of what it means to be free, to make an ideal real, to redeem a promise, to—in the words of Gandhi that Martin Luther King personified—become the change that we wish to see in the world. It is in short our story. It is the story each of us experiences as we make our moral ascent. And God bless Jock Smith for having the courage to share this story with us so that each of us in our way may better climb life's ladder.

JAN RICHARD SCHLICHTMANN is the environmental lawyer portrayed in the book and film, A Civil Action.

CLIMBING JACOB'S LADDER

I

'They're Still Ahead, but We're Gaining'

H E WAS CHRISTENED Jacob Abraham Smith, a name at once Biblical and as American as apple pie, and although he was known to most as Jacob, he would answer to any number of nicknames. Some of his business associates in the dizzying world of justice and high finance, down among the skyscrapers of Lower Manhattan in New York City, knew him cordially as "Jay," or "Jake" or "Jack." My mother and our relatives and many of our closest friends preferred "Smitty." But to his only son, who absolutely idolized him as I was growing up in Queens, New York, during the 1950s, he was simply "Daddy."

In order to understand just what a pioneer he became, we must recall the period of American history in which he lived. He had been born in Kansas City, Kansas, in 1922, not the best of times for an African-American to come along in the United States. Raw segregation and blatant racism were rampant in the Deep South, where the Ku Klux Klan was enjoying its heyday, lynchings and routine humiliations of black people being a way of life in the dominant white culture of the old Confederacy. In the rest of the nation, where segregation wasn't officially sanctioned, the African-American nevertheless was regarded as a second-class citizen. There were two societies in the country back then, one black and the other white, and it wouldn't be a stretch to say that Jacob Smith was destined to impact that situation from the day he was born.

17

In the border states such as Kansas, stuck out there in the middle of the country, far away from the old slave states, it was possible at that time for a black person to better himself by attending college. Among those who determined to do just that was the young black couple from Kansas City who would become my parents. Jacob Smith wanted to become a lawyer, Bettelou Bowers an artist, and in pursuit of their dreams they enrolled; he at the University of Kansas in Lawrence, she at Kansas State University in Manhattan. They had first met in Kansas City, their hometown, and, once they realized they were in love, they laid their plans. They would finish college, marry, and then begin their life together in that great metropolis located halfway across the country, the place where dreams could come true, New York City.

Then came the outbreak of the Second World War. Like other Americans, Jacob and Bettelou had to put their dreams on hold. While his bride-to-be stayed in Kansas to finish college and do volunteer work on the home front, Jacob swore in with the U.S. Army for what would turn out to be a six-year hitch. He was assigned to the Medical Corps, joined the famous all-black Buffalo Soldiers, rose to the rank of captain, won three battle medals during the campaign in Europe, and finished his tour of duty as a member of the peacekeeping force in the rubble of postwar Germany. Upon his return to the States, Jacob finally was able to marry Bettelou and effect the rest of the plan. They moved to New York and set up housekeeping in a segregated neighborhood in Queens, on Long Island. With his wife at home, wondering what to do with her art degree, Jacob enrolled at Brooklyn Law School. He graduated there in 1950, with the highest honors—a tall, handsome, baby-faced charmer with great gifts of persuasion, a man born to argue in court for the underprivileged— and soon he was helping to form Wilson, Carter & Smith in an office on Lower Broadway. It's important to note that this was the first black law firm in Manhattan not to have originated in Harlem. Pioneers must unearth the grounds and level their own playing field, which is exactly what they set out to do.

∾

I was born June 10, 1948, little more than a year after Jackie Roosevelt Robinson joined the Brooklyn Dodgers to break the color line in major league baseball, one of the major milestones in the long history of the African-American struggle for equality in this country. There is more than a little irony in that fact, for it was the game of baseball and the strides toward racial parity that would become two of the major forces that forged the unique relationship between my father and me.

Although I retain some vague memories of our family's living in an all-black neighborhood on 170th Street in Queens, where we made many lifelong friends, it seems as though my real life began somewhere around 1955 when we moved several blocks away to Nashville Boulevard, a formerly all-white enclave in Springfield Gardens. The family had been needing more room since the addition of my sister, Paula, four years after my birth. Now, with Daddy's financial status greatly improved (his clients included Count Basie and the National Association for the Advancement of Colored People), we could afford to move up in the world. The house we moved into wasn't commodious, by any means—just a three-bedroom red-brick ranch, with a basement used only for the washer-and-dryer and storage—but it certainly marked upward movement. To tell the truth, we simply felt that the time had come.

It was an important decision, and Daddy knew it. Just as Branch Rickey had counseled Jackie Robinson, a refugee from south Georgia who was being asked to break the cycle of racism in America, my father pulled me aside one day, when I was barely seven years old, to make certain that I understood what we were doing and why. He said, "Everything's about to change, son." He explained that from now on, all of our neighbors would be white. My playmates would be white. My schoolmates would be white. "You're going to have to be perfect. People are going to be watching every move you make. They may call you names, refuse to let you play with them, maybe throw rocks at you, whatever. But you can't back down. Be on your P's and Q's. Do the best you can." If I complained or looked uncomfortable about the uncertainty of more or less starting over at such a tender age, he wouldn't hear of it. "We're making history, son, and I want you to always keep that in mind, no matter what happens." End of discussion.

The fact is, I never once heard the "N" word during my lifetime at 197-62 Nashville Boulevard. For one thing, my father was a prominent lawyer, a dignified black man, as successful as anyone on the block, someone the whites of the neighborhood must have known would never stand for that kind of talk. For another, they knew that my mother was also well-educated and, more to the point, quick of tongue, not one to trifle with, a woman who could wither them with scorn in the proverbial New York minute. Their children, Paula and I, wore the best of clothes, had the best of playthings, spoke the language properly, minded our manners, and comported ourselves with pride. Our parents fully understood the pitfalls and the obstacles that would confront us as African Americans, and they were preparing us to meet them.

Indeed, rather than seeing our new white neighbors run from us or peer at us through closed curtains, it was the other way around. In due time, when Daddy staked out a rudimentary softball field in our big back yard, kids came from all over the neighborhood to play ball with us and to laugh with him over the hitch in his swing. Fathers and sons, black and white—integrated softball right there in my own back yard was great sport. I'd heard from a family friend that Daddy had been quite a basketball player during his high school days in Kansas City, and before I knew it he was punching the bottom out of a peach basket and nailing it to the telephone pole in front of the house so we could all play, using the street light if necessary so we could continue into the night. He still had all of the moves—driving, hesitating, dribbling behind his back and through his legs, using the head fake of a good fighter before going for the makeshift "hoop"—and he was loving every minute of it.

Jacob Abraham Smith, in fact, loved every minute of every day. There wasn't a challenge he didn't savor, didn't figure he couldn't conquer, and there were many: charming and convincing a reluctant jury, beating the establishment at its own game, winning against all odds, further tearing down color barriers even though New York was officially "desegregated," winning arguments with friends about baseball or politics or music or something as mundane as women's fashions. He was a man of great charisma, someone who could enter a room and take it over, the center of attention wherever he went. He was a pioneer, a seer, one who always insisted on striving for excellence. I can still remember his coming home to Nashville Boulevard at the end of a long day in Manhattan, taking off his top hat and his overcoat, putting them in the closet at the front door, then turning to greet his wife and his children. "How you doing, Smitty?" my mother would say. "How was your day?" And he would say, with a mischievous wink, "White folks are still ahead, but we're gaining."

∾

The offices of Watson, Carter & Smith, Attorneys at Law, were located at 305 Broadway, on the corner of Duane Street, in an old building in Lower Manhattan, near City Hall and all of the various courts. My father's partners were achievers and visionaries in their own rights: Lisle C. Carter, a graduate of the Yale Law School, a "genius," as my mother would later describe him, who later would become president of Atlanta University; and James L. Watson, another Buffalo Soldier from the Second World War, who was a senior judge on the United States Court of International Trade upon his death in September of 2001. They had proven themselves to be pioneers when they became the first all-black law firm in that part of New York. I remember going down there many times as a child, crawling around on the checkerboard linoleum floors, seeing the black-and-gold lettering on the frosted panes of the front door, looking out the windows for a breathtaking view of the city, marveling at the bookcases crammed with law books. In retrospect, I like to think that my father, by taking me to the offices as such an early age, hoped that one day I would follow in his footsteps by becoming a lawyer.

Daddy was their trial man, flamboyant and persuasive, a showman in the courtroom. Over the years, my mother would tell me many stories of his successes. In one of them, the white judge called him to the bench at the end of a trial that he'd had no business winning: "Mister Smith, that's the best presentation I've ever seen in my courtroom. Though the law didn't appear to be on your side and you shouldn't have prevailed, I felt that, after all of the hard work and legal skills that you've exhibited, I had to award you the decision." Obviously, he won a lot of cases with his preparation and coolness under pressure and his innate charm, all of which attracted an increasingly large following among his peers, men as diverse as Adam Clayton Powell and Malcolm X.

Ultimately, Jacob Smith answered the call to run for the New York State Assembly. Among our friends in the old segregated neighborhood where we lived before the move to Nashville Boulevard was Guy Brewer, who ran the United Negro Democratic Club in Queens, whose aim was to put up the first black officials to run for public office. Guy Brewer presented an unforgettable image—spats, flashy suits, cigars, conked hair, yet a sophisticate with quiet dignity—and was the most politically active African-American in Queens at the time. He had taken a real liking to Dad and pushed for him to become the first African-American from our district in Queens to be elected to the state assembly. Count Basie's wife became a chief fund-raiser. He was endorsed by the *Amsterdam News*. The outlook was good. I still have an old campaign ad that I can quote, word-for-word, by heart: *What are we waiting for and why? Is there any good reason why one-hundred thousand Negro citizens in Queens don't have a single Negro elected official? Must we always take a back seat: a back seat on the bus in Montgomery, Alabama; a back seat in the political life of Queens?* That's very inspiring for me, that my daddy was talking about Rosa Parks even as he was campaigning for the New York Assembly. (Ironically, I would marry a woman who had joined the bus boycott in Montgomery as a child.) That ad shows a man who was aware of history, a man who knew what was going on in the world, a man who understood the plight of African Americans everywhere.

I've been told that Jacob Abraham Smith should have won that election, that he was the right man at the right time to become the first black from Queens elected to the New York State Assembly, but it didn't happen. They got him on a technicality having to do with district lines, disqualified him from being on the ballot, with the claim that he didn't live in the proper district. As it happened, the honor of winning that office would go later to Guy Brewer, Daddy's best friend, who had always felt that the only people in the United Negro Democratic Club with any really good sense were "Smitty" and himself.

❧

None of that was important to me at the time. All I knew was that my daddy was about the best a boy could ask for: a pal, a firm hand, a counselor. He seemed to be more excited about Christmas morning than were his two young children; rising well before daybreak, excitedly shaking us awake to announce that it looked like maybe Santa Claus had come, hustling us into the living room, watching with tears in his eyes as we tore into our presents (more of them, you can be sure, than at any other house on the block). On another morning, as Daddy and Paula and I sat in the kitchen, laughing and banging on special silver cereal bowls filled with Cheerios and Wheaties, my mother rushed in to see what was going on. He told her, "Sorry, Red"—his pet nickname for her, based on the beautiful shade of her hair—"but you can't interrupt us right now. We're in the middle of a meeting of the Cereal Club." She said, "Smitty, you've lost your mind." He had been looking for a way to make sure his kids started each day with a good breakfast, and this was it. Another time, while we were left in the care of my great-uncle Marion Smith, known around the house as "Kansas City Smitty," so my parents could go out to a movie or dinner or something, I lost my temper and broke a pinball baseball game; picked it up, slammed it to the floor, tore it apart. Uncle Marion tried to cover for me when my parents came home, sharing the blame, saying it was "an accident," but I got a spanking and a lecture before being ordered to bed. More importantly, to teach me a lesson both about being a good loser and taking care of possessions, Daddy never did replace that pinball game.

Everywhere, it seemed, there were lessons to be learned. He stayed home from work one day just so he could drop in at my school, P.S. 15, to check things out personally and see how I was doing in school. During his visit, he noticed a list of all the students, some with stars beside their names, but none by mine. Afterwards, he asked me what the stars meant. "I don't know," I said, "good work, attendance, stuff like that?" He looked me right in the eye and said, grimly, "From now on, I want to see stars beside your name." And I remember a Saturday when I got into a scuffle with one of my best buddies in the neighborhood, a white kid named Dickey, and when he whacked me in the head with a good right I took off running for the house. "Jock!" It was Daddy, who had happened to see the fight and was standing at the screen door. As I ran into the house, hauling my backside to safety, I was slapped to the floor by the palm of his hand. Standing over me, without a glimmer of a smile, he shook his finger at me: "Never run, son. Don't be a coward. Be a man. Stand your ground, no matter what."

In the manner of any good parent, as I now can understand, nearly every move he made had a larger purpose that was intended to prepare me for the struggle awaiting me when I entered adulthood as a black man in a white world. Most of the enlightened black parents of that time knew that they had to try harder than white parents if their children were to make that difficult climb to success. It was not going to be given to them, as it might to a child who happened to be born with white skin. It would have to be earned. I would have to be tougher, more studious, more dedicated—in a word, Daddy's word, "perfect"—if I were to amount to anything.

And so, with these goals in mind, he and my mother did everything they could to prepare us to meet the challenges. They created a stable, loving home for their children, a safe haven brimming with tranquility, amiable friends, achievement, learned discussions around the dinner table of race and politics and the sweep of history. They were confident and caring, in love with each other and the challenges of life, perfect in their own right. *They're still ahead, but we're gaining. Time for the Cereal Club meeting. I want to see stars beside your name.* We retained our membership at the all-black Calvary Baptist Church, in the old neighborhood on Merrick Boulevard—a rousing house of

God known for the fire-and-brimstone sermons dished out by the Rev. Walter Pinn—to remind us of our blackness and our soul. But there we were now, pioneers living on Nashville Boulevard, breaking ground as we went about our daily business.

∾

My father and I were united in our love of baseball. The Fifties may have been the grandest decade in the entire history of the game. There were only sixteen teams in the two major leagues then, and three were located right there in New York. To a kid my age, it was like living in a candy store. It was the time of *The Boys of Summer*, of Bobby Thomson's "Shot Heard 'round the World," of Yankee Stadium and the Polo Grounds and Ebbets Field, of the emergence of such Hall of Fame players as Mickey Mantle and Willie Mays and Jackie Robinson, of intense rivalries affecting every borough of the great, sprawling metropolis. You were either *for* the Yankees (or Dodgers or Giants) or you *hated* them; no waffling.

Most African Americans at that time were fans of either the Dodgers or the Giants, for the simple biased reason that not until 1955 did the Yankees hire Elston Howard, the first black man ever to wear the pinstripes, while the Dodgers' and the Giants' lineups were brimming with the first wave of black players to make it to the majors. Here is where my dad and I split. For whatever reasons, I had become a huge fan of the Dodgers, he of the Giants. The good-natured wrangling between us never ended. While I raved about the virtues of the Dodgers and Ebbets Field, of "Jackie" and "Campy" and Don Newcombe and Joe Black and the regal "Duke of Flatbush," the white Duke Snider, he similarly went on and on about his Giants and the joys to be found at the Polo Grounds: Willie Mays, Monte Irvin, Bobby Thomson, and Hank Thompson. So it was that we followed our heroes on radio and television—we even argued about which club had the best announcers—and, more times than I can recount, went together to see them in person.

The games were enough fun in themselves, whether at Ebbets Field or the Polo Grounds, more than enough to keep a little boy's interest, but my father took it further. He taught me the beauty of the game itself, its history and its intricacies, and in the process showed me that baseball, more than any other sport, was a metaphor for life. *There's where Thomson's homer went out,* he would say on a visit to the Polo Grounds, pointing at the 257-foot-deep leftfield foul line. *I ever tell you about the time the white fans were booing Jackie and Pee Wee Reese, this white Southern boy, mind you, walked over during the game and put his arm around Jackie to shut 'em up?* he said during a game at Ebbets Field. Baseball-as-metaphor: *It's a team sport, see? Sometimes a perfect bunt is as good as a homerun. You got to hit the cutoff man, steal the base, give yourself up to advance the runner. One man doesn't win a pennant; it takes all nine of 'em. Okay, son, watch now, he's got him set up for the changeup.* Little did I know it at the time, but as the years went on I would cling to the game of baseball as an infant would to a blanket and eventually become one of the most avid collectors of baseball memorabilia in the world. All because of my dad.

And finally, after years of falling short, there came the '55 season when the Dodgers went up against the Yankees in the World Series. All throughout black America, this was as big as they could get: the Dodgers of Jackie Robinson against the haughty uptown Yankees, the mighty Bronx Bombers, just now getting around to having their first black player. It was so big, in fact, that my Uncle Wilson Smith came all the way to New York from his home in Portland, Oregon, just so he could be there with my dad to watch it all unfold. They went to a couple of the games in person, as I recall, but what I remember most clearly is the seventh and deciding game, at Yankee Stadium. Our house was filled with friends and relatives that day, everybody gathered around the black-and-white television set, as the game went on and the tension mounted. It was 2-0, Dodgers, two outs in the bottom of the ninth, one more out to go, Johnny Podres on the mound, Elston Howard at the plate. There was a grounder to short, Pee Wee Reese coming up and throwing, Gil Hodges stretching to take the throw at first before leaping into the air in celebration. *The Dodgers win! The Dodgers win the World Series! The Brooklyn Dodgers are champions of the world!* I looked across the room to see that those three men, my father and his two brothers, were breaking down and crying like babies. Minutes later, when the crying and the whooping had subsided, my father looked over at me and said, with a wink, "Well, Jock, you finally won something, didn't you, son?"

There was no reason to think this idyllic life wouldn't last forever. We lived in the center of the universe, as far as I knew, where my father reigned as a superstar and my mother was a beauty queen. My little sister had inherited those good looks and I had begun to get stars beside my name at school. Even in New York, at that time, people thought nothing of leaving the doors unlocked when they left the house. Jacob Abraham Smith and his family, the only blacks on the block, were as good as anybody and better than most. We were living the American Dream, an *African*-American Dream, and only unforeseen disaster could bring it tumbling down.

2

Murder in Manhattan

THE DAY WAS April 24, 1957, and it seemed to me like any other perfect spring morning in Queens. I was eight years old, soon to turn nine, and life was wonderful. The only problem in my world, in fact, was that this would be the last baseball season for both the Brooklyn Dodgers and the New York Giants as we knew them. The Dodgers were scheduled to move to Los Angeles and the Giants to San Francisco once the '57 season ended, provoking all sorts of anger throughout New York City. ("The three greatest threats to mankind in this century," wrote the columnist Pete Hamill, "are Hitler, Stalin, and [Dodgers owner] Walter O'Malley.") What my father and I would do when our idols were gone, I didn't know, although in my worshipful eyes I trusted that Daddy was so powerful he probably would work something out to keep them from going to the West Coast. In the meantime, with the season already underway, I was looking forward to a long summer of afternoons and nights at Ebbets Field and the Polo Grounds.

It was business as usual around the house that morning. Daddy had been down with a cold for a few days, and while I was dressing for school I overheard my mother trying to talk him out of going into the office that day. He being a man who loved his work, this wasn't an easy thing to do.

"But Smitty," she was saying, "you really shouldn't be going out with a cold like this."

"Don't worry," he said. "There's just this one appointment."

"Can't it wait?"

"No, we've got to close this case. It's been dragging on too long as it is. As soon as we settle, I'll be back. I promise."

"Well," she said, "I might go in to Gimbel's."

"See you later, then."

He put on his top hat and coat, kissed everybody good-bye, and walked out the door to the driveway. That would be my last image of my father alive: at the wheel of his black '57 Ford Fairlane, backing out of the driveway, waving good-bye, then driving away toward his office in Lower Manhattan.

∾

The case he was tending to that day was a divorce settlement involving a policeman and his wife, Edward and Beryl Pegram, a black couple with a three-year-old son who, as it happened, shared the same birth date with me. This in itself was a departure for my father, who, as far as I know, had never handled a domestic case. He was the trial man for Watson, Carter & Smith, a great trial lawyer, specializing in criminal law and civil litigation. He had more or less inherited this case from a friend, fellow lawyer Lawrence R. Bailey, whose offices were in Harlem. Apparently, Bailey had encountered a conflict in his representation of Mrs. Pegram and she had asked him for a recommendation. And so Daddy took the case not only as a favor to Bailey but also because he remembered that Beryl had been a strong supporter and a volunteer worker during his campaign for the state assembly.

The Pegrams had met in 1950 at a political gathering where she was a volunteer worker and he was a uniformed officer assigned to security (she offered him a pamphlet, which he had to refuse, but that led to dinner together that night), married in '52, and gave birth to the son, John, in '54. He was a much-honored policeman with the NYPD, working mostly in Harlem, recipient of six commendations during his career, and she was a $60-a-week switchboard operator. The marriage began to flounder soon after the birth of their son, and in September of '55 she had filed for a divorce through her attorney, Lawrence Bailey. Edward Pegram (known as "Eddie" and "Peg") had fallen badly behind in his payments to his wife, under the terms of a temporary settlement. Now, in the spring of '57, with my father representing Beryl and the equally famous Percy Sutton representing "Peg," they were all getting together for what they hoped would be a final settlement.

It's not as though my father hadn't been warned of possible trouble in the case. Custody of the child had become a major issue. The father had been granted temporary custody until the boy reached the age of seven, but now his arrearage in payments might threaten that. During the first week of April, in fact, Eddie Pegram had shown up at my father's office, without his attorney, for what later was called a "stormy" meeting.

Pegram was worried about being sent to alimony jail and, worst of all, losing his son. Even as my father was insisting that they shouldn't be talking without Percy Sutton present, Pegram pulled out his billfold and produced snapshots of his boy, John, ice skating. A father bragging on his son; Daddy couldn't resist. "I didn't know they could skate at that age," he told Pegram.

"I taught him how. You know how it is."

"Of course I do." With that, Daddy pointed out the photographs of his own children, Paula and me, displayed on his desk. "I know exactly how you feel, Peg."

"Well, why are you trying to take my son away from me, then, Smitty? That's what I want to know. Why would you want to do that?"

"I wouldn't do that, Peg. That's not what this is all about."

Pegram was steaming, highly perturbed, and in short they had to show him the door. Over the next few days, word would reach Daddy that Edward Pegram had been making veiled threats toward him. Said Guy Brewer, the state assemblyman and Daddy's close friend: "Jacob told me there had been threats, and I warned him about that." Said James Watson, Daddy's law partner, who was out of town on Wednesday, April 24: "I should have been there with him. I told Smitty not to go there by himself to that office." But this was Jacob Abraham Smith, who had received many threats during his career as an aggressive lawyer and had chosen to ignore them. He was an attorney at law. He was simply answering the call to duty.

They gathered together at half-past noon in my father's office on the tenth floor of 305 Broadway—Edward Pegram and his attorney Percy Sutton on one side of the desk, my father and his associate Lisle Carter with their client Beryl Pegram on the other—and tried to hammer things out. Although there remained some issues to be settled, everything seemed to go smoothly at first. "Peg" had brought along blueprints of two lots the couple owned jointly in Westchester County, New York, and was proposing to sign over one of them to his wife. He had borrowed $1,700 from the NYPD credit union and was prepared to pay the arrearage and attorney's fees and even to increase the monthly payments. Money wasn't the problem. Clearly, the real issue to Edward Pegram was that he retain custody of the boy, who was now living with him and his mother in a garden apartment in Queens. There was a brief timeout while Pegram and Sutton went off into another office for a private talk, another while the husband and wife tried to reason with each other. Then, suddenly, Beryl hardened and my father was obliged, as her attorney, to follow her wishes. Voices were raised for the first time.

"If I go to jail, what happens to Johnny?" Pegram said to his wife.

"If you do, you won't be in long."

"Who's going to keep him while I'm gone?"

"The lady who owns the apartments. What do you care, anyway? You'll be in jail, remember."

It was one o'clock by now, and everything appeared hopeless. Percy Sutton had another appointment to keep, and Daddy had promised he would return home early to nurse his cold. To continue seemed fruitless. Sutton said, "Well, Jack, too bad we couldn't work things out. Come on, Peg, let's go." He got up and shook hands with my father and left the room, assuming that his client was following, until, like a bolt of lightning, all hell broke loose.

Edward Pegram had worked until midnight, rushed home to tuck in his son, cleaned his apartment, gotten three hours' sleep, missed breakfast, delivered his son to a nursery, shopped for groceries, rushed downtown for this meeting, and now this. In retrospect, it is clear that he had reached the breaking point. He shouted at his wife, "Nobody sends me to jail! I'll kill you first!" Bolting up from his chair, he threw open his coat and pulled his .32-caliber Colt police revolver from a holster on his belt and began to shoot. As Lisle Carter would say, some months later: "It was like a tableau, a picture you see, a point in time."

Bam-bam-bam! Three shots hit Beryl Pegram in her face.

Bam-bam! One bullet slammed into my father's head, another into his heart.

There was pandemonium in the room and in the outer offices. Percy Sutton, having reached the reception area, spun at the sound of shots being fired "like a cap pistol." A secretary hid behind a thick bookcase. A clerk had the prescience to take an elevator to the street-level drugstore and buy a store of bandages.

"You're killed my partner!" said Lisle Carter as he charged Pegram with a folding chair and began wrestling with him over the pistol.

"Carter, I don't have anything against you!"

Sutton: "You gave me your word, Peg!"

Pegram: "My God, Percy, what have I done? What have I done? Pick up the gun, pick up the gun!"

The pistol was on the floor now, hot and smoking, and Sutton picked it up and put it in a desk drawer while he was calling the police. Pegram stumbled out of the office and calmly told a terrified secretary, "I won't hurt you, miss, I just want to call home so I can talk to my son for the last time." When the clerk arrived with the bandages, he rushed into the office and found that my father was facedown on the floor, dead from the shots to the head and heart, and then he bent over Beryl Pegram to sop at the pool of blood covering her face. The police arrived within fifteen minutes and found Edward Pegram in a state of shock, sitting there, as though waiting for an appointment.

ॐ

I knew nothing about any of this, of course, and wouldn't find out until years later when Lawrence Bailey, Beryl's original attorney, presented us with a full transcript of Edward Pegram's jury trial for murder. All I knew at that point, sitting at my desk at school in Queens, was that everything was fine. Life went on.

Our friend from around the corner in the old neighborhood, Earnestine Robinson, my "Aunt Earnie," had agreed to look after my sister Paula at our house on Nashville Boulevard that morning while my mother went shopping at Gimbel's in Manhattan, so it was she who answered the phone when the police called. They would tell her at that point only that there had been an accident, that Jacob Smith had been shot, and asked if she could get word to his wife, Bettelou. Frightened, expecting the worst, Aunt Earnie flew into action. First, she called Gimbel's and had my mother paged, telling her when she called back that both Paula and I were sick; nothing serious, but she should take the subway home right now to be with us. Then she put Paula in her car and raced to P.S. 15 to pull me out of school. Finally, she drove to her home, left us there with her husband, my "Uncle Bob," and then headed to the subway stop.

My mother thought little of it when she was met at the subway, her concern being that her children were sick, but when Earnestine drove not to our house but to hers and Mom saw Paula and me happily playing in the yard as though nothing had happened, she stiffened.

"Wait a minute," she said. "It's Smitty. Something's happened to Smitty. You have to tell me, Earnie. What's wrong? What's wrong?"

Earnestine said, as calmly as she could, "Bettelou, Smitty's been shot."

"Oh, my God. Oh, my God. Is he all right? Is he alive? Is he living?"

"We don't know yet."

The next few hours are a fog to me, to this day. I remember my mother arriving, in a state of shock. The house began to fill up with friends and neighbors. The phone kept ringing. Sitting on the couch, feeling the chill in the air, watching the others breaking down and consoling my mother and hugging my sister and me, I knew that something very bad had happened. I remember being lost in a sea of nothingness, not knowing exactly what to do or what to say. The adults were showing more emotion than I because I don't think I really comprehended what was going on. I went into a shell.

It wasn't long before it became apparent to me, either through direct word or through body language, that my dad had died. Surely, at some point, my mother would have told me, "Jock, your daddy is dead." I remember staying at the Robinsons' house for several hours. I remember newspaper reporters coming around, asking questions. I remember sitting on the couch, watching the six o'clock news, seeing my father's face on the screen, hearing about the death of this "prominent black lawyer."

Not until a couple of days later did it finally sink in that my father had left me. His body lay in state at a funeral home there on Merrick Boulevard, and Paula and I were taken there by our family doctor, a black female named Pearl Foster. We stood before the open casket. Beside it was a sign reading, "Jacob A. Smith, At Rest." A service was held the next day at Calvary Baptist Church, Rev. Walter Pinn presiding, nearly a thousand mourners attending; many of them prominent African-American leaders from the worlds of law, politics, and government. Immediately following the service, we all got on a plane and flew with the body to Kansas City, where my father was put to rest in the family plot. Only then did I know for sure. My friend, my hero, my mentor, my father, was gone from this world forever. I would never be the same.

3

Little Boy Lost

ITH MY FATHER suddenly gone from my life, I fell into years of struggle, confusion, and underachievement. Nothing would be the same for quite a while. No longer would there be his joyous returns home at the end of the day, with the confident observation that whites might still be ahead "but we're gaining." No longer would there be his patient counseling that we must be "perfect" in an integrated society. No longer would there be his insistence that stars should be beside my name at school. There would be no more journeys downtown to his glamorous office in Lower Manhattan, nor any more father-and-son treks to watch our baseball heroes perform at the Polo Grounds and Ebbets Field. The hole left in my life following his assassination—and to this day that's the only word I can use to describe his premature death—was tremendous.

During the murder trial for Edward Pegram in late 1957, the whole sordid mess came out in great detail: the crumbling marriage of Eddie and Beryl Pegram, the divorce proceedings, that last day of the negotiations when Pegram finally snapped and killed Jacob Abraham Smith. It was pointed out that NYPD officers were *required* to carry their firearm even when off duty, negating any argument that he had come to the meeting with premeditated murder in mind. If Pegram had made threats before, they had not been reported ahead of time to the police. With Pegram continuing to "forget" whether he had fired the pistol, and a series of expert witnesses speaking of trauma and temporary insanity, the charges were reduced to manslaughter. Eddie Pegram received a sentence of eight years, served only four, and later was rumored to be a policeman in Puerto Rico. My mother filed a $500,000 lawsuit against the NYPD for negligence, but because my father had never reported the threats it was dropped. I would never hear another word about the widow, Beryl Pegram, or their young son.

Daddy was only thirty-five years old when he was killed, a rising star in New York's African-American community, both socially and politically, and I wasn't the only one to suffer his loss. The firm of Watson, Carter & Smith all but dissipated after he passed, although Lisle Carter and James Watson would do quite well for themselves individually. It was a setback, as well, for the United Negro Democratic Club in its ongoing attempts to promote the first waves of black individuals running for public office. And Daddy also would be dearly missed at the Calvary Baptist Church, where he had been strongly entrenched, a deacon, large in the church. Here was a charismatic young future leader cut down well before his time, much as would be the case soon after with Martin Luther King, Jr., and John and Robert Kennedy, and that loss would be felt for years to come.

Memories of just how powerful and influential he was would be brought to my attention at every turn. I remember when I got out of law school, in 1973, and was interviewing for jobs. One interview was for the Center for Constitutional Rights, then headed by William Kunstler, the white lawyer famous for defending the Chicago Seven. In the middle of the interview he paused and said, "Wait a minute, are you Jacob Smith's son?" When I said yes, he said, "Oh, my goodness. Your daddy was a hell of a man, a hell of a lawyer, a pioneer. I've got to stand up and shake your hand." The interview was stopped in its tracks.

Somewhere in the early Eighties, I was summoned to New Orleans by Fred Gray, the Alabama lawyer who had represented Martin Luther King, Jr., and Rosa Parks during the bus boycott in Montgomery in the Fifties. Fred was running for National Bar Association president, and since I was president of Alabama's Black Lawyers Association at the time he wanted me to help him get votes from the New York delegation. When I walked into that room, here came Lawrence Bailey, Daddy's lawyer friend from the New York City days. "Let me tell you something," he said to the others. "Do you know who this is? This is Jacob Smith's son." Soon they were all telling me Jacob Smith stories.

And I recall having James Watson, Daddy's former law partner, as a house guest on the night Jesse Jackson made his ringing speech before the 1984 Democratic National Convention. He was Judge Watson by then, the first African-American to sit on the federal bench as judge of the United States Customs Court on Chambers Street in New York. While we were watching television, we began talking about various leaders. "Hey, did my daddy know Adam Clayton Powell?" I asked, and he said, "Yes, we were all close." How about Malcolm X? "Of course, of course. We all respected him." I asked about this guy and that guy. "Yes, yes, he knew all of them." Then, suddenly, in the middle of Jesse's speech, probably the greatest he had ever delivered, Judge Watson suddenly got up out of his chair as though to leave the room. "I can't watch any more of this," he said. "Why?" I asked. "Because that should have been your daddy."

૨

Even so, no one missed him more than the family he left behind. It took my sister, Paula, a long time to get over his loss even though she had been too young to carry vivid memories of him. My mother would remarry many years later, to a fine man in his own right, but the memories and the loss of Smitty could never be replaced. Now and then she would up and say, out of nowhere, "Think about this, son. Your daddy filed a lawsuit to desegregate the Pierre Hotel downtown. Did you know that?" Or she would start talking about his charisma, how he could walk into a room and take it over. She's never discussed April 24, 1957, with me in much detail. I think it's much too painful; that she knows she's been robbed of a life that could have been. She did say to me, years ago, "I didn't realize how strongly your dad's death affected you kids as I know now, but I understand now why Smitty had to die." I asked her why. "If he had lived, you would've had everything handed to you on a silver platter. You probably would have been a Harvard lawyer who walked into a multi-million-dollar law practice. But I guess that just wasn't what God ordained. He wanted you to earn it, to go out and show that you could do it yourself. Smitty died so you could live."

I became a hard case, a difficult child, one who had miles to go before I would recover from such a devastating loss. It wasn't as though I was headed toward a life of crime or drugs or anything like that, although one can never tell how things might turn out. I simply didn't *care* anymore. I was a zombie. I had lost my dad, and with him the will to live and to win. There were no more stars beside my name at school.

It's not as though there weren't plenty of friends and family members to help me out of this. The men, particularly, seemed to understand what a bond baseball had been between this father and this son, so I didn't miss much of that pivotal 1957, the last anyone would ever see of the New York Giants and the Brooklyn Dodgers. Bob Robinson ("Uncle Bob," Earnestine's husband) made sure that I took in some games. Reverend Pinn of the Calvary Baptist Church took me a couple of times, bless his heart, and my Uncle Gene took me to a few games. Later, when the two clubs had moved to the West

Coast, I would burrow beneath the covers and tune my new transistor radio to hear how the Dodgers were doing at Chavez Ravine in Los Angeles and the Giants at Candlestick Park in San Francisco.

And then there was my great-uncle, Marion Smith, "Kansas City Smitty." He lived on 151st Street in Amsterdam, and before we'd leave for a game he'd take out this skillet and put the grease in and then he'd start tossing pancakes up in the air and catching them. "Son, that's why they call me 'Flapjacks.' Eat 'em up so we can get to the ball game." We'd walk up the hill and then down an incline to the subway, put in a dime, get a token, first stop the Polo Grounds, second stop Yankee Stadium. He didn't care much for the Yankees, just thought Mel Allen was a great announcer, so he baptized me, introduced me, to Yankee Stadium. He'd look out at centerfield and point at Mickey Mantle. "Now son," he would say, "*that's* the big leagues." Kansas City Smitty. We became big buddies. The last time I saw him alive was in '62, when the New York Mets were about ready to open their first season, and they took me in to see him in his hospital room. "Hey, Jock," he said. "Soon as I get out of here, boy, we're gonna go see the Mets, now, just you and me. National League baseball again, son, right here in New York City." He died two weeks later, never getting to see the Mets play.

❧

Soon after Daddy's death, Mom had to go to work outside the home for the first time. She had gotten an art degree at Kansas State University, but never pursued painting as a profession. When she and Dad married and moved to New York, she put aside her creative genius and settled into the role of housewife and mother. After Dad's death, she went on to work at various jobs, the best one being as a reservations clerk for Eastern Airlines, where she worked for many years. She was a strong woman, secure in her Christian faith, the first of many who would come along in later years to save me from wallowing in self-pity and utterly losing my way.

The best part about Mom's job at Eastern, at least for my sister and me, was the free travel it afforded if we were willing to wait on standby. We went back and forth many times to Kansas City, of course, to visit our parents' families, but Mom made sure that Paula and I got to see at least a little bit of the larger world: Mexico City, Cancun, Nassau, Acapulco, wherever we could go with our standby tickets. I remember going on a trip to the Bahamas one time with a group that included Jackie Robinson. I have a vivid memory of Jackie on a golf course, getting ready to tee off. I knew he was great, a significant figure in African-American history, but I was too young at the time to fully appreciate the moment. It was during that trip that I had lunch with Jackie's daughter, Sharon, and after our little lunch he came by and dropped some money on the table to take care of the bill. I was only eleven or twelve years old and I still remember that, even though I've never talked with Sharon Robinson since. At any rate, my mother exposed me to things like that. She was a very hard worker, and I never heard her complain about the work she had to do to put bread on the table after Dad's death. She symbolized courage and steadfastness in terms of what lay ahead.

With Dad gone and Mom having to work, my day-to-day rearing from the third grade through high school was more or less turned over to my maternal grandmother, Rebecca Bowers. I'd never met either of my grandfathers and had spent only a little time with Dad's mother, Lula Smith, on trips to Kansas City. But after my father's death I spent most summers in Kansas City, staying with Grandma Bowers and my mother's sister, Aunt Elaine French, on Hickam Drive, and during the school year Grandma would come to live with us in Queens. Grandma Bowers really taught me some things during those summer nights in Kansas City and those winter days in New York, things that have stayed with me to this day.

Grandma's husband, the Rev. T. A. Bowers, had been a Methodist preacher in Kansas City, and she was sold out to Jesus. She read the Bible every day, quoted from it all the time, and told me I should do the same. She was a great lady, with blue eyes and golden-silver hair, and when she wasn't quoting from the Bible she was passing on other words to live by. Out of nowhere, she would say, "The bigger they come, the harder they fall," leaving me with something to chew on. Or, "Never get too big for your britches." One time she said, "A fool and his money are soon parted. You know why that is, Jock? You ever think about that?" When I told her I really hadn't given it much thought and asked what it meant, she said, "Because he's a *fool*. Doesn't realize the value of *anything*." That stuck with me.

Anything I was into, Grandma was into. She even got into baseball. When the Mets finally came to New York, filling the void left by the Dodgers, I became a huge fan of theirs and Grandma fell in line behind me. She taught herself baseball, learned the lingo, got to know the names of the players. I'd rush home from school when they had played an afternoon game at the Polo Grounds, still sweating, dying to know how things had turned out. "What happened, Grandma, what happened? Is it over?" "Well, it just ended," she would say, always holding out. "What happened?" She would say, "*Nothing* happened, that's what happened. Skunked. Two-to-nothing. They ought to be ashamed of themselves. Those old ornery devils. Tying runs on base, two-to-nothing, and Marvelous Marv strikes out. Didn't even come close. I'm through with them. I don't want to discuss it anymore." I suspect that Grandma knew all along what I was up to in my bedroom when the Mets were on the road and it was past my bedtime—under the covers, listening to Ralph Kiner and Bob Murphy and Lindsey Nelson from Chavez Ravine, Mets and the Dodgers—but she never let on to my mother, God bless her, that I was breaking the curfew.

Being a total loss at school, the only thing I was good at in those days was baseball. I had drifted away from the Calvary Baptist Church and those wonderful sermons by Rev. Pinn to join the St. Albans Presbyterian Church, mostly because of its Boy Scout troop and its baseball team. Both were integrated. I guess that was the seed that began my understanding of integration, why it's important, and why today I go to an integrated church. The St. Albans Presbys, as we were called, were the only integrated team in the league. The Yankees' "M&M Boys," Mickey Mantle and Roger Maris, were wreaking mayhem on the American League in those days. So I wore Mantle's number 7 and played centerfield while my best buddy, my next-door neighbor Charles Tolbert, wore Maris's number 9 and played right field. I was learning, early on, what it must have been like for Jackie Robinson to be a black guy on a white baseball team. And I was good. I could go get any ball, right-center or left-center, the way Willie Mays and Mickey Mantle and Duke Snider used to go get the ball. I guess I knew, if nobody else did, that I was really going to get the ball not so much for myself but for my father. I wanted to believe he was watching me all the way.

Maybe that's what enabled me to quit running from bullies. About a year after Daddy's death, while I was still feeling deep remorse and just moping through my paces, I became the daily target of a gentleman by the name of Robert Osborn. He was the school bully, the greatest fighter in the history of P.S. 15, and he began taunting me every day from the opening bell to the last. It got to where I dreaded getting dressed and going to school every morning. But then it was almost as though I heard my father talking to me, repeating what he had told me some years earlier on the day he slapped me to the floor after watching me run from a fight: *Never run, son. Don't be a coward. Be a man. Stand your ground, no matter what.*

There came a day, then, when I'd had enough. With all of my friends looking on, Osborn started in on me again one afternoon—taunting me, jumping in my face, talking trash—and this time I fought back. I hauled off and hit him with one of the greatest rights the school had ever seen, or at least the greatest that Robert Osborn had ever seen, and it took several minutes to break up the fight that ensued. I didn't win, but I held my own, and the great Robert Osborn never bothered me again.

Classwork, now, that was another matter. My trek through the school system from the third grade through the tenth had been little more than going through the motions, a listless journey to find some reason to achieve. Remember: when my father was alive he visited P.S. 15 with me and said he wanted to see stars beside my name. Now there were no more stars, just passing grades. My mother was deeply worried, so one day she took off from work and went to see an academic counselor at Andrew Jackson High in Cambria Heights, Queens, which happened to be the same school where the great basketball player, Bob Cousy, graduated. Based on my grades and general inattention, I had been taken off of the academic track and placed in vocational classes. She had been so busy working, leaving my raising to Grandma, that this was news to her. *Bad* news. The counselor was a Mr. Stein.

"What?" she said. "*Vocational* classes?"

"That's where he seems best suited, given his work."

"But my son's going to college."

"Not with these grades, he's not."

Mom exploded. "What are you talking about? This is Jacob Smith's son. He *will* go to college, and that's it."

He said, "Look, Mrs. Smith, I wouldn't be so upset about your son's performance. Not everybody's capable of doing academic work. Who knows? He could turn out to be a fine garbage worker."

Now my mother was furious. "How *dare* you make an evaluation like that of my son? You don't know what he's gone through. You have no idea of what he's capable of doing."

She stormed back home, where Grandma and I were waiting, and she was madder than I had ever seen her. She told us what "this Mister Stein" had said. "A *garbage worker!*" Then she lit into me. "I can't stand up and defend you anymore, Jock. If you want to do nothing and don't want to go to school, if you don't want to have an opportunity to go to college and to make anything out of your life, I can't make you. I'm through, son. I fought your last battle for you today." And then she broke down for the first time since my dad's death, broke down and cried right in front of me. I realized then that I was letting everybody down, especially my mother, who was working so hard to keep us going. Worst of all, I was tarnishing the memory of my father and everything he stood for. Somewhere deep in my resolve, I determined that day that I would get up off the mat and make something of myself if it meant doing it one day at a time.

A year later, when I was in the eleventh grade, a miracle occurred. I had somehow managed to enroll in a public-speaking course. I was still placed in vocational classes and this was an academic course—to this day I don't know how I pulled it off—and discovered that I enjoyed public speaking. There came a day for each of us to stand up and deliver a speech. The white kid just ahead of me, very gifted, very dramatic, delivered a recitation of a famous speech, "O Captain, My Captain," just about scaring me to death as I listened and waited for my turn. I have no memory of what I recited, except to recall that it was delivered extemporaneously, but when I finished and sat down I heard the white teacher say, simply, "Excellent. You have a gift, Jock. You need to exercise it." That was the first good thing anybody had said about me in the school system for eight years, since the day my father died. *Maybe I'm onto something,* I thought. If there was a turnaround in my life, that was it.

In speeches I give before groups of kids who for some reason haven't had an opportunity to participate in the American Dream, I love to tell that story. Always, at the end, I say, "Mister Stein, how am I doing now? I want *every* person to know that if there's a Mister Stein in your life, what he says is not your destiny. Your destiny is determined by *you,* not someone else. Your will to win, your willingness to practice excellence, means everything. It's your willingness to pay a price; to sacrifice, to learn, to become educated so that you can develop a craft, a profession, or something that will serve humanity and serve your own personal economic needs." The Mister Stein story is replete with negative connotations, but maybe that's what makes it work.

4

Tuskegee

WHEN I FINALLY graduated from Andrew Jackson High, in June of 1966, it was time for me to think about college. This was going to be a problem, given my poor academic track record during those years following my father's death. Except for my A's in public speaking, my grades were doleful. There would be no Harvard knocking at my door, nor any other blue-chip university clamoring for my services, greatly impressed by my promise. It was my fault, nobody else's, that I was more or less at the remedial level when it came to academic achievement. There had been some truth to Mr. Stein's assessment of my lack of achievement, after all. What I needed was a small place where I could be nurtured, brought along slowly, until I could catch up.

This is where an old friend of my mother's came into my life. His name was Walter C. Bowie, whom Mom had known during her undergraduate days at Kansas State University. Now he was *Doctor* Bowie, a professor of veterinary medicine at Tuskegee Institute in Tuskegee, Alabama, about halfway between Montgomery, Alabama, and Columbus, Georgia, on the plains of east Alabama, near Auburn University. As small as it was, with only about three thousand students, Tuskegee was big in the hearts of most African Americans at that time; the place made famous by Booker T. Washington and Dr. George Washington Carver around the turn of the twentieth century and, later, by the heroic Tuskegee Airmen of the Second World War, the first all-black flying unit in United States history.

Dr. Bowie happened to be in New York on business about that time, and he called my mother and invited her to lunch. She told him of my father's death and my ensuing struggles in school, everything that had happened since their days in Kansas, and he seemed to grasp my situation. "Look," he said, "Tuskegee might be just the right place for Jock. Don't worry. I'll look after him. The Montgomery airport's about forty miles away. I'll pick him up there every time he's coming back from spring break, summer vacation, or the holidays. Send him on down there, Bettelou. In a little place like Tuskegee, he might find himself."

She came home with the news that I was to apply to Tuskegee immediately. Tuskegee? *Alabama?* A little black college in the "Heart of Dixie," as the state's license tags proclaimed? For a black kid who had grown up comfortably in integrated surroundings in New York City, the center of the universe as far as I was concerned, that seemed to be a million miles away. I had little choice, of course, so I mailed off my application, such as it was, and waited for a response. I was accepted, no doubt with a push from Dr. Bowie, but on certain conditions. I would be admitted to the pre-freshman summer program, and if I did well I would be accepted as a full-time regular freshman in the fall. My mother and I packed my things and got on a plane, headed for the Deep South of Bull Connor and the Klan and George Wallace. I was one nervous kid.

I remember well that first day in Tuskegee, when we had flown into Montgomery, driven to the campus, and checked in. It was the dead of the summer in Alabama, heat and humidity like I had never experienced. As my mother and I were walking from the men's dormitory to the cafeteria, we passed a couple of young women who were coming from the opposite direction. Both of them said, "Good afternoon." I was shocked. Having grown up in New York City, where it wasn't cool to so much as acknowledge another human being passing on the street, I'd never imagined such a thing. "Good afternoon," I said back to them. *Wow,* I thought, *this is going to be something else.* It was my introduction to Southern hospitality, and I liked it.

Hunkered down in my dorm room during that sweltering Alabama summer, a Yankee boy alone in this strange new environment, I worked hard in my remedial studies and somehow qualified to enroll as a *bona fide* freshman student in the fall quarter. During that freshman year, having decided to major in history, I got by with a C-plus average, earning a 2.4 grade-point average on a 4.0 scale. It was nothing to write home about, but I knew I had to take things one step at a time, day by day, lesson by lesson, test by test, in order to climb out of the hole I had dug for myself. I *had* to make it through that first year if there was going to be a second and, miraculously, there was. I began to get the hang of it. During my sophomore year my grades improved immensely, and from that point on I made the Dean's List every single term, my undergraduate career culminating in a perfect 4.0 GPA in my final semester, the highest in my major.

Dr. Bowie and my mother had been right all along: Tuskegee was, indeed, the perfect place for me to find myself, to restore dignity to my father's legacy. Virtually all-black, with only a smattering of white students and faculty, Tuskegee was and still is a place of great pride to African Americans. It was founded in 1881 as Tuskegee Normal School, for the training of black teachers, on the site of a 100-acre abandoned cotton plantation. A black teacher by the name of Booker T. Washington was hired as the school's first president (or "principal"), and when he spoke of a program of "self-help," he meant it literally. Most of the original buildings were built, by the students themselves, of bricks handmade of clay dug from an area of high ground known even today as Brick Hill. The campus, and therefore the institution itself, came to be a point of great personal pride for that first generation of children born to freed slaves. Among Tuskegee's alumni would be Daniel ("Chappie") James of the Tuskegee Airmen, America's first black four-star general; and Ralph Ellison, whose *Invisible Man* made him the first black to win the National Book Award. But the most famous of all Tuskegee men remains George Washington Carver, son of slaves from Missouri, whose work in agricultural sciences early in the twentieth century produced hundreds of industrial uses for the lowly peanut, inducing Southern farmers to raise crops other than cotton as a defense against the onslaught of the boll weevil.

∾

If this little college stuck off in a forlorn corner of the Old South seemed like a foreign country to me, in the beginning of my stay, it soon became a home, a refuge, an incubator. I threw myself into everything: playing baseball and running cross-country, participating in campus politics, joining the same fraternity that my dad had belonged to, studying black history and the great philosophers, inviting powerful speakers to campus, joining in on some campus escapades, even writing a thesis on the revolutionary philosophy of Malcolm X that remains on file in the university archives today. In a way that only a small college can, Tuskegee helped me to grow and taught me to think and stand on my own two feet. It gave me a sense of knowing, a sense of identity, a sense of belonging. It gave me a high level of raging confidence that has never left me.

In the classrooms, some in those same old red-brick buildings fashioned by the first group of students, I sopped up everything offered in philosophy and history. It was a means of taking a long view of the world, the entire sweep of mankind's development, something we seldom have the time or the inclination to do once we settle into our careers and our daily lives. That, of course, is what college is all about. In the philosophy courses, for example, we studied the greats— Aristotle, Plato, Socrates, Hobbes, and many others—and I remember the three schools of thought: idealism, realism, and pragmatism. Learning about myself as I went, I soon found myself categorized as an idealist, one who strives toward a perfect world. My favorite philosopher became Socrates, a man of great wisdom, who went through the villages of Athens asking what the greatest good was. Although he got great answers from lawyers and doctors and other leaders—diamonds? jewels? gold?—he still felt empty until he decided, in the end, that the greatest good is wisdom.

Many professors would influence me. Among them was a white philosopher by the name of Dr. Ramer, a nonconformist who was clearly sympathetic toward the Yippie and Hippie movements of the time. Although their attributes were tolerated in the Sixties but tended not to produce lasting results as far as how one should live his or her life, he made a good case for the philosophy, "I think, therefore I am." His knowledge of the philosophers was everlasting. He taught us, on the other hand, of social Darwinism, the idea that pragmatism drives society. Socrates, Aristotle, Plato, he taught them all. And all of this think-tank energy that he drummed into our heads would become most useful in my life; particularly as a lawyer in a courtroom, where thinking spontaneously on one's feet is the only credo for success.

Another professor who had a lasting influence on me was Dr. Frank Toland, an expert on slavery ("that peculiar institution," he called it). We studied John Hope Franklin's *From Slavery to Freedom*, Nat Turner's slave rebellion, Malcolm X, and John Brown's raid on Harpers Ferry. Dr. Toland gave unforgettable recitations on slavery and those fighting it in their time. He told us that black people were second-class citizens in America because, for one thing, they hadn't come over on the Mayflower; and, therefore, echoing what my father had always taught me, we had to be better than our white counterparts. It was for Dr. Toland that I produced my senior thesis on Malcolm X, knowing that I had to bring some critical and creative thinking to the table in order to get an "A" in the course. His teachings were invaluable to me. The same could be said of Dr. Velma Blackwell, who became my counselor and mentor.

All along, I was being looked after by our old family friend, Dr. Walter Bowie. He had plenty on his plate at the College of Veterinary Medicine, which now produces more than seventy-five per cent of the African-American veterinarians in the world, but he always had time for me. During my four years at Tuskegee, he would speak to me at least two or three times every semester, asking how I was doing and providing me with pearls of wisdom, treating me like a son. Even today, retired but living in Tuskegee, he still calls me from time to time. In fact, after I became partners with Johnnie Cochran, I had a very interesting conversation with him about how to handle my newfound fame, helping to run a national law firm in association with someone the likes of Johnnie.

This was the late Sixties, remember, a time of great tumult in American life. While the Cold War with the Soviet Union continued apace, there were more immediate concerns: the Vietnam war, the assassinations of the Kennedys and Martin Luther King, regressive Republican administrations in Washington, white backlash to Black Power, major cities on fire, student activism throughout the nation.

Tuskegee, this little predominantly black college in the middle of Alabama's Black Belt, became a mecca for African-American leaders of the time. SNCC (Student Nonviolent Coordinating Committee) workers were everywhere. Wearing black pride on our sleeves, our hair done up in Afros, wearing anything from colorful dashikis to torn jeans, we loudly applauded a procession of notable black leaders to the campus: Dick Gregory, Vernon Jordan, Stokely Carmichael, H. Rap Brown, and the poets Gwendolyn Brooks, Don Lee, and Nikki Giovanni. They would come to Logan Hall, the basketball arena, to display their oratorical skills. I especially remember the appearance of Adam Clayton Powell, Jr., the black Congressman from New York, resplendent in a black short-sleeved turtleneck with a huge silver medallion around his neck, a giant in the black community, imploring us to "keep the faith, baby!"

And there was the memorable night when Julian Bond came to the campus. There was another packed house for Julian, who had been a leader of the student movement for civil rights and against the Vietnam War and was by then a state representative from Georgia, a handsome and charismatic young man wearing a three-piece suit. When he took to the podium, fiddling with the watch chain protruding from his pocket, he said, "I've come here tonight to read to you the accomplishments of President Richard Milhous Nixon." The crowd booed, then grew quiet, wondering what this was all about. Bond produced a tiny scrap of paper from his pocket and stared at it for a full fifteen seconds, tilting it this way and that, squinting, scratching his head, saying nothing. Then he crumpled the scrap of paper, tossed it away, and said, "I'm finished." Needless to say, he got a standing ovation.

They were heady times, especially for a young black man from Queens who was just beginning to feel his oats, and at the end of my junior year I decided to run for vice-president of the Student Government Association. I felt that my grades were good enough and that I had something to offer. Since the seed had been planted back in the eleventh grade that I had a gift for public speaking, I knew I was ready. I put together a campaign committee, plastered the campus with posters, and began speaking each night in the men's and women's dormitories.

I got standing ovations everywhere I went. Part of it was for the style and passion I brought to the table, talents I had begun to sharpen, but some was due to my campaign platform. Generally speaking, I was for empowering the students' rights to control their destiny. Specifically, I was for improving dormitory visitation rights, giving students more input about the choices of classes and courses to be offered, and for the abolition of compulsory ROTC and compulsory attendance at chapel meetings. Of the latter two, ROTC was a natural, this being at the peak of the Vietnam war; but the complaint about being forced to make chapel, though popular at the time, would become a source of embarrassment years later when I returned to the Christianity I had been raised to embrace. At any rate, I won the race without a runoff against four opponents, and compulsory ROTC and chapel attendance became things of the past.

More importantly, my tenure as vice-president of the student body in 1969 and '70 introduced me to the exercises of power and diplomacy. Since the titular SGA president had more or less chosen to be a no-show, leaving a void in leadership, the burden fortunately fell upon me. I was the only student representative on the education and executive councils, which included the deans of all the schools, the dean of student affairs, and, of course, the president of the university, Dr. Luther Hilton Foster. Just being in the meetings gave me a front-row seat to observe how decisions are made at the highest level. Dr. Foster would step into a heated discussion among the deans about some controversial matter dealing with school policy and say, "Well, gentlemen, I think we need to table this one right now. Let's reflect on it and come back to it later when cooler heads might prevail." Silence would enter the room, almost as though the emperor had spoken. These were great lessons for one who would become a lawyer involved in negotiations between warring opponents.

Ultimately, as the year progressed, I went before these giants to make the proposals I had campaigned on. I won the abolition of compulsory ROTC and chapel meetings, but there was some resistance to allowing men to visit the dormitory rooms of their girlfriends. (Not that I would know much about that. By this time I had married a young lady I had met during my freshman year, Janice Cheek, of South Boston, Virginia, and we were living in married-student housing on campus.) At any rate, as Bob Dylan was singing, the times, they were a-changing, and my job was to convince these older heads.

"Mister Vice-President," I remember Dr. Foster asking me, "do you think the students are mature enough to handle this now?"

"Dr. Foster," I said, "I've given this great thought and lamented on this and I really believe we're ready."

"All right, then. I'm calling you if there are any incidents."

And that was it. I won. Coed visitations became a part of campus life at Tuskegee and the policy has worked well ever since. I had learned some more lessons that would serve me well in later life.

∾

The evidence was all around me that confrontation, just for the sake of it, doesn't necessarily get the job done; that cool heads will almost always win the day. The year before I was elected vice-president of SGA, the student leaders at that time locked up the members of the Board of Trustees, at the old Dorothy Hall Guest House where they were meeting, and allowed them only bread and water for two full days. The issues were the same ones I would win the next year; basically, a bill of student rights dealing with tuition and courses of study and dormitory visitations. The demonstrations and lockup were led by a student named Michael Wright, an articulate leader and poet, and for forty-eight hours there were speeches in front of Dorothy Hall while the trustees waited helplessly inside. Soon, Gov. George Wallace sent in the state police and the Alabama Army National Guard to storm the Lincoln Gates.

There had been a lot of shouting and posturing on the part of the students, but now they were eyeball-to-eyeball with an armed state militia. Little Tuskegee Institute seemed to be the center of the nation at that moment. Anything could happen. But into the midst of it all came Dr. Foster, the school's president, who so far had been unable to calm the students and resolve the matter in a peaceful nonviolent manner. I remember being torn between the memory of my father's advice many years before—"Stand up for what's right, even though you may lose the battle"—and what I was seeing in front of me. More than that, however, I remember how Dr. Foster met the challenge. Calmly and courageously, he walked to the Lincoln Gates and literally stood up to the tanks. *You will stop here, and we will work it out*, was his message. Within minutes, it seemed, the students had fled, the tanks had turned around, and the trustees were allowed to walk free. And most of those issues that had led to the lockup were solved a year later through sober negotiations with the council of deans.

That didn't keep us from protesting the war in Vietnam, of course. With body bags returning from Southeast Asia by the planeload, a disproportionate percentage of them containing the remains of young African Americans, we had seen the war for what it was: a misguided attempt to "stop the spread of communism" by sticking our noses (and bombs and napalm and gunships) into another culture's business on the other side of the world. During my tenure as vice-president of the student body, I led several marches against our involvement in Vietnam, finding that I was able to galvanize the bulk of the student body simply by calling a meeting and speaking in front of White Hall. With only an hour's notice, I could rally 2,000 of the school's 3,000 students into marching downtown in protest. Now that was *power*, and I loved the feel of it.

∾

Traditionally, Greek life has been extremely important to African-American students, men and women alike. This was particularly true in the Sixties, a time of emerging black power in a country still dominated by a white power structure. You were, in a sense, what fraternity or sorority you belonged to. College-educated white people had always benefited from the friendships and contacts made during their campus days—the old-boy network constructed at, say, a place like Princeton or Harvard or Yale—and we needed that advantage as much as anyone. It was extremely important that we become empowered through the brotherhood and the "networking" (before that word was coined) that would result from membership in a fraternity or a sorority.

My father had become a member of Alpha Phi Alpha fraternity during his days at the University of Kansas. APA was America's oldest black fraternity, founded in 1906 at Cornell University in Ithaca, New York, by seven gentlemen remembered as "the seven jewels." Alpha had expanded across the United States and is represented on most college campuses today. Its members have included Martin Luther King, Jr., Frederick Douglass, and Thurgood Marshall, to name a few. Because it was my dad's fraternity and because it was known as a fraternity for intellectuals (I was a bookworm in those days, buried in history and philosophy books, preparing myself to become a worthy participant in the black revolutionary movement), I felt that Alpha was the only fraternity for me.

I remember going to a smoker, during Pledge Week of my

sophomore year, where the brothers would speak on the benefits of pledging Alpha. The speaker that night was a gentleman by the name of Lee Trillo Watts, a veterinary student from California, and I remember being mesmerized by what he had to say and how he said it: "Pledge Alpha, the way Michelangelo painted. Pledge Alpha, the way Jackie Robinson played baseball. Pledge Alpha, with fanatical fanaticism." That was it. No more convincing was necessary. I had found a home at Alpha Phi Alpha fraternity.

Subsequently, I became the historian of the local chapter, Gamma Phi Tuskegee, which meant that I would teach courses on the history of the fraternity to Alpha pledges until I graduated from the Institute. In order to become a member of Alpha, each pledge had to pass my written exams. Just to demonstrate how these connections we establish during our college days tend to stay with us forever, my student pledges included Milton C. Davis, a native of Tuskegee. Milton went on to become a fine attorney and recently completed his four-year tenure as national general president of Alpha Phi Alpha, whose inspiring speech was a highlight at the ceremony celebrating his investiture. It did my heart good to know that a general president of Alpha had once been a student of mine. Milton and I remain the best of friends today; his law offices are next-door to mine on North Main Street in Tuskegee. He has been a light in my life, a man who exudes great moral character and leadership qualities, reminding me of what the Apostle Paul says in Philippians, that we must "press toward the mark of the high calling in Christ Jesus."

My experiences in Alpha Phi Alpha were invaluable. Many of the brothers during that time were high academic scholars, achievers, people who were mentors. I remember a sign on one brother's dormitory room: "Alpha Phi Alpha. Goodwill is the monarch of this house." That line comes from the poem, "The House of Alpha," from the history book I once used while teaching my pledges (page 408, as

I recall). It was goodwill that helped me understand the importance of being agreeable and of good cheer. It was Trillo Watts's "spirit of fanatical fanaticism" that continues to drive me in all of my pursuits, whether it be as an attorney or a Christian or a collector of sports memorabilia. Alpha Phi Alpha has been my extended family for thirty years and counting.

∾

As my undergraduate years wound down toward graduation, I found that I had learned many things from many different sources during my days at Tuskegee.

When Ronald Reagan came to speak, during his Presidency, the students came prepared to tar and feather him. He was a conservative Republican, thought to be not particularly friendly toward African Americans, but there would be no tarring and feathering that Sunday morning because Reagan came prepared. The heart of his message was that George Washington Carver had done more for the Southern planter and the farm industry in the old agrarian South than any other individual in America. Thus, like him or not, Reagan had befriended a potentially hostile crowd by telling them what they wanted to hear; and with the facts to back him up. He was shrewd, well-informed, and charming; nothing like the students had expected. I learned a lot that morning that would serve me well in later years. To wit: you can turn a jury around in a minute if you have the facts and the ability to present them in a convincing way.

I also learned firsthand about the power of the ballot. During my studies of Malcolm X, I had heard a recording of one of his key speeches, about how if the black man didn't get use of the ballot he would remain powerless and, therefore, out of a feeling of hopelessness, might turn to violence in order to achieve equality in America. I saw a living example of that in Tuskegee during the many citywide elections held while I was a student. The candidates who were wise came onto the campus to galvanize the student vote—recruiting campaign workers, making speeches, even taking students downtown to register as voters—and, as a result, the "swing" vote in local elections was actually the Tuskegee Institute vote. In fact, right after I left the school, in 1972, the city of Tuskegee got its first black mayor when Johnny Ford upset the longtime white mayor, C. M. Keever, thanks to the college turnout.

On a less serious note, but one that nevertheless had a bearing on my development, I began to think about the image I wanted to present as an attorney. Among the black leaders I brought to speak on campus was Earl Graves, the founder and editor of *Black Enterprise* magazine. I was struck by the stunning appearance he cut—cream-colored trousers, brown jacket streaked with cream checks, fancy tie, shoes to match—and I told him afterwards that if I ever got any money or achieved any success I intended to dress just like that. I remembered from my childhood days in Queens the family friend and political leader Guy Brewer, who bore an unforgettable aura: cigars, conked hair, two-tone spats, colorful suits; a man who at first glance looked like a pimp but spoke with sophistication and quiet dignity, oozing success. At any rate, many years later, having become known for my flamboyant dress, I ran into Earl Graves at a function. Although I've toned it down a little since joining Johnnie Cochran, I still have a flair for the dramatic when it comes to dress. I may have been wearing green that day, or maybe royal blue right down to the matching alligator-skin shoes, I don't recall. Whatever, I told Mr. Graves of my vow some thirty years earlier as a poor student at Tuskegee, and he fell out laughing. "The way you're dressed tonight," he said, "it looks like you must be doing pretty good for yourself."

The number and variety of people from whom I learned valuable lessons during my undergraduate days at Tuskegee is unending. The list certainly includes Tom Joyner, a smalltown boy from Tuskegee, a C student at best, who told me that grades didn't mean all that much. Tom's gifts were to communicate, to get along with people, and in his role as a coordinator of student activities he brought onto campus such groups as the Impressions, the DelFonics, and the Miracles. He told me one day that he would become wealthy from his ability to recognize musical talent, and he turned out to be right. Today, some ten million people across the United States listen to the syndicated "Tom Joyner Morning Show." Not bad for a C student.

∾

And so the four years I spent away from Queens, far away from home in the heat of the Civil Rights days, down in the belly of the Heart of Dixie, had produced amazing results. Not a day passed when I didn't miss my father dearly, but now I had learned to turn that loss around and use it in a positive manner. Every book I read, every exam I took, every extracurricular activity I joined—indeed, all of my plans and dreams for the future—all of it was now dedicated to the memory of Jacob Abraham Smith. I had truly become my father's son.

One day toward the end of my tenure in Tuskegee, I drove over to Montgomery to meet my Uncle Gene, Dad's youngest brother, who was flying down for a visit. Uncle Gene had spent his entire adult life in New York. All he knew of the South was what he had seen on television over the years, George Wallace and Bull Connor and the violence of the Civil Rights years, and when he bounded off the plane it was with some cockiness. "Come on, Jock," he said, "let's go get something to eat."

We entered the restaurant at the airport, this young black student and his uncle, a pugnacious New Yorker convinced that the South was full of heathens. The white lady behind the counter said, in a strong Southern drawl, "What'll y'all have?"

"A hamburger," said Uncle Gene.

"What you want on that?"

"A bun. Y'all have any buns in 'Bam?"

It not only was embarrassing to me, it evidenced the divide that still existed between the North and the South, which seemed to remain as wide as it was during the Civil War. Among the many things I had learned was that the situation wasn't all that simple, that there are good people and bad people on both sides of the Mason-Dixon line. My basic training was over, if we could call it that, and now it was time for me to move on to a larger world.

5

Notre Dame Law School

DUE TO MY grades and campus leadership at Tuskegee and, for all I know, being the son of Jacob Abraham Smith, I received a three-year scholarship to attend Notre Dame Law School, the oldest Roman Catholic law school in the United States. I would need some financial help from both my mother and my new wife, of course, but this was an exciting prospect. Notre Dame! Touchdown Jesus! The Fighting Irish! South Bend, Indiana, was a long way from the Queens I had known as a child and the Black Belt of Alabama I had just experienced as an undergraduate at Tuskegee, and I was looking forward to this new adventure. With its liberal Catholic image and the fact that its president, the Rev. Theodore Hesburgh, was chairman of the Civil Rights Commission, I figured Notre Dame would offer a hospitable atmosphere for an African-American graduate of little Tuskegee Institute in Alabama. How little I knew.

Of the 212 students in my entering class, only eight were black, and I had gotten a taste of what might lie ahead when one of the eight told me he was having trouble finding housing in South Bend. He had four or five children, as I recall, but that wasn't the problem. Every time he responded by phone to a newspaper ad, he was told that there was a vacancy; but when he showed his black face at the house or apartment, the vacancy, curiously, no longer existed. Before he had attended a single class, he was gone.

I ran into this brand of racism on my first day on campus. While standing in a line for registration, I noticed a white student eyeing me. He came over to me after a while and introduced himself. Then he said, "I'm afraid I've got some bad news for you."

"Yeah," I told him, trying for a joke, "this line has no end."

"No, I'm serious. Odds are, you probably aren't going to make it."

"*You?* Who's *you?*"

"Blacks," he said. He leaned in, as though he had a secret to share. "Just about every black over the last two years has flunked out of law school."

"Not me. I'm not going anywhere."

"Just a warning, understand."

He got my goat, all right. "If law school is that tough, with all of these people failing, maybe I'll wind up taking *your* spot. Me, I intend to graduate." He backed off, with a shocked look on his face. That encounter served as my introduction to Notre Dame and—fair warning—Notre Dame's introduction to Jock Michael Smith.

Although I had come out swinging, I could see that this wasn't going to be easy. I learned that half of the fourteen African-American students in the previous class had, in fact, flunked out. I learned that there was a military atmosphere in the law school, and if you didn't dance to their drumbeat you would be history in a hurry. They let you know this from the very beginning. I remember having barely settled into my seat on the first day of classes when Les Facio, a professor in criminal law, looked out over the crowd and said, "Look to your left and look to your right. Two of you three won't make it. Law school isn't for everybody. Not everybody is smart enough to be a lawyer." *Wow,* I thought. *Such encouraging words.*

Some of the students folded their tents early. On another first day of class, this one in real property, a professor named Conrad Kellenberg scared the dickens out of us. He started using all kinds of foreign and antiquated legal terms, saying we were going to study *"fee simple, fee tail,* the doctrine of Worthier Title, and the rule in Shelly's case." There was coughing and shuffling in the hall. Suddenly, the white student sitting next to me began gathering his books, and turned to shake my hand. "I'm out of here," he said.

"Where you going?" I asked.

"Home, to Nashville."

"But we haven't even gotten started."

"I don't have to take this crap." His dad was a prominent physician, his mom a professor at Vanderbilt. "They'll take care of me. I don't have to graduate from Notre Dame Law School." He was another classmate I would never see again.

Quitting was never an option for me. To paraphrase Martha and the Vandellas, I had no place to run, no place to hide, as this gentleman did; not with my mother working hard to make ends meet and my grandmother keeping house and raising my sister back home. This was my one chance to make it through a law school, and I had to make good.

Consequently, I threw myself into my studies with every ounce of my strength. There was a contracts professor by the name of Edward J. Murphy, who had written the book we were using, *Studies in Contract Law.* Ed Murphy may have been a right-wing William F. Buckley-ite, but he was scholarly and smart as a whip, and I got along with him very well. Since he had invited students to go by his office after class if there was something they didn't understand, I visited with him so often that he took a keen interest in me and this unlikely friendship steadily grew over the years. There was another professor, Peter W. Thornton, who taught civil procedure. Thornton, I soon learned, had taught my father at Brooklyn Law School many years earlier, around the time I was born. Every time he called on me and I failed to give the correct answer, he would cluck and smile and inform the class, "His father would have known that answer." Thornton rode me hard, but the experience taught me good work habits and further strengthened my resolve.

❧

Racism was alive and thriving at Notre Dame, in spite of the strides toward tolerance that had been made in the Deep South during the Sixties, and I'll never forget an ugly incident at Notre Dame Stadium early in my first year. I'd always been in awe of Notre Dame football, the legacy of Knute Rockne and Touchdown Jesus overlooking the end zone and Rockne's perhaps apocryphal "win-one-for-the-Gipper" speech. Each student received one ticket for each home game, and I intended to make use of mine. During the third home game of the '70 season, I was seated in the stands with a few of my fellow black law-school classmates when the Irish coach, Ara Parsegian, sent a black quarterback into the game. The offense began to sputter. Suddenly, from a white student about five rows behind us, there came a bloodcurdling cry: "Get that nigger out of there!" I was stunned to find that this was still happening in America. With dismay and hurt in our hearts, my black friends and I left the stadium. I attended very few games after that.

And then, in the spring of '71, there was Ali–Frazier I, the fight for the world's heavyweight championship at Madison Square Garden in New York. I had become a fanatical follower of Muhammad Ali, the former Cassius Clay, who had converted to the Muslim religion, changed his name, and been stripped of his title for refusing military induction during the Vietnam years. Now he was back, thanks to the United States Supreme Court—the new black man, tired of the white man's chicanery and skullduggery—going up against Joe Frazier, a less political Negro from another era. Since the fight was being carried on closed-circuit television at a movie theater in South Bend that night, I attended with a blond-haired classmate from California named Allen Enwich, a friend from the law school who was the most liberal white man I had ever met. Ali lost to Frazier, leaving us in tears, but the worst was yet to come. When Allen and I arrived for our contracts class under Ed Murphy the next morning, at about ten minutes before eight o'clock, we saw that many of our white class-mates were all huddled together. They seemed tickled to death that Ali had lost. "He got his due," I heard one of them say. "Yeah, all of that bragging," said another. They paid little attention to us as we sank into our seats with much dismay.

Acts of discrimination went beyond sports. We African-American students had learned early on, for example, that seldom was a black student called upon if he raised his hand during a question-and-answer session. It was when he did *not* raise his hand that he was asked to respond; as though the professor was hoping we would be unable to give the right answer. We eight black students met and talked often about the indignities we were suffering. I remember one classmate in particular, Clarence Martin, from Savannah, Georgia, an older student, who always had pearls of wisdom about how to "get through this sucker," as he called Notre Dame Law School. "Smith," he said, "there's two kinds of law. There's the one they teach here, the one that's supposed to be fair and just. Then there's 'nigger law,' the kind that's used when it's *not* fair and just. That's when we take the law into our own hands. That's Newark and Watts and Chicago." I told him I'd had some personal experience with that in Tuskegee, when radical students took the board of trustees as hostages.

∽

The racism became so blatant that I felt compelled to make some inquiries as to what we might do about it. When I learned that there were chapters of the Black American Law School Association at many of the law schools around the country, but none at Notre Dame, I knew what my mission was. I called a meeting of all the black students in the law school and suggested that we should form a BALSA chapter. The first-year students were all for it, full of fire, but most of the second- and third-year students were appalled. *Boy, they'll run us out of here,* was their thinking. *We can't do anything like that.* Attending that meeting was the president of the Student Bar Association, a black man, and he lambasted me; I was a fool, he said, and things were just fine.

We knew better, of course, and ultimately we formed a chapter of BALSA at Notre Dame Law School. We held a protest, holding up classes, to bring attention to our concerns about discriminatory treatment in classrooms. Soon we were taking it to the faculty, arranging for a sensitivity session that lasted four or five hours. I was the chief spokesman for the students. All of the professors were there, including Edward J. Murphy, and for the most part they acknowledged that it simply hadn't occurred to them that they might have been discriminating against their black students. The meeting went surprisingly well, I thought, and I had the feeling that we had brought the law school to its knees. The atmosphere in the classrooms improved remarkably after that sensitivity session, although it was anything but perfect.

I suppose I should have felt some vindication later in the year by what happened one night after I had given a speech in the main auditorium of the university. I was on the podium as the man from BALSA. I gave an impassioned talk about why we had felt the need to form a chapter on campus, the resistance to it, how we did it, and how we felt it was going. Little did I know that standing in the back of the room, taking in every word I said, was Father Theodore M. Hesburgh himself, president of Notre Dame, whom I was yet to meet. He came up to me afterwards. "Mister Smith, I'm proud to have you at Notre Dame," he said. "You remind me of Julian Bond. You're going to make a fine lawyer. Carry on."

Nevertheless, I felt like a marked man after the formation of BALSA. By then, every professor in the law school certainly knew who Jock Smith was, and it became clear that I would have to do better than my white colleagues if I were to pass those examinations during my first year. Again, I could not run and had no place to hide. I could hear my father's admonitions on the day we integrated Nashville Boulevard in Queens: *You're going to have to be perfect. People are going to be watching every move you make. Don't back down. Do the best you can.* Now I bent over my books like never before, determined to show them I could do the work, and although my daily work placed me somewhere in the middle of the class academically I began to excel in moot court arguments. That's where you argue an appellate case by drafting a brief and arguing a mock case before "judges." Having fully realized my strengths as a speaker, the powers of persuasion I had inherited from my father, I began placing first in the arguments. Now I knew that I was destined to be a trial lawyer. I wanted to finish what my father had started, to live out his dream.

∾

All along the way during those three years at Notre Dame there were numerous fellow students whom I befriended, black and white, male and female. Law school was no cakewalk, especially against that background of discrimination, and we had to stick together in order to make it through to graduation. That white student who had challenged me on the very first day of registration, warning me that most blacks wouldn't succeed, had made his point. Five of the seven black students in the class preceding mine by two years had, indeed, failed out of law school. But with the help of BALSA, I like to think, seven of our eight *did* graduate and, for the most part, went on to stellar careers in varied fields of law. Yes: the times, they really were a-changing.

There were so many who helped me make it through by their friendship and encouragement during some years that would have been bleak otherwise. I was probably closest to Stella Owens, one of the first women to be admitted to Notre Dame Law School, and an African-American woman at that. Stella had finished her undergraduate work at Hunter College, giving us a special bond as New Yorkers, and we inevitably wound up sitting next to each other in classes; complaining throughout our three years together, serving as life support to each other. Clarence Martin of Savannah, Georgia, the one who told me of the "two kinds of law"—fair and just, and "nigger" law—brought a certain levity to our class because he was older, having been manager of a Kmart store before coming to Notre Dame. If I had a mentor during those years, it was Paul Cole, who had done his undergraduate work at Talladega College in Alabama. Though Paul never became an active member of BALSA, being a third-year student when it was formed on campus, I don't know if I would have survived without his encouragement: *Study, study, study. Close yourself off, Jock. Nobody's going to give you anything. There's a whole lot of hell being caught around here by everybody, no matter the color.* Paul went on to a distinguished career as an attorney in New York City for Mobil Oil.

Two of the more interesting classmates were Clark Arrington and Ann Williams. Clark was from Philadelphia, a graduate of Penn State University, a down-to-earth brother who always had a high level of energy and enthusiasm for black causes, whether inside or outside the law school. "Right on, brother, right on," he was always saying. "We got to fight for the people, got to look out for our interests." He hasn't changed; he still wears his jeans and heavy boots, involved with a community action group in Boston, still working for African-American rights. Ann is from Detroit, smart and good-looking (when I first saw her, I thought, *Wow, this lady's going to be a superstar*), and she hasn't disappointed. She spent time at the United States Attorney's office in Chicago after graduation and then was appointed as a federal judge by none other than Ronald Reagan, our conservative right-wing President, and what has struck me is how she has managed to assimilate so well; surviving in the white community while, at the same time, not losing respect in the black community.

My heart still aches when I think of two other classmates who were special friends during those days: Allen Enwich and Alford Perry Williams III. Allen, you recall, was the most liberal white person I had ever met, the one who accompanied me to the closed-circuit telecast of the Ali-Frazier fight at a South Bend movie theater. I got a call from him on the day when student grades were being posted at the end of the first year, telling me there was good news and bad news. "You passed," he told me. And the bad news? "I failed out of law school, Jock. I won't be a lawyer, after all." That was my lowest point until the day before we were to graduate, in May 1973, when news of what had happened to Al Williams hit the campus. Al was a curly-haired African-American graduate of Michigan State, with the greatest spontaneity of articulation I had ever heard, someone who could spend the morning working as a community-action leader, walk into class without having read up on the case being presented in class, and yet rap out precepts as though he had read every line and verse. He had a great gift for gab and a tremendous commitment to community service. He was driving back to South Bend for graduation day, having registered to take the Michigan bar, when he was killed in an automobile accident. I couldn't believe it when I saw the newscast that night. I remember Al's father coming over the next day, accepting his son's degree on his behalf, and receiving a standing ovation.

∾

The graduation ceremony was muted due to Al Williams's tragedy, but life went on. There were two significant moments for me that day. One was that my mother and my grandmother, these two strong women who had raised me following the death of my father, were able to attend. I especially remember Grandma, Rebecca Bowers, coming up to me afterwards, her pretty blue eyes shining, kissing me and saying, simply, "I'm so proud of you." After all we had been through together while she nurtured me, this lost little boy who had lost his father, it was more than I could handle. It was probably the most meaningful thing anybody had ever said to me: *I'm so proud of you.* And during the ceremony itself, the graduation speech had been given by Paul R. Moote, our professor in uniform commercial code. "Love the law," he said. "Practice law with fidelity. "Even though Professor Moote has since passed, I remember those words as if he said them yesterday. Every time I enter a courtroom, in fact, I whisper them to myself as a sort of mantra. *Practice law with fidelity.*

Sitting there with my fellow black graduates, I smiled to reflect on a recent conversation I'd had with Dr. Thomas Schaffer, the dean of the law school, a very liberal white man for whom I had the utmost respect. "Dean, I'm getting ready to graduate," I said, "but I'm still concerned about the dwindling scholarships being offered African-American law students. And I'm concerned about the failure rates and the future of blacks at this law school." He said, "Jock, I understand what you're saying, but you've got to consider something. We didn't admit a single black student until Martin Luther King was assassinated in '68. But some of the professors here said they felt sorry for African Americans after the assassination and that's what began black enrollment in this school."

"Wait a minute. Felt *sorry* for us?"

"I don't know how else to put it."

"Brought us to your attention might be better."

"I suppose so. At any rate, in my opinion Notre Dame has come a long way since then. With qualified representatives like you going out onto the highways and byways of life, I feel that Notre Dame has already made a significant contribution to African Americans."

I didn't agree with him—it sounded condescending to me and completely overlooked the work of BALSA in overcoming the daily indignities we had endured—and our meeting came to an abrupt end. But I suppose, looking back, that he had made a valid point. The situation for black students at Notre Dame Law School had improved considerably during my three years there, and felt I could take some credit for that. We had stood up for our rights as American citizens, and we had endured and prevailed. We had, as they say, seen the elephant and heard the owl.

Years later, in the Eighties, I was touched to be invited back to the law school as a speaker at the traditional Brown Bag Luncheon, where students literally bring a brown-bag lunch and listen to speakers in the auditorium of the law school. I spoke that afternoon about "imaginative advocacy," and felt honored to be there. That evening I spoke at the BALSA banquet, sharing the platform with the Rev. Andrew Young, the great civil rights leader, and I recounted our travails in 1970: the racism prevalent at the time, our protests, the formation of a BALSA chapter on campus, and what it had all meant to Notre Dame. The response was phenomenal, most gratifying. Up to the podium afterwards came Prof. Edward J. Murphy himself, with tears in his eyes, embracing me and saying, "Jock, that was one of the finest speeches I've ever heard. You are Notre Dame. You will always be Notre Dame. You are the embodiment of what we're about, what we've become."

6

'Doctor Jock'

NOW WHAT? ARMED with a doctorate degree from the Notre Dame Law School, but lacking any practical experience that might ultimately lead to the practice of law, I wound up making a few pit stops, as it were. I needed a job, any job, so I grabbed the first one available: a staff position with the NAACP's Civil Rights Project in Binghamton, New York.

Binghamton was a cold and lonely place for me. Here I was, a young black man who had grown up amid the excitement of New York City, been exposed to an all-black culture in the Black Belt of Alabama during the heat of the civil rights days, stirred up a tempest at Notre Dame over the rights of African-American law students; stuck, now, in an isolated outpost far away from anything I had ever known. Binghamton, with a population of some 47,000, had a branch headquarters for IBM but not much else. Its favorite son was Rod Serling, writer of the popular television series "The Twilight Zone." The city was plopped out there in central New York State, in low hills overlooking the Susquehanna and Chenango Rivers, just over the Pennsylvania line, a three-hour drive from the Big Apple.

I'll say this: the NAACP certainly had its work cut out for itself if it wanted to uplift the barely visible African-American community in Binghamton. Broome County's population was 200,000, only one per cent of it black, and those 2,000 blacks seemed too busy making it through the day to get stirred up about such matters as gaining the vote or fighting racism. The numbers simply weren't there. I did what little I could, under the circumstances, but after six months I left the project to take a job across town as a professor at the State University of New York-Binghamton.

∾

Except for the hours I had spent tutoring my Alpha Phi Alpha fraternity brothers at Tuskegee, this was my first experience as a teacher. I was assigned to teach a full-credit course entitled, "Race, Racism, and American Law," and drew a full house, the students evenly divided by race. I chose to use a textbook, written by Derrick Bell, with the same title as the course, which covered the period from the *Dred Scott* decision in 1857 (wherein Chief Justice Kennedy ruled that blacks had no rights, that although Scott had escaped to a free state he was in fact still a slave and therefore remained the property of his "owner"); to *Muhammad Ali v. the United States* in 1971, which vindicated Ali for his refusal to accept military service on the grounds of his religious beliefs. We studied many of the pivotal Supreme Court rulings on civil rights in between: *Brown v. Board of Education, Gomillion v. Lightfoot, Baker v. Carr, Reynolds v. Sims, Miranda v. Arizona,* and countless others.

I found my first job as a college professor both invigorating and entertaining, an opportunity for me to strut my stuff as a speaker, a law-school graduate, and one who had spent considerable years tracking the course of law decisions through the rise of black empowerment. The white students, at least, seemed very active and interested in the subject matter. But, much to my chagrin, the same couldn't be said of the African-American students. I was shocked to find that many of my black students couldn't care less about any of this. It was my first clue that there was a new generation of blacks, kids who now were reaping the gains of the bloody Civil Rights movement and yet were totally disinterested in academics. It was, to say the least, deeply disheartening.

At the end of the semester, I required a term paper rather than a written final exam. I collected some of the most beautiful essays one could wish for from most of my white students and from a couple of the African Americans. But the bulk of the black students turned in papers that were little better than trash; fish-wrappers, maybe, or birdcage liners. I was astonished.

One young black woman, for example, came to me and personally handed over her term paper—three pages, handwritten, on regulation notebook pages—and made her plea: "Sorry I couldn't do any better, but I'm upset. My boyfriend and I broke up and he stole my black-and-white television set. I hope you'll excuse me and give me an A or a B." (I gave her a D, but should have made it an F.) Another black student turned in a paper that seemed brilliant, at first reading, but something smelled. I began poring through my massive library of African-American books and there it was, copied word-for-word. He got an F, of course, and was extremely upset when he came to see me about the grade. "It's so well-written, how could you give me an F?" he said. I explained plagiarism to him, but he still didn't get the point. "Yeah," he said, "but I changed a couple of sentences here and there. What's the big deal?"

Like the cold winter in central New York State itself, the days were becoming longer and colder and less hospitable as time went on. And by now, after nearly five years of marriage, Janice and I were discovering that our union had not necessarily been made in heaven; it was, in fact, beginning to crumble. With no one to share my hopes and disappointments at home, and an almost invisible black community on the streets of Binghamton and in the fields and villages of Broome County, life became an unbearably lonesome tour of duty for me. I began to think fondly of my second home, Tuskegee, the unlikely place where I had found myself.

❧

In an exploratory visit, I first went to see Fred Gray, who had been the dean of African-American attorneys in Alabama since representing Rosa Parks and Martin Luther King, Jr., during the Montgomery bus boycott in the Fifties. He had no openings in his office, he said, and no one else was likely to until I became a member of the Alabama bar. Notre Dame Law School or not, that wasn't going to be easy for me. There were only fifteen African-American members of the Alabama bar at that time. Hat in hand, thanking "Mister Gray," as his stature certainly demanded, I left his office, wondering what to do next.

As it turned out, word got out that I was back in town and I was advised to go by the college to see Dr. Howard P. Carter, who was still dean of Tuskegee Institute's College of Arts & Sciences. He had held that position when I was vice-president of the student body, serving on the educational executive council and thus privy to all of those high-level meetings, and he seemed to remember me fondly. After we chatted for a while, mainly about my adventures since graduating from Tuskegee, he threw a fastball into my wheelhouse. Would I like to teach political science right there at Tuskegee Institute? *Would I?* This was like a dream fulfilled: going back to my alma mater as a professor, teaching in those same old historic red-brick buildings where I had only recently been a student.

For the next three years I would wind up teaching all of the law courses in political science, plus a full load of others that included constitutional law, public law, international law, and African-American politics. Lecturing in Room 212 of Huntingdon Hall, a place I knew like the back of my hand, I took to my new calling like a fish craves water. All of my classes were over-registered, packed to the rafters, and in some cases the hallways outside would be lined with students who had been unable to enroll in the class. Sometimes, when I would reach a crescendo with the dramatic final point in a lecture—*Brown v. Board of Education*, say, or Muhammad Ali's vindication in front of the Supreme Court—we would hear outbursts of applause rolling in from the hallway.

Because my given name happened to be Jock and I had a doctorate degree, and also wrote a column called "Dr. Jock's World of Survival" in the Tuskegee *Voice,* I became known around campus as "Doctor Jock." And I must say that Doctor Jock was thoroughly enjoying himself. I was still young enough to be able to relate to kids of that age, and not so far removed from my own undergraduate days at Tuskegee that they didn't know stories about me, so it worked both ways. I enjoyed most of all my course in African-American politics, which generated a lot of excitement within the student body, these kids still being politically motivated. I used such disparate books as the poet Don Lee's *From Plan to Planet,* Earnest Patterson's *Black City Politics,* and Robert Allen's *Black Awakening in Capitalist America.* Having already learned a thing or two for myself, although still only twenty-six when I took the teaching job, I was able to stick in some personal experiences and observations; some of them, you can be sure, having to do with my father and friends of his like Guy Brewer and Judge James Watson as they strove for racial equality in the Queens of the Fifties.

The greatest reward in teaching college is seeing your students go on to successful lives through something you might have taught them. There were three of those, in particular, with whom I remain in contact. Moses Daily was from Beatrice, a tiny town down in the old cotton country of south Alabama, a dirt-poor kid who was rough around the edges but could cook a mean meal. He had played high school basketball with John Drew, who was having a great career with the Atlanta Hawks of the National Basketball League until he ran afoul of drugs, and Moses wanted to know everything, especially how to become an empowered black man. Today, he is big in the entertainment business in Atlanta—managing groups, putting together recording deals—and he tells me that everything he learned about Malcolm X, W. E. B. Du Bois, Frederick Douglass, Martin Luther King, Jr., and the rest, he learned in my classes. Another student, Janice Spears, got so good that I hired her for the Tuskegee office of Cochran, Cherry, Givens & Smith. She enrolled in all of my law classes at Tuskegee, became a lawyer in her own right, says that watching me perform in court left her "spellbound," and helped me win a jury verdict of $1.8 million over a washer-and-dryer. And there is Janice Franklin, a brilliant student who has gone on to a coveted job as head librarian at Alabama State University in her hometown of Montgomery.

There were some disappointments, as well. As I had discovered at SUNY-Binghamton, now we were seeing a new breed of African-American student who was not as, well, *intense* as those who had preceded them. In talking with other professors, I found that this was happening all across the country. This generation just didn't identify with the black revolutionary movement of the Sixties as the earlier one had. On top of that, their knowledge base was weak and they lacked the willingness to learn; a bad mix all the way around. I remember giving a test in an African-American politics class during my last year at Tuskegee. In the identity section I gave the name of the college president, Luther Foster, a "gift" question, I thought, but when I inserted his middle name it completely threw them off. They had no idea who this Luther Hilton Foster was. Some guessed he was a follower of Elijah Muhammad, some the founder of the United Negro College fund, others a leader of the anti-slavery movement. First, I lay on the floor laughing. Then I cried.

And there was another phenomenon developing on campuses at that time. Precisely when we were pushing our young African-American women to reach for the stars, to think beyond fun and games and marriage, to aspire toward politics and the law and medicine, too many in this group were up to the same old bag of tricks: swapping sexual favors for whatever it was they wanted, in this case grades. It was always the student who seldom came to class and now, suddenly, wanted an A. I remember one, an F student if there ever was one, coming by to see me one afternoon, wearing tight "hot pants," making overtures from the moment she wiggled into the office. "I find you gorgeous and irresistible," she said, cooing, moving in on me. "Well, I really appreciate that," I told her. I stood up and locked the door, then turned to her. "Before we do it, though, let me say that the grade's still an F." She jumped up and stormed for the door. "But I'm gorgeous, irresistible, and you want me," I called after her as she fled the office. "Where are you going? I'm shocked, truly shocked." The lesson I learned from that was that I'm not so adorable and irresistible, that only an A would have made me so. I could be flippant and quote Bob Dylan here—"It ain't me, babe"—but this was academic prostitution of the first rank, and I wasn't going to be a part of it.

During that same period, from 1974 through 1977, I took on an additional job that proved invaluable: as an assistant to Alabama's progressive Attorney General, William J. Baxley. I needed the additional income, for one thing, but more importantly I needed the practical experience. It's instructive, how I came about getting the job. Back when I was vice-president of the student body during my undergraduate days at Tuskegee, I had been contacted by a black civil rights leader named Connie Harper, asking if I could help raise a crowd for an appearance on campus by Dr. Leon Sullivan, founder of the Opportunities Industrial Center. I saw to it that thousands turned up to hear Dr. Sullivan, and, apparently Mrs. Harper, director of the Montgomery branch of the OIC, never forgot it. When she heard I was back in town, teaching at Tuskegee, she recommended me to Bill Baxley and I was hired within thirty days. The AG's office had never been integrated prior to Baxley's election. Ironically, my certificate was signed by Baxley's arch rival, Gov. George Wallace.

Bill Baxley was turning out to be a major pain to Wallace. He was hiring bright young African-American lawyers right and left, all of them on their way to great success. Myron H. Thompson went on to become a United States District Judge; Daniel Thompson a counsel for South Central Bell in Atlanta; Milton Davis, the dear friend whose law offices are now next door to mine in Tuskegee, one of Alpha Phi Alpha's national general presidents; Vanzetta Penn McPherson a U.S. magistrate judge; and Charles Price a circuit judge of Montgomery County.

Each of us was given an opportunity to do significant tasks while at the AG's office. My jobs included writing briefs and handling criminal appeals. Milton Davis really struck it rich when he played an important part in obtaining pardons in the historic case of the Scottsboro Boys, a group of young black men falsely accused many years earlier of raping a white woman. Baxley's *tour de force* turned out to be his reopening of the 1963 bombing of Birmingham's Sixteenth Street Baptist Church, a heinous crime in which four black girls died. White law enforcement officials at the local, state, and federal levels had failed to arrest and convict anyone for the crime at the time, but when Baxley became attorney general he doggedly pursued the case. In 1976, a former Klansman, Robert "Dynamite Bob" Chambliss, was convicted as a result. Baxley also convicted a notorious white supremacist, J. B. Stoner, for the 1958 bombing of another black church, a crime which had also gone unpunished in an earlier era of Alabama "justice." Cases like those were bringing fame and notoriety to Alabama's young attorney general.

A man of immense integrity and considerable personal charm, Baxley might have become Alabama's governor if not for hardball partisan politics in the 1986 elections. Alabama had historically been a "one-party" state, with the Democratic primary essentially deciding who would become the next governor. In 1986, Baxley, by then lieutenant governor, was challenged for the Democratic nomination for governor by Charles Graddick, the incumbent attorney general. Graddick was a former Republican and was as conservative as Baxley was liberal. Graddick beat Baxley, but it soon surfaced that his margin of victory was from Republican voters who "crossed over" and cast ballots in the Democratic primary. A nasty battle followed within the Alabama Democratic Party and in the state courts. The result was that Graddick was essentially disqualified by the Democratic Party as their nominee and a new election was held. However, the public was evidently so disgusted by the raw politics involved that in the general election that fall they elected instead a relatively obscure Guy Hunt, who was a probate judge, Primitive Baptist preacher, and conservative Republican. That election became a major milestone in the balance of politics in Alabama. The state's Republican Party had been dead for more than a century, but now it had sprung back to life and remains the dominant force today. (Hunt, incidentally, was later removed from office for corruption.)

We had our moments, Bill Baxley and I, but one of my favorites has to do with the fight between Muhammad Ali and George Foreman in Zaire, in '74. Bill was a great sports fan, and there was no way he was going to miss seeing the fight on closed-circuit television at the Montgomery Coliseum. I was among the group of five lawyers accompanying him that night as we walked across the parking lot to join the crowd. "I've got ten thousand dollars on Foreman," Bill said. "Mister Attorney General, you're going to lose your money," I told him. "Jock, you're crazy. Foreman's too big, too strong." I was the only black man in the group, and I disagreed on the grounds that Ali would come up with something. Had he forgotten what Ali had said of Sonny Liston? *You gon' lose yo' money/If you bet on Sonny.* He used his rope-a-dope strategy that night, barely throwing a punch until the seventh or eighth round, but when Foreman began to tire from all of that whaling away Ali jumped all over him and finally put him down for the count to regain the title. Even Howard Cosell had been wrong about Ali, indicating that he hoped Muhammad would get out of the bout alive. Baxley was disconsolate afterwards, cracking open his bottle of J&B Scotch to forget the loss of $10,000. I needled him about how he had made a career of siding with the underdog but had messed up on this one.

There's no doubt in my mind that Bill Baxley was the most able and courageous Attorney General in Alabama history, a man's man and a lawyer's lawyer, a perfect example of how to be an excellent attorney while standing up for "the least of these" at the same time, further enforcing what my father and many others would tell me over the years. *Don't be a coward, son. Stand up for what's right.* Bill Baxley fought, and he's certainly not a coward, no matter the odds against him. Today he is practicing law in Birmingham, with the same fire and determination he had as an attorney general. He set a new standard for that office that isn't likely to be equaled anytime soon.

❧

With politics in my blood, I decided for some strange reason to run for the Tuskegee City Council in 1976. I was virtually unknown in the community at the time, seeing as how my duties as a professor restricted me to the campus, but I worked day and night in my campaign. I had campaign posters slapped up all over town and the campus: *Teach the Truth* and *It's a New Day* and *The Man with the Direction.* Much to my surprise, I was the top vote-getter during the primary, right alongside Mayor Johnny Ford and a funeral director/ city councilman named Frank Bentley.

But then Ford made a critical mistake that cost me the election. Without asking our permission, Johnny, who had already been elected, decided to endorse a slate of candidates that included me. When he did that, I knew it was the kiss of death. In smalltown politics, folks don't like being told who they should vote for, and it usually backfires. That certainly was the case here. Whereas I had been only about a hundred votes short of winning outright before the runoff, after Johnny Ford's "endorsement" I lost the seat I sought on the Council by two hundred votes. All of us learned that oftentimes politicians' coattails aren't very long. That was my one and only attempt for political office.

As it turned out, that campaign became a blessing for me a year later when I opened my law practice right there in Tuskegee. In going door-to-door to meet the citizens of the town, in the passionate nature of my campaign, I had managed to endear myself to many of the people. Name recognition is everything, whether in politics or opening a new business, and I would have had little of that if I hadn't run in that campaign. Apparently, the voters liked what they had seen, a spirited man who would fight to make little ol' Tuskegee a better place, and they saw no reason to think I wouldn't do the same for them in a courtroom.

7

Attorney at Law

I WAS SWORN into the Alabama bar in April of 1976, the bicentennial of the United States of America, only the twenty-seventh African-American so certified in the history of Alabama, and it was clear that the prospects were phenomenal for a black lawyer with talent. Blacks had been serving on juries for a decade now, just beginning to get the hang of it, and there was a need to be filled. John Brown, Jr., the founder of SEASHA (Southeastern Self-Help Agency), had noticed me during my campaign for a seat on the Tuskegee city council. Soon he was pointing out to me that the only black law firms in town were those of the distinguished Fred Gray and my friend Milton Davis, who had just opened his offices, and he was strongly recommending that I begin my career right there in Tuskegee.

On the first day of March, 1977, I hung a shingle reading "Jock M. Smith, Attorney at Law" outside the SEASHA Building. Mr. Brown was kind enough to provide me with free rent and assistance from SEASHA's secretarial pool for the first year of my practice so I could get out of the gate and have a chance to make it. One of the first phone calls I received on that first day was from Judge James L. Watson, my father's law partner and closest friend from the days at Watson, Carter & Smith in Manhattan, by then a federal judge with the United States Customs Court. He wanted to congratulate me and lend encouragement, he said, but most of all he wanted to say that my daddy would be proud.

Like anyone opening a new business, I had much to learn. I had no money left in the bank, having spent my last $1,500 to begin a law library, so I had to generate some income. Even as I was trying to find my way to the bathroom, I was spending hours at the nearby Macon County Courthouse: getting to know the clerks, learning about probate work, studying famous cases, learning the proper style of draftsmanship. During that first year as a *bona fide* attorney, I must have handled just about every sort of transaction known to man. I searched titles in order to make a few dollars from land transactions. I pursued court-appointed criminal cases, treating them as though I was pleading before the U.S. Supreme Court, even though the fees were ten dollars an hour out of court and twenty dollars an hour in court.

Some clients did trickle through the front door during that first year, locals who knew my name from my futile run for the city council, most with complaints in the areas of automobile accidents, domestic relations, slips-and-falls, that sort of thing. My second year of practice was a little better as I continued to learn the ropes and build a following, such as it was. But then, in my third year, I got my first real break when a famous criminal lawyer named Robert Cheek—a white man, by the way—came and asked me to assist him in a sensational local murder case known as *State of Alabama v. Ethel Henderson Reed.*

The gist of the story was this. Mrs. Reed was charged with the murder of her husband, Fred Reed, an officer with the Tuskegee Police Department, after she allegedly found him in his car with another woman at five o'clock one morning. The state was claiming that she engaged her husband in a high-speed chase that ended with her slamming into the back bumper of his car, causing it to tumble over an embankment, killing him in the crash. The supposed mistress escaped, unscathed, and walked away from the scene.

From my vantage point, as co-counsel for the defense in the case, I was able to learn from Bob Cheek what the trial court is all about. Right off the bat, he had pushed me forward and asked me to present the opening statement, telling me that it was all right to argue the evidence when he knew that was improper; you can't *argue* the evidence, only *present* what the evidence will show, a big difference. So I got up there, this fiery young attorney, arguing the evidence with all my might, and the district attorney was objecting right and left, all of his objections being sustained. After about five minutes of this, thoroughly frustrated, I got into a shouting match with the DA. When I returned to the counsel table, I noticed that Bob Cheek was grinning from ear to ear. Ultimately, after a day-and-a-half of deliberations, the jury found Mrs. Reed not guilty. What nailed it was Cheek's bringing in the back bumper of Fred Reed's car, which showed little damage in spite of the state's claim of an eighty-mile-an-hour chase.

Bob Cheek's passion for his client had been so admirable that I remember thinking, *Wow, I want to be like this guy one day,* but I didn't know what that ear-to-ear grin had been all about until a few months later when he invited me to breakfast with him at a well-known local haunt known as Mr. G's Restaurant. We ordered coffee and then he said, "You've got guts, young lawyer. You passed your first test with me." He was talking about my shouting match with the DA that day. "I've pretty much decided to retire from this business," he went on, "and I'm going to turn it over to you. I said that if I could find an African-American that I felt would be honest, the right man who could bring on a new legacy in Macon County, I'd retire. I have identified you as such a lawyer. You've got the guts, young lawyer."

By the time that breakfast meeting was over, Cheek had put me through school on the challenges that lay ahead. He went right down the list of every lawyer who was practicing in the county at that time, one at a time, evaluating the strengths and weaknesses of each man and advising me on what it would take to win against them. He even predicted how many years this would take. He was extremely high on my talents and gave me every reason to believe I would succeed. That, coupled with what I had learned through my father, gave me the intestinal fortitude to move ahead in my practice and to represent my clients with complete enthusiasm. The time had come for me to follow the advice of Prof. Paul Moote of Notre Dame: to "practice law with fidelity."

∾

Not long after that, around 1979, I was in court one morning when Circuit Judge James Avery took the bench. Judge Avery, a Princeton man who was in the habit of wearing khaki trousers and having a supply of maybe eight cigars crammed in the pocket of an ordinary open-collared blue shirt when he checked in for duty—no judicial robe for him—stared down at a frightening apparition: a large, menacing black man, about six-four and at least 260 pounds. All of the other lawyers, veterans at this game, could sense what was coming and stampeded toward the exits. I was just about out the door myself when I heard Judge Avery call my name: "Jock, come here." I knew I was in trouble. "I'm appointing you to represent Darnell Williams," he said. *Oh, my goodness,* I thought, swallowing hard. Everybody already knew that Darnell Williams was charged with the rape, robbery, and kidnapping of a white woman. I did not want this case. It was a sure loser, and I would be the next victim of it.

Having no choice, I "accepted" the case. "Ask Mr. Williams how he pleads," said Judge Avery, and the arraignment began. Williams and I conferred, if we would call it that, and when Judge Avery asked if he was waiving the reading of the indictment Williams flew into a tirade: "What *indictment?* It's a fuckin' piece of paper! It'll burn, won't it? You got a fuckin' match?" The 'F' word was flying through the courtroom, over and over again, and I was so embarrassed about my "client" that I was shaking. The judge maintained his decorum, however, and had the deputies haul Williams away.

Later in the day, hoping that he had cooled off a bit, I went to see Darnell Williams in his jail cell. No such luck. As soon as he looked up and saw me standing outside the cell door, he exploded: "What in the hell are *you* doing here? I don't need a lawyer like you, I need a *real* lawyer. You got no guts." That got me angry. I stood my ground. "Look, Williams," I said, "you're charged with rape, robbery, and kidnapping a white woman. An agent for the ABI [Alabama Bureau of Investigation] has already told me that if they don't fry you they'll lock you up and throw away the key. If you don't want me, fine, I'll tell that to the judge. I don't think I want your case, anyway. But I'll tell you this: if you want a lawyer who'll fight for you, you'd better keep me." That gave Williams pause. Soon we were huddled there in his cell, the accused and his attorney, having a relatively civilized conversation that lasted for an hour or so.

I prepared intensely for the trial. Even though I hadn't wanted the case at all, any more than my future partner, Johnnie Cochran, would want the O. J. Simpson case many years later, I knew that this could be a big one in my career. I would be up against a worthy warrior in Tom Young, a highly qualified district attorney, in a major trial that was being closely followed by the media. In my preparations, I found out that Darnell Williams had been convicted of rape in another state some years earlier, but had served his time. I also discovered a key discrepancy in the story told by the victim in this case, the white woman allegedly raped and beaten and kidnapped by Williams, and for the first time in my career I planned to employ a set-up question to throw her testimony out of whack.

Up to a point, both Darnell Williams and the "victim" agreed on what happened that night. They had met at a truck stop on the edge of Montgomery, where he solicited her for prostitution. Agreeing on a fee, they checked into a motel. Williams had a fifth of Johnny Walker Red scotch with him, drank it all up, paid his money, and then, before consummating the tryst, promptly fell asleep. When he awoke, his money was gone and so was the woman. He remembered her telling him that she was headed for South Carolina, so he got into his car and headed north and east on I-85, hoping to catch up with her. He spotted the car somewhere around the Tuskegee exit, and when he motioned for her to pull over, she did. Here, their stories diverged. He said that he then yanked her out of the car in a swoop, wrested his money from her, and drove away. She said that he drove her car off the road, pulled her out of it, beat her half to death, robbed her, and then raped her.

I planted the set-up question early on. The woman was on the witness stand, giving her version of the events, and somewhere during her testimony, in the midst of some fairly mundane questions, I asked her, "When were you first in fear of Mr. Williams?"

Without hesitating, she said, "Oh, back at the motel."

"When he caught up with you, you stopped, is that correct?"

"That's what I said. Yes."

"Voluntarily."

"Sure."

"Well, let me ask you this. If you had been afraid of him back at the motel, why would you even think about stopping then? You'd already driven for thirty miles, trying to get away from him."

There wasn't much that Tom Young, the DA, could do about this but seethe. He went berserk, though, when I got Williams on the stand later on. Williams went through his version of the events, which everyone had heard, of course, but there was something else I wanted to plant in the minds of the jurors.

"Have you ever been convicted of a crime before this?"

"Yes," Williams said.

"What was it?"

"Rape."

"How did you plead?"

"I was guilty." There was some rustling in the courtroom. "I was guilty, I admitted it, and I served my time like a man."

"Are you guilty in this case?"

"No, sir, I'm not."

I had stolen the state's thunder, disarmed them, and they knew it. It didn't take a Clarence Darrow to know that they had intended to make a big deal out of Williams's past criminal record during their cross-examination. Now the DA was jumping up and yelling at the top of his lungs, pointing at Williams, calling him "a rapist, a robber, a kidnapper!!!" I was objecting, Judge Avery was hitting his gavel, and three of us were talking at once. Young had made himself look like an overeager prosecutor, hell-bent on destroying a man who was now admitting to the jury that, yes, he had been guilty once but had paid his dues to society "like a man."

My *coup de grace* was delivered during my closing statement. In between two animated sentences, I stuck in these words: "We all remember the Scottsboro Boys case. Enough said." The DA objected and the judge sustained, rightfully so, but it was too late. The jury had gotten the point. When they found Darnell Williams not guilty, Young went berserk again.

∽

Though still rough around the edges, like a rookie in major-league baseball, I felt that I had turned a corner. I had defeated a formidable adversary in Tom Young, a qualified district attorney of long standing, in a case that had attracted a great deal of attention in the press.

My success in the Williams trial marked the beginning of a seven-year run in criminal law where I won case after case, or else got charges significantly reduced, often clearing my clients on charges as serious as murder and rape. The more I won, the higher my confidence level soared, but at the same time I was learning a hard fact known to most attorneys: criminal law doesn't pay. And now, around the time of the Darnell Williams victory, my personal life was taking an abrupt turn.

8

Strong Women

I T HAD BEEN obvious to Janice and me for some time that our marriage wasn't working as we had hoped. Having met during my freshman year at Tuskegee, in the fall of 1966, a time of great excitement for African-American students all over the country, we were husband and wife, living in married-couples housing, by '68. We were too young, to begin with, and much had happened since then. There had been the three difficult years of study at Notre Dame Law School, the bleak year in Binghamton, three more years back "home" in Tuskegee as a professor and an Assistant Attorney General under Bill Baxley, and finally the stressful early days of trying to make it on my own as a young attorney at law.

The marriage had held up for nine-and-a-half years, through some very hard times, but by the late Seventies we both felt that there was nothing either of us could do to save it. We had simply grown apart, begun heading in different directions. I still felt an enormous obligation toward Janice—she had, after all, worked to help keep us afloat during the three years at Notre Dame—and I intended to repay the favor. I helped put her through Atlanta University, two hours up the interstate from Tuskegee, where she ultimately received a master's degree in social work. The marriage ended shortly after that.

On a night in the fall of 1978, during the time while my divorce was pending, I happened to be attending a convention of the Alabama Democratic Conference in Montgomery when I was introduced by a mutual friend, the niece of Joe Reed, founder and chairman of the conference, to a woman named Yvette Smiley. She was vivacious and attractive, an independent African-American in her own right, and I was immediately attracted to her.

When I asked her what she did, she launched into a breathless ten-minute version of her life: daughter of one of Martin Luther King, Jr.'s deacons at the Dexter Avenue Memorial Baptist Church in Montgomery; a participant in the Montgomery bus boycott as a child; *summa cum laude* graduate from Hampton University; first black female to work for Arthur Andersen, one of the "Big Eight" accounting firms in Atlanta; first black female to receive a certificate as a Certified Public Accountant in the state of Alabama; currently director of the trial staff of the Alabama Public Service Commission; and was the divorced mother of an eight-year-old daughter. When she asked me what I did, about all I could do after hearing a resume like that was to mumble, almost apologetically, "I practice the law with fidelity."

Later that evening, joining some friends at the American Pie restaurant, we had a wonderful time. This was a formidable woman, no doubt about it, and I was hooked on her from that first moment when we met. We stayed in touch off and on over the next few months, while my divorce case worked its way through the courts, and when it was finalized I finally told Yvette one day that I had made up my mind about something.

"What is it?" she said.

"We ought to get married."

"You can't be serious."

I said, "Why put off until tomorrow what we can do today?"

As the brothers in the street say, after going through the litany of a woman's physical attributes—they are either a "butt man" or a "chest man" or a "leg man"—Yvette attracted the "face" men. She had what they call the Jane Kennedy look, the rarest and most perfect of all, and on top of that she had intelligence and financial independence. When she said yes to my proposal, I found myself thinking *Yip-yip, skippity-do, time to get on with the ceremony.* My divorce was finalized in April of that year and we were married on the third day of June, 1979. We lived in an integrated neighborhood in Montgomery, whence I would begin commuting to my office an hour's drive away in Tuskegee.

༄

Early in the marriage, I would discover that I was practically a neophyte in the push for civil rights when compared to Yvette Smiley-Smith. I had been a child wallowing in self-pity over the premature loss of my father in the mid-Fifties, a crucial period for black people demanding equality in America. But at that precise moment in history, more than a thousand miles from Queens, New York, little Yvette had been a trouper on the front lines, right there in Montgomery, the Cradle of the Confederacy. She was the child of Gloria and Marion David Smiley, educated people who had taught her strong Christian values and how to sustain herself in a recalcitrant white Southern society brimming with racism. Both her father and her uncle, Richmond Smiley, served as aides for Martin Luther King while he pastored in Montgomery, which is what led her to join the bus boycott as a little girl, and she remembered seeing crosses being burned in the yard of the family's home at 3372 Mobile Highway.

She had vivid memories, as well, of a meeting in her uncle's house in March of 1965 two weeks following the Selma-to-Montgomery march, the one that had led to violence at the Edmund Pettus Bridge in Selma. Dr. King was staying with them that night, as he often did when he came to Montgomery, and he was joined by many of the most powerful African-American leaders of the Civil Rights movement. They were discussing the mayhem of that day at the bridge, were planning the continuation of the march now, a fortnight later, and some of those present were wondering how much longer they could practice nonviolence. Yvette remembers Dr. King speaking to them: "I understand what each of you is saying, but let me say that we must continue. God has called us to this day and time and place for us to march peacefully, to integrate the South. There may be police dogs and water hoses and all that you suggest, but no matter what violence is perpetrated upon us, we cannot retaliate. We are here to change society. God has called us."

She walked down the hall and went to bed after King had spoken that night, but that memory lasted and became her life's blood as she went off to college and then returned home to become a trailblazer for justice in her own right. I had already learned that Joe Farley, the head of Alabama Power Company, called her his most worthy adversary while she was with the state's Public Service Commission; a determined, well-prepared, uncompromising opponent, the last person the utility company wanted to see enter the room when a questionable rate increase was on the table. She had God on her side, something I wouldn't understand for some years to come, and that made for quite a package. A beautiful woman of God, armed with the truth, determined to win, is well-nigh unstoppable.

Not lost on me was the fact that in marrying Yvette I was continuing a pattern, going back to my childhood, of being nurtured by strong women of Christian faith. How else could I describe my mother and her mother, who raised me after my father's death? It was Bettelou Smith who took on the callous school counselor who told her that her son "might make a fine garbage worker someday." And then went to work to support her two young children in the bad days to follow. It was Rebecca Bowers, Grandma, who took over as my surrogate mother while her daughter spent long hours on her feet as an airport reservation clerk. Here came another one now, my second wife, to hold me up while I found my way.

$\sim$

Like those other strong women in my life, Yvette had already responded to the responsibilities of raising a fatherless child. Her first marriage had been rocky, ending in violence. She had escaped it at three o'clock one winter morning in Atlanta, fleeing into below-freezing temperatures with her baby daughter, Janay, wrapped in a blanket. Janay's separation from her natural father was not only physical but financial and emotional as well, the father seldom seeing her and never paying court-ordered child support after the divorce.

For me, the new kid on the block, I had a tough row to hoe. Understandably, I wasn't exactly welcomed with open arms by Janay. We had spent little time getting to know each other before the wedding. She had enjoyed her mother's complete attention for all of her eight years, so now here came this stranger threatening to divert that attention. I was immature, myself, and for a long time there was a tremendous tug-of-war between the two of us over Yvette's love. It was a battle I couldn't win, of course, since a mother's love for her child will win out every time. For several years, Janay and I walked around the house, speaking only to her mother, seldom to each other.

Time, though, has a way of taking care of some things. I had been a miserable failure as a father from the beginning, too preoccupied with my law practice and too busy trying to sop up all of Yvette's love for myself. But Janay did some maturing herself as the birthdays rolled by, and so did I. There's no doubt that a major turnaround in our relationship occurred in 1986, when I was born again, returning to the Christianity I had abandoned as a teenager. At the same time, as I became a better stepfather with God's help, she was blossoming as president of her class, a member of the honor roll, and point guard and captain for the basketball team at Jeff Davis High. By the time she had graduated from high school, we found ourselves sitting beside each other in front of the television on Sunday afternoons, rooting for her Dallas Cowboys and my New York Giants (except when they played each other, in which case we watched separate sets in separate rooms). Yvette's unconditional love for Janay and me was the glue that kept us together as a family until our father-daughter relationship came to fruition.

I'm jumping ahead of myself a little here, but I'm dying to report on Janay's unqualified success that followed those early days of cat-and-mouse games between the two of us. She had been saying, even during her high school days, that she wanted to be a lawyer, but one day she came home from school and announced that she wanted to become an engineer and inventor. Remembering how she had always been Ms. Fixit around the house as a child, able to repair everything from ice-makers to washers and dryers, I was all for it. But Yvette, being the more conservative and dealing from the perspective of a protective mother, showed little excitement for the idea. Lawyers make money, inventors don't, was the crux of her argument. I pointed out that in a recent year only two or three African-American lawyers in the whole state of Alabama had made more than six figures. Yvette came around, agreeing that in the end you have to let your children fly with their own wings, and before we knew it Janay was studying mechanical engineering at Howard University.

Once she had graduated from Howard on a full academic scholarship, she set her sights on Stanford University, in California, where she wanted to pursue a master's degree in product design engineering, the only such program available in the country. Stanford's policy was to admit fewer than eighteen students to the program in a given year, and getting into it wasn't an easy thing. Knowing of Janay's tenacity and zeal, Yvette and I joined her on her mission to reach Stanford. It would be necessary for her to do further study in the design arts in order to qualify for the program, so she got a job with Ford Motor Company in Detroit during the day while attending classes at night. It took her two years, but she made it, winning a full academic scholarship to become the first African-American female to do so in her program in the rich history of Stanford University.

Her chosen profession suits her perfectly. Today, she is the only product design engineer at the Gillette Technical Center in Boston, in the oral care products division. She travels a lot, both inside the country and overseas, and I'm humbled and deeply grateful that she has become one of my most steadfast supporters. She is always showing up for major events in my career—trials, conferences, appearances—and if she can't make it she calls to say, "Daddy, I'm proud of you." That same kid with whom I competed for her mother's attention has shown uncompromising love, respect, and gratitude to me as a father. And it works both ways; I've learned to appreciate that more than any multi-million-dollar jury verdict I might receive. There's no doubt that my relationship with my daughter is without peer. Yvette often complains that the two of us gang up on her, outvoting her on family decisions. Honestly, Janay and I do see things in remarkable synchronicity. What can I say? She's a smart kid.

∾

For much of my adult life, I had been separated from my only sibling due to geography. Paula Elaine Smith is five years younger than me—she was only three when our father was killed and has few memories of him—and as the years passed we found ourselves on opposite sides of the country. I was all over the place for a while, in Indiana and central New York State and finally in Alabama, and in the meantime she had settled in North Hollywood, California, working for an attorney while pursuing a career as a singer and songwriter. We would exchange birthday greetings and phone calls now and then, only occasionally seeing each other at family gatherings, but all of that changed around the time I married Yvette.

Men have a bad habit of not staying in touch, and I was as guilty as anyone about that. My climb up Jacob's ladder was often lonely and all-encompassing, made worse by my not having an immediate family member by my side to share the dream. I was too busy doing what I had to do to succeed—learning the law, establishing a practice, finding happiness in marriage—to understand that help was there if only I asked for it. Little did I know that Paula had been there all along, a strong woman in her own right, just waiting for the opportunity to come back into my life if I needed her. That moment came in a time of crisis.

Yvette had been suffering from a disabling bladder condition for some time, often requiring surgery, and when we called Paula for help she came running. Yvette was going in for more surgery, just at a time when my practice was beginning to flourish, and managing everything at once—caring for my wife, still trying to forge a relationship with little Janay, keeping our house in Montgomery in order, driving to my office in Tuskegee every day—seemed to be a monumental chore, too much for me to handle alone. Taking leave from her job and putting her musical career on hold, Paula flew to my side and immediately took over.

She was a trouper, and much more. With Yvette incapacitated upon her return from the hospital, Paula cooked and cleaned, running the house as if it were her own, and somehow managed to console the three of us: Yvette, Janay, and me. I learned a lot about my sister in the process. She also had chosen a difficult profession, Hollywood being a very cutthroat environment even for a talented singer and songwriter, but her drive to make it remained intact.

Although she would have liked to have more *things* in her life, as our mother and our grandmother would have preferred when they were raising us in Queens, she had never been a materialistic person. Often we are judged by our peers on the basis of what kind of car we drive, what kind of clothes we wear, what kind of house we live in, and I found that I was guilty of responding to that. Trial lawyers too often see only the million-dollar verdict, not the values that lie beneath: principles, morality, courage, steadfastness with family members, and a relationship with God.

Paula had found spiritual salvation many years before, in a Pentecostal church in New York, and now was talking Jesus as she went about her chores. For my part, I just couldn't make that breakthrough, couldn't understand where she was coming from, since I still thought that Jesus was pretty much for people who were broken and down on their luck. I tried to connect the fact that there was some recent upward movement in her musical career, and maybe she was crediting this Jesus for it, but she told me that isn't how it works. "The Bible says that Satan is the god of *this* world," she told me, meaning the world we live in, "but not of the spiritual world, the one that counts the most." As I watched her move about the house, taking care of the spiritual needs as well as the mundane, I began to see for the first time that there must be something I was missing. The seed had been planted. It would take years to grow, but there it was.

9

The Least of These

I HAD BEEN in practice for only five years when a case that would increase my faith in justice and direct my destiny as a lawyer literally came right to my doorstep. In 1980, my law office was still housed in Tuskegee's SEASHA Building. The Southeast Alabama Self Help Association's mission was to improve the economic and social lot of black people throughout twelve counties in southeastern Alabama. John Brown, Jr., SEASHA's founder, had struck a deal with me. His organization was looking for a lawyer to help set up a practice for disenfranchised black people, who had been long-term victims of the legal system. In exchange for an office and secretarial help, I would pledge my support to the SEASHA cause when needed.

Then one day Brown came by the office and asked me to become involved in a case in Tallapoosa County, right down the road from Tuskegee. He told me that a number of black families in the county were being taken advantage of, through immoral and illegal foreclosures, and that those families were in need of my immediate intervention. He also made it quite clear that SEASHA had very little money to pay for my services and that he was asking me to do it as a favor to him and to blacks. In my heart, I knew that I had to agree.

After interviewing several of these families at my law office, I determined that they were in serious danger of losing their homes. The legal instrument at issue was a "Bond For Title." In effect, this is a document stating that one receives a deed only after an entire indebtedness to the owner is paid off over an extended period of time. At that time, Bonds For Title were typical of the way many wealthy landowners would conduct business with poor folks. In some instances, landowners hoped that poor families would default somewhere along the line by making an untimely payment or two, so that immediate eviction from the premises would be legally in order. When I determined that all of these families had Bonds For Title rather than deeds to their respective homes, I became disheartened because I realized that the chances of winning their cases were slim to none.

Initially, the cases against these families were filed in the District Court of Tallapoosa County. The District Court does not allow a trial by jury, but a trial before a sitting judge who is duly elected by the people of the county. Given the politics of Tallapoosa County and the political clout that the landowner carried, I knew that we would not prevail. Ultimately, we would have to appeal the case to the Circuit Court of Tallapoosa County, where we would request a trial by jury. The presiding judge confirmed this when he asked me to lunch. On our journey back to the courthouse, he informed me of all the reasons why he intended to rule against me. I was quite unmoved by his recitation, as I had predicted it. In fact, the appropriate papers to appeal the matter to the Circuit Court of Tallapoosa County were already in my briefcase.

After the case was docketed with the Tallapoosa County Circuit Court via the appeal, I immediately entered defenses to the case under the legal theories of the Part Performance Doctrine and Estoppel. That is, these families had been making irregular payments on and off for twelve- to fifteen-year periods. Under Equity law in Alabama at that time, if these families had partly performed and were led to believe by the acceptance of partial and/or late payments that the owner had accepted such a payment schedule, then the owner might be prohibited from foreclosing the property. With regard to Estoppel, Alabama law said that once the Part Performance Doctrine was proved by the defendants, the same possibly gave rise to the owner being stopped from evicting the individual with whom he was transacting business over the years. Though the defenses might seem cogent to the layman, keep in mind that Tallapoosa County was and is a predominantly white jurisdiction, which did not have a history of justly protecting black folks like my clients. Thus, my outlook was pessimistic.

∾

I remember on that hot summer day in 1982 the striking of the jury for our first case as though it happened yesterday. Two entrenched local white lawyers represented the plaintiff, who was the wealthiest landowner in the county. Here I was, representing a poor rural black family who had purchased their home approximately fifteen years earlier. There were thirty-six people in the jury pool, five of whom were black. Each side had twelve strikes. The landowner's counsel used up their first few strikes by excluding every potential black juror. As they made each strike, they would direct a grin in my direction as if to say, *Son, you don't have a chance. We're going to impanel a white jury who will seal your clients' doom before a word in the trial is spoken.*

Keep in mind that this was proper jury selection at the time. Not until years later did the United States Supreme Court determine that striking jurors along racial lines without race-neutral reasons was unconstitutional.

During the *voir dire* of the jury, I spent most of my time asking the potential jurors questions about whether they could be fair to my clients even if it meant deciding against the wealthiest white landowner in the county. I also inquired as to whether they could be fair to me in that I was a black lawyer, something that just did not exist in Tallapoosa County. Though no jurors raised their hands informing me that they would not be fair, it was clear to me from the chilly atmosphere and the stone-faced responses I was receiving, that my clients and I would be the victims of a race-based ruling. After the jury was chosen, I noticed that the only person remaining in the court-room to view the trial was an elderly black woman with a cane, who seemed very attentive throughout the proceedings.

∾

Shortly into the trial, the circuit judge informed the counsel as to how he intended to instruct the jury. He told us that he was going to inform them that if the landowner won, then my clients would be immediately evicted from the property and the jury would only have to determine the reasonable value of the rent due the landowner. The judge went on to say that if my clients prevailed, then they would own the homes outright and the eviction and/or foreclosure process would be avoided. Once the judge pronounced this, it was clear to me that part of my job was to have the value of the property in question assessed as low as possible in case we did not prevail.

The landowner called the most recognized and experienced real estate appraiser in Tallapoosa County as a key witness. The landowner's counsel got the witness to admit that he was well familiar with the homes in question. He testified that the homes were built in or around 1957, and that he had engaged in many real estate transactions involving these homes over the years, offering many appraisals. The witness also testified that the value of the property had gone up tremendously since 1957.

Accordingly, the witness certified that my clients owed a substantial sum in past-due rentals, under the Bond For Title. The witness went on to proclaim that a reasonable rental in 1982 for the properties in question was substantially higher than the payments that my clients were even required to make under the Bond For Title agreement.

As bleak as the case appeared, I didn't give up. At the tail-end of my cross-examination of this witness, I asked a series of questions that could have only come from the Master above, had I been so enlightened at the time.

"Sir," I began, "you have quite an impressive resume. Would it be safe to say that you are the real estate guru of Tallapoosa County with regard to property appraisals?"

"Yes."

"Would it be safe to say that you are the Alpha and the Omega, the essence and quintessence of real estate transactions and property values within the four corners of Tallapoosa County? Is that not so, Sir?"

"Yes."

"You indicated that you are very familiar with the history of the property that is the subject matter of this lawsuit. Right?"

"Yes."

"Let me ask you this. What was the racial makeup of the community in 1957, when these homes were first built?"

There was an extended pause before he finally answered, "It was all white."

"And please tell me, sir, what is the racial makeup today?"

Another long pause. "It's all black."

At this point the trial judge was sitting back in his seat, almost choking on his cigar, smiling as though wondering whether I would have the courage to ask the last and final question that needed to be asked. After much reflection, I put it to the witness.

"Sir, is it not a pragmatic principle of Alabama real estate that when us folks move in [pointing to myself] the value of property goes down?"

This time the pause lasted a full minute. "That is right."

"Thank you, sir. That ends my cross-examination."

The judge called me to the bench, a big smile on his face. "I would have never believed that you had the guts to ask those questions," he said. I told him that it was my duty as a lawyer to represent my clients to the fullest extent of my duties, even if it meant rehashing some of the racial issues of the past.

During my closing argument to the jury, I informed them that I was foolish enough to believe that the ink had not yet dried on the Declaration of Independence in Tallapoosa County, and that noble precepts of justice pervaded the county. I also said that I was foolish enough to believe that while my client and I were black, and that while the landowner was not only white but the richest and most powerful landowner in the county as well, each of the jurors would still keep the promise they had made under oath to be fair and impartial and decide this case based solely on the evidence. Looking straight at their detached faces, I asked this all-white jury to pray before they rendered a decision in this case.

After about an hour and a half of deliberations, to everyone's surprise, the jury returned a verdict on behalf of my clients on every issue in the case. I believe the members of the jury searched their hearts and consciences and rendered a decision that they felt was just and fair. They came down on the side of truth and resisted the temptation to come down on the side of prejudice. As they filed out— very quietly—I noticed that they were all looking at the ground, as if they themselves were in shock over the verdict they had just reached.

On my way out of the courtroom that evening, the elderly black woman with a cane in her hand, who had been sitting on the back row throughout the trial, approached me. She extended a handshake and said, "Son, I never thought I'd see this day come to Tallapoosa County. God is going to bless you for what you have done here. If you continue to handle your cases this way, you'll always be in His care and receive His abundant blessing."

"Ma'am," I said, "I'm not so sure that I thought I would ever see this day, either. But I'm very proud to have been a part of it."

I was eternally rewarded and grateful for not only the outcome of the trial but for what it signified. Those twelve unknown souls of the Caucasian race rendered a verdict of hope on the hot summer day in deepest Alabama. Their verdict represented the best of what America has to offer in its allegiance to the principles expressed in our Declaration of Independence, that "all men are created equal, that they are endowed by their Creator with certain unalienable Rights, that among these are Life, Liberty and the pursuit of Happiness."

This case affected families to whom Jesus referred as "the least of these." Now that two decades have gone by, there are many Rivers of Jordan still to be crossed on behalf of the least of these, but I believe that one must first step into the water to truly understand the possibilities contained within. The first step to becoming a great trial lawyer is a true understanding that the unseen world is more powerful than the seen world. Representing these families increased my faith and hope in the future, and relieved my despair. It showed me that a just cause *can* be won against all odds. It inspired me to try to help many other people since then and it will always remain part of my reason for practicing law.

10

Moon Money

THE VICTORY OVER DA Tom Young in the Darnell Williams rape case, followed by the successful representation of
the poor black homeowners of Tallapoosa County, had left
me feeling flush and full of myself. I was on a roll now, with the media
beginning to pay attention, winning case after case as a criminal
lawyer representing the poor. I was thoroughly enjoying my years as
a criminal lawyer and would have continued for the rest of my career,
but for the sobering fact that it just didn't pay any money. Face it: the
people who commit such crimes as burglary, robbery, and receiving
stolen property are in a fix precisely because they lacked financial
resources. They have committed their crimes in order to survive.
Thus, it became apparent to me that I couldn't make a really good
living by continuing to practice criminal law in the Deep South.

Soon after winning the Tallapoosa County case, I was able to
move out of the old SEASHA Building and set up my practice in a
building at 119 East Northside Street in downtown Tuskegee, just
four doors from the Macon County Courthouse. I purchased the
building from T. Dudley Perry, Sr., an attorney and a state senator at
the time. Dudley sold it to me at a very good price, even assuming the
second mortgage himself, and the location of my new office was
perfect for my plans to look into the pursuit of civil law.

I began to drop in on trials as they proceeded at the county
courthouse, in order to watch some of the great lawyers as they tried

cases. The most notable of these was Fred Gray, famous for his work in civil rights with Rosa Parks and Martin Luther King, Jr. Later, of course, Gray would serve as counsel for the plaintiffs in the infamous Tuskegee syphilis study, wherein patients were "observed" as they succumbed to painful deaths, *a la* the Third Reich; and went on to become president of the National Bar Association. I watched everything Fred did—his line of questioning, his tactics, his pauses, his body language—and it was clear to me after watching several of his trials that he had mastered how to get to the psyche of an African-American juror. He was cagey and crafty and skillful in a courtroom. I walked out of the courtroom one day and thought to myself, *You know what, I can do this, I can become a great trial lawyer myself.* With a new wife and daughter at home, meaning there were more bills to pay, I pointed myself in that direction.

I got a chance to try my first civil case, right off the bat, and I was taken to the woodshed by the great Fred Gray himself. It was a breach-of-contract case, *Mary Mullins v. Wilbur Harris*, a mistake all the way around since I was representing Mary Mullins, my secretary at the time. I was extremely confident as I entered the courtroom, certain I was going to win overwhelmingly—had I not been peeking over the master's shoulder all of this time?—but I was in for a big surprise. Fred jumped on me like a chicken on a Junebug, winning every motion, every objection, every point.

At the close of my evidence, Fred moved for a directed verdict, to have my case dismissed. I had done such a poor job that I hadn't even realized that I hadn't given the jury enough evidence to rule on the case. The judge was James Avery, the cigar-smoking Princeton man, the same one who had assigned me the Darnell Williams rape case as though to see what I was made of, and now he was coming to my aid.

He looked down at me and said, "Do I hear a motion to reopen your case?" I said, following his lead, "Your Honor, I make a motion to reopen my case." He said, "Granted," and then walked me through the questions I needed to ask in order to prove my case. In the end, the jury returned a verdict of $3,300 for Mary Mullins, but it had taken blood, sweat, tears, and a kindly judge to get it.

Although I felt the verdict was just, I also felt the jury had almost given it to us out of pity. I had been humiliated in my first civil case, administered a whipping, and I vowed never to let that happen again. From now on I would have to do my homework, come to court prepared, and above all never underestimate my opponent. I learned that from Fred Gray when I dropped in to visit him after the trial. "What did I do wrong?" I asked him. "You weren't prepared," he said. "Never come to court unprepared." I've never been unprepared since.

Not long after that, I had another chance to go head-to-head against Fred. It was very important for me to see how I would do this time, as a way of measuring my progress. It was sort of like a rookie hitter, fresh up from the minor leagues, being blown away by Nolan Ryan's fastball the first year, and again the second year, and then reaching the third year and thinking *Hey, wait a minute, here's Nolan Ryan and that ninety-eight-mile-an-hour fastball. I've seen this sucker before. I've got to hit it if I'm going to stay in the big leagues.* I was representing a kid at Debra Cannon Wolfe High School who had been slapped by an ROTC colonel for chewing gum, and this time the result was a hands-down victory for me over Fred Gray. I got a $25,000 verdict. We called that "moon money" in those days, a far cry from today's verdicts.

∿

It was sometime in the late Eighties when I learned of a gross injustice being perpetrated on an employee of the Seaboard Coastline Railroad. I first heard of the situation from my sister-in-law, Marielle Munnerlyn, who told me that a man who was married to a cousin of Yvette's needed some legal help. Clayton Wellman was a train operator who had fallen to the ground because Seaboard had failed to remove the ice from a flight of fifteen metal stairs at its Nashville facility. He had already run up medical bills totaling about $14,000, and a top African-American psychiatrist had gone on record as saying that the fall had affected his mental stability.

Since cases of that nature could be filed in any county where a railroad has tracks, and there were plenty of railroad tracks running through the Tuskegee area, Macon County had become a favorite venue during those years. Lawyers had been flying in from all over the country to file FELA cases—Federal Liability Employee Act—and many such cases had been settled or won outright. Fred Gray, with his national reputation, had won more than his share. When Clayton Wellman hired me to represent him, meaning I would finally have a railroad case, Fred visited me to ask if he could get involved in Wellman's case against Seaboard. I told him that I appreciated the offer, but I really needed to find out for myself, once and for all, whether I was ready to litigate large civil cases; with his assistance, I wouldn't be able to find out exactly where I stood on the learning curve.

By then I had returned to the church, been "born again" after many years' absence, and I did a lot of praying over *Wellman v. Seaboard*. The railroad was well-represented by Walter Byers and Wanda Devereaux and a host of others from the Montgomery firm of Steiner, Crum. As a new Christian, I was in constant prayer while driving to a pretrial conference with the Seaboard lawyers and Judge Howard Bryan, Jr., just hoping that my case would be sustained through the system so I would at least have a chance to argue it. I was literally shaking in my boots when I arrived at the courthouse in LaFayette, Alabama.

When Walter Byers began to present his argument about how I had no case, I saw the image of Jesus occupying the empty chair beside me, as though I weren't there alone after all. I had also recently put a thousand dollars in the plate at my new church in Montgomery as a faith pledge, having learned that Jesus will give you a hundredfold return if you obey in your giving. That seemed to be the best thing I had going for me until suddenly, when Byers had finished his argument, Judge Bryan turned to him and said, "Jock's got a great case. He's got a good venue and a great client. You all need to go and settle this case." Before I knew it, we were settling for $325,000. The way I looked at it, we were reaping the harvest of that seed I had planted at Christian Life Church.

After *Wellman,* I felt I had a better handle on civil litigation but still knew that I had an awful lot to learn. Then came *Lucy Turner v. Southern Life and Health Insurance.* Lucy Turner was a poor black woman who held two insurance policies with Southern Life, one on her life and the other on the life of an aging aunt, and when the aunt died she phoned a man named Richard Perry, who had recently taken over the debit route for the insurance company. "I need to cash this policy so I can bury my aunt," she told Perry. He said, "I'll be over tomorrow, no problem." When Perry came by, though, he told Mrs. Turner that he would have to have all of her insurance papers so he could process the check. Little did she know that he intended to destroy the records and then claim that the policy had lapsed due to nonpayment of premiums.

Southern Life took that position and refused to pay off. But then Lucy Turner got lucky. She had been complaining about how she couldn't even bury her aunt, so one day Richard Perry went by her house to make a deal. Unknown to Perry, a man named Miller Efram, whom she was seeing at the time, happened to be seated in an adjoining room and heard the ensuing conversation. Perry said, "Mrs. Turner, I checked with the boss man and we can get you five hundred dollars a month for three months so we can fulfill our obligation of this fifteen-hundred-dollar policy. We're going to pay you in cash, too, but you can't tell anybody." When the agent left, Miller Efram stormed into the room and told Lucy, "Look, you've got to do something about this. Something isn't right here." She still didn't understand what had taken place, just felt it wasn't fair, so they went down to the State Department of Insurance in Montgomery and reported Southern Life and Health. Then they retained me as their attorney. When the general counsel for the insurance company rejected my settlement offer of $50,000, telling me they would pay $3,000 or $4,000, no more, we filed suit.

The case came to trial about a year later, in December of 1988, and on cross-examination the agent, Richard Perry, came off as confident to the point of pomposity. He felt there was no way we could prove our case against him or the company because (as he did *not* say) he had confiscated all of the payment booklets and policies. But I had instructed her to make a thorough search of her house, and in a desk drawer she discovered one portion of one payment book that she had failed to turn over to Perry. Although it was on her policy, not the one for her aunt, that scrap was enough to show that Perry had been over to her house on certain days, collecting premiums, while now he was claiming that he had not been coming around anymore because the policy had lapsed.

In the middle of the cross-examination, I produced the payment card and handed it to the court reporter, to be filed as an exhibit, and then showed it to Perry. He seemed shocked to see it. Before I could even ask him to explain, he jumped in. "Oh, I forgot," he said. "She did pay on the other policy, but she didn't pay on this one."

"Wait a minute, Mr. Perry," I said, "you're changing your story. Now you're saying you *were* at Mrs. Turner's house during those months."

"Yeah, I was there, but, see, she didn't have all the money."

At this point, Perry was looking very bad. As I continued to press him, he finally blurted out, "I'm not a racist. I did a favor for a black man one time."

"And what was that?"

"Well, I used to own a grocery store. I remember one time, I let a black man buy a six-pack of beer with food stamps."

"What kind? Bud, or Miller? That's about all we drink."

I didn't have to say another word. The jury was stunned, as was Perry's own attorney, and soon they fell out laughing. Perry mumbled something, but it couldn't be heard over the laughter. The man had made a fool of himself. The die was cast.

In my closing argument to the jury, I argued from John 10:10, that Jesus said Southern and Perry had come "as a thief in the night, to kill, steal and destroy," and that, furthermore, you [the jury] have been chosen to give my client "the abundant life." Miller Efram, the witness who had overheard Perry's self-incriminating "offer" to buy off Lucy Turner, had died before the trial, but fortunately we had taken a deposition from him before his death. For some reason, the famous story about Knute Rockne's "Gipper" speech to the Notre Dame football team came to mind—legend has it that George Gipp's last words from his deathbed were for Rockne to tell his teammates to "win one for the Gipper"—and I exhorted the jury to "win one for the Miller," because Miller Efram was looking down on the proceedings, expecting them to do the right thing. Still in a poetic mood, looking over at my client, Lucy Turner, I said, "You know what? I think you'll all agree with me when I say this. 'I love Lucy.'" The members of the jury broke out laughing. Then I looked at the bank of lawyers at the defense table arrayed against me and said, "I have brought my slingshot to court today, and I intend to slay Goliath." And, finally: "You don't need any more than thirty minutes to decide in favor of Lucy Turner. Besides, it's getting late in the evening and I need to get home so I can watch Dwight Gooden pitch for the New York Mets. We've got better things to do than to deliberate half a night over a case that's clearly an outright fraud." I asked the jury for five million dollars, not a penny less.

Five million dollars!? That was beyond moon money, to most of us, and to some it was downright ridiculous. But the jury was back in only twenty minutes to announce that that was exactly how much they had decided to award Lucy Turner. It was the largest verdict ever returned to an African-American attorney in the history of the state of Alabama. I remained at the counsel's table when I heard the decision, stunned, trying to let it settle in, my whole life flashing across my mind. I heard that school counselor telling my mother that I might turn out to be a good garbage man one day. I saw Tuskegee Institute and Notre Dame and my hard-working mother and all of the others who had helped me along the way. I looked toward the heavens and whispered, "How am I doing now, Daddy?" As I was leaving the courtroom, I felt that Jacob Abraham Smith and Jesus were applauding me from heaven for a job well done in representing the least of these.

I did slay Goliath that day. "Macon County Woman Receives $5M Verdict" read the banner headline in the little Tuskegee *News*, and I was the toast of the town for a while. That was gratifying, to say the least, and it certainly paved the way for me to pursue other major civil cases in the coming years. But I had made a grave miscalculation, as it turned out, one that is common to people who are relatively new to Christianity. I had assumed that it was I who had done this wonderful work for poor Lucy Turner; I, me, Jock Michael Smith, myself. What I did not yet understand was that Jesus, not Jock Smith, was the one responsible. I had to let go of the notion that God, not I, was Master of the Universe.

Born Again

EVEN THOUGH MY family's move when I was a child to
Nashville Boulevard in Queens put us smack into the all-
white environment we had sought, we nevertheless retained
our membership at Calvary Baptist Church several blocks away on
Merrick Boulevard in the neighborhood we had left. I suppose that's
because we simply felt more at home at Calvary, where most of our
best friends still lived. It was a traditional old-fashioned black church
known for its lively choir and the emotional preaching of the Rev.
Walter Pinn. Located as it was right around the corner from the
United Negro Democratic Club, where my father and such civil
rights leaders as Guy Brewer had begun to empower black voters in
Queens, Calvary was political as well.

My father had been heavily involved there, as a deacon and as the
church's lawyer, and I have only the fondest memories of attending
Calvary as a child: wearing my Sunday-best clothes, being moved by
Rev. Pinn's vivid sermons, watching the choir members as they strode
down the aisle, two-by-two, singing "Take It to the Lord in Prayer" to
close the service. It was an exciting time, an exciting place, where the
civil rights movement was just beginning to stir.

But then Daddy was killed, and with him went my passion for
church. Rev. Pinn was one of the men who tried to play surrogate
father, taking me to Ebbets Field and the Polo Grounds during that
summer of '57, much appreciated to this day, but after my father's

death I went to Calvary Baptist only a few times, as though afraid that going there would remind me of the daddy I had lost.

To the surprise of many, I soon began attending First Presbyterian in St. Albans, a mostly white church that was only a ten-minute walk from our house. Looking back, I suppose I was lured there by two of my best pals, Irvin Culpepper and Chuck Tolbert, who were in the Boy Scout troop and on the church baseball team. We three, in fact, were the only blacks on the mighty Saint Albans "Presbys" baseball team, who got as far as the Queens semifinals before getting clobbered by a team called Carter Community. That was the year when Chuck and I, two black kids, pretended to emulate the Yankees' white "M&M" Boys, Mickey Mantle and Roger Maris, by playing center and right, and wearing their numbers 7 and 9.

St. Albans Presbyterian was the first integrated church I had ever attended. I went so far as to attend Sunday school and take convocation and pass the written test required for membership, ultimately joining the church, as did Irvin and Chuck, but I must confess that we were regarded by some as "the unholy three." Our church attendance was sporadic, to say the least, Sundays often finding us playing baseball or stickball rather than sitting in the pews where we should have been. The truth is, the Presbyterians were laid-back and conservative—in a word, white—and I missed Rev. Pinn's stirring sermons and the soulful singing and everything else about Calvary Baptist. Had I stayed there, I don't believe I would have strayed so far away for so long.

ॐ

By the time I checked in to begin my studies at Tuskegee Institute, in that summer of '66, I had drifted far from organized religion. Neither my mother nor my sister had yet been truly saved, and my God-fearing grandmother was more than a thousand miles away in

New York City, leaving me all alone to form opinions for myself. School was all that mattered to me at that point—studying, partying, dating, finding a career path—and religion was something that seldom crossed my mind except in the most negative sense. It galled me that all students at Tuskegee were required to attend religious convocation, and I maintained minimum attendance, at best, simply to remain in school. Being a child of the Sixties, with my hair in an Afro and a dashiki on my back and my fist clenched in a Black Power salute, I had adopted the stance of a radical.

It seemed clear to me that both the military and the church were evil institutions of a white man's government, controlling spirits put in place to disenfranchise the African-American. I never quite came out and claimed that Christianity was led by a white Jesus, anymore than I became a Muslim, but I'm sure that in the recesses of my mind I felt that way. Otherwise, went my thinking, why is this Jesus allowing more black people than whites to be killed in Vietnam and in cities all across America? It was an easy step for me to campaign for the vice-presidency of the student body as a man who would see to the abolishment of ROTC and mandatory attendance at chapel meetings, both of which I accomplished while in office.

I was studying Dr. Martin Luther King, Jr., and his philosophy of nonviolent protest, of course, apparently without listening, for it was the other black leaders who were having the greater impact on my young mind: Frederick Douglass, W. E. B. Du Bois, and especially Malcolm X. Black Power! That seemed to be the answer. Instead of reading the Bible, or paying closer attention to the life of Dr. King and his Christian movement, I was immersed in the philosophies of the militant black leaders. In my mind, all preachers were the same, be they black or white: con artists who drove big Cadillacs, slept with every woman in the pews, robbed the collection plates, and ate all of the fried chicken their parishioners could put in front of them; all in the name of some Jesus fellow who did black people no favors.

∾

These negative feelings I had toward religion held fast during my various sojourns following graduation from Tuskegee—the three years at Notre Dame Law School, the fitful year in Binghamton, and upon my return to teach and then to set up a law practice in Tuskegee—but they began to wobble when I married Yvette in '79. Up until then I had felt that those who proclaimed Jesus were generally weak people without financial resources, folks who were leaning on a crutch to justify their existence, suckers for any con man who came along. That description certainly didn't apply to Yvette and her parents, all of whom had known Dr. King and his movement intimately; nor did it apply to my sister Paula, now born again and letting me know all about it on the occasions when she came in from California to help out while Yvette was coping with her illness. Together, they would jump in the car and run off to witness a Kenneth Copeland revival; my response was to drive to Atlanta for a Braves baseball game.

My mother had drifted away from the church, herself, and I remember looking forward to holiday visits to the old house on Nashville Boulevard in Queens because of the good times I could have with her and with my stepfather. Wade Nance had been one of the few black maitres d' at the famous Plaza Hotel in Midtown Manhattan for thirty-five or forty years, had even known my father from the days when Dad worked a side job at the old Forrest Hills Inn while a student at Brooklyn Law School, and he was great company. Both Wade and Mom smoked and drank during the late Seventies. When I would hit town, the three of us would sit around talking and drinking for a while, and then Wade and I would go out on the town. I remember he was a Dewar's scotch-and-soda man, a Parliaments smoker. We would go bar-hopping, just drinking and talking trash in the local taverns of New York City, staying out until five or six o'clock in the morning. Obviously, nobody had any plans to make church on Sunday mornings.

Then, on a visit in 1982, I found that everything had changed. As soon as I had entered the house and hugged Mom and Wade, I looked around and said, "Okay, where's the scotch? Where's the bourbon?" They looked at each other, as if to decide which would be the one to break the news. It was Wade who finally spoke up: "We don't do that anymore, Jock."

"No liquor? I can't believe it."

"We've given our lives to Jesus, son," Mom said.

I was flabbergasted. I couldn't believe that two people who had been such staunch drinkers would give up their habits for anybody. I was speechless. Then, when Sunday morning rolled around, there was a great bustle around the house. They were getting ready to go to church, of all things. A part of the tradition whenever I visited was that Wade and I would gear the whole day around watching the Giants or the Jets playing their National Football League game on television. On that particular Sunday, in fact, the Giants were to play the Philadelphia Eagles.

"But what about Big Blue [the Giants]?" I asked Wade.

"Son, that's why they made VCRs," he said, grinning and setting the VCR to record that day's game. And then they were off to church, leaving me at the house to watch the game alone. I wasn't yet converted to this Jesus, but I must say that these small evidences of faith and trust in a mysterious larger power were beginning to have an effect on me.

∾

The hits just kept on coming. About a year later, during a holiday trip Yvette and I had made to Las Vegas, that sprawling city of sin, I found myself standing in the middle of Caesar's Palace. I looked across the casino floor and, lo, there came the famous television evangelist Kenneth Copeland, one of Yvette's heroes, striding my way with his wife and a couple of aides. I thought, Ah-hanh, there you go. He's just like the rest of 'em. I couldn't resist.

"Mr. Copeland," I said, "I'm a lawyer in Alabama. Jock Smith. My wife is a devoted follower of yours, gives money to your ministry every year."

"I see," he said.

"She's upstairs, asleep. I've got to tell you, she'd have a fit if she knew you were down here right now. I've a mind to go get her. But, of course, you'd probably be gone before I could get back."

"Well, you know," he said with a smile, "the last I checked, you can't find a decent hotel in Las Vegas that doesn't have a casino. The fleas come with the dog, so to speak."

A likely story, I thought. But somehow I got drawn into a conversation with the man, indicating to me, after these many years of denial, that maybe I was willing to open my heart and to hear more. I virtually blurted out the fact that most of the people dear to me—my wife, my daughter, my sister, my mother, and her second husband— had heard the call of Christ. Ultimately, he asked me where I stood with Jesus. I told him I had no standing whatsoever; that Jesus was not in my life because I didn't want to give up the finer things like the vices that go along with hanging around casinos. He was patient with me. "You don't have to give up anything for God," he said, boring into me with his eyes as only Kenneth Copeland can do. "It's a voluntary decision that any man will make once he really understands who Jesus is."

"Well, I don't know about that," I said.

He introduced me to his wife, Gloria, and then startled me by saying, "You're coming one day. You've got too many people praying for you. Your mother's been saved and she's praying for you. Same for your wife, your step-dad, your sister. And I'm proclaiming here today that you're going to be one of the greatest soldiers of the Kingdom that's ever lived because what you believe in you'll fight for. You're coming, all right, Jock Smith. It's just a matter of time." And then, with the slot machines whirring all around him, Kenneth Copeland took his wife's hand and they walked right out of Caesar's Palace, off to do the Lord's work.

∾

The moment that was bound to come finally occurred during the Christmas holidays of 1985, when Yvette, Janay, and I went back home to Nashville Boulevard to be with Mom and Wade. By now, of course, I was resigned to a holiday without whiskey and saloons and football on television. But I rebelled when Mom announced the plan for New Year's Eve: we would attend the ceremony at her new church, Redeeming Love Christian Center in New York, pastored by Clint and Sara Utterbach, and then continue afterwards to someone's home for the New Year's Eve celebration. That meant everybody, she said, me included: "I don't care how old you are, Jock, as long as you're under my roof you'll do as I say."

The ride over to the church, which must have taken forty-five minutes, was a quiet one. I was seething, feeling like the little fatherless kid I once had been, not understanding why my mother wouldn't let me hang out with the boys and watch the big ball come down at Times Square. I couldn't understand how she could feel that this church service had any relevance to the strange and interesting behavior I wanted to share with my old pals, one that was so traditional for any New Yorker. I must admit that I enjoyed the service that night, what with the inimitable BeBe and CeCe Winans wailing in the spirit, but not enough to answer the ensuing altar call.

Soon we were walking into a New Year's Eve celebration like none I had ever experienced. It was being held at the home of one of the church's deacons. At least 150 people were swirling about the rooms, devouring chicken and barbecue ribs, washing it down with punch and lemonade and soda. What really got to me was that everyone seemed so jovial and happy, laughing and fellowshipping and thoroughly enjoying themselves, and yet nobody had a drop of alcohol in their glasses.

At some point, leaving Yvette and my mother and stepfather to their own devices, I drifted into a room that served as a library. There, on a shelf, I noticed a book that I knew held my name but that I had never read, much less purchased, because I couldn't afford it when it came out. It was a leather-bound copy of Who's Who in American Colleges and Universities, 1969-70. I pulled the book from the shelf, opened to my page, and there it was: "Jock Michael Smith, Tuskegee Institute, Alabama," extolling my achievements while in college.

As I was reading, reliving some of the moments from my years as an undergraduate at Tuskegee, I felt the presence of someone looking over my shoulder. "I'm Aaron Knight," he said, an assistant pastor at the church. He took the book from my hands, read my biography, then handed the book back to me. "I'm a friend of your parents," he said, "and I know how proud they are of you. You've accomplished so much for such a young man. I understand that you're a very outstanding attorney in Alabama. You're to be congratulated." This was nice to hear, and I thought that would be the end of our conversation. But Aaron wouldn't let it go at that.

"Tell me," he said, "where do you stand with Jesus?"

I was shocked that a stranger would ask such a personal question. I gave him the usual rhetoric, hoping that he would go away—I had no standing with Jesus, I said, because the preachers steal the money and sleep with the women and drive the Cadillacs—and he simply smiled patiently as I finished my spiel by saying, "They just aren't living right."

"I admit that some are like that, and it's wrong," he said. "But let me ask you this. Do you believe in the Bible?"

"Of course," I said, though a bit shakily.

"If I show you something in the Bible, will you believe it's true?"

"Sure."

He reached for a Bible and took it from the shelf. I was thinking What kind of crank is this? I'm big stuff back home, got a great wife, great practice, just won my first moon money. I'm no kid. "Here it is," he said. "Read this." He pointed to a passage of scripture saying that we should keep our eyes on Jesus, not keep our eyes on men.

"What do you think now?" he said.

"I was wrong. I thought we were supposed to keep our eyes on men."

"Well, then," Aaron said. "Are you ready to receive your salvation?"

"My salvation."

"Yes. Are you prepared to accept Jesus Christ as your Lord and Savior?"

"When?"

"Now."

I wanted to suggest that we wait a while, like sometime next week or next month, but I could see that he was going to be unrelenting. I had no good reason left by then not to accept Jesus as the Lord of my life because Aaron had just shown me an absolute truth in the Bible that refuted everything I had been believing for years.

That night, or more precisely in the early-morning hours of January 1, 1986, I got saved. I sat and repeated the sinner's prayer, with people standing all around me, my mother and my wife and my stepfather included, the house as quiet as a church. I hardly realized what had happened to me. I walked out into the night as a new man, a born-again Christian, feeling as though I were wearing new clothes. On the drive home, my wife and my mother began to exalt and told me how fortunate I was and how blessed they were to have been there at that very moment. They were so happy, they cried.

∾

Returning to Montgomery after the holidays, ready to go back to the old routine of driving every day to my office in Tuskegee, I didn't know what I would do with my new life as a born-again Christian. I wondered what you're supposed to do: run an ad in the newspaper to announce your salvation? knock on doors like a Jehovah's Witness to gather converts? rout the heathens from the bars? Yvette had her own Christian home, a local Catholic church, but I had none. I remembered a day many months earlier when my mother was visiting us and she and I were driving along what is known as the Bypass, a wide boulevard that routes traffic around Montgomery, and we passed a glassy modernistic building proclaiming itself as Christian Life Church. The marquee out front announced "Jerry Savelle Coming Sunday." I had no idea who this Savelle fellow was, but Mom practically jumped out of her car seat. "Son, son," she said, "that's a great man of God, one of the world's great evangelists. It's a sign. This is the church for you. This is where God will place you." Yeah, sure. Church was the last thing on my mind. I kept on driving until we reached the house.

Despite my mother's plea to promise I would start attending Christian Life Church when I got back home, I did nothing about it for the entire month of January following my salvation. Frankly, I was frightened and confused, totally without any sort of plan. But then, on the first Sunday of February, I fell into a late-afternoon depression that had become all too familiar. All of the televised sports events had

(continues on page 161)

Left, my maternal grandfather: Rev. T.A. Bowers of Lane Chapel C.M.E. Church in Topeka, Kansas.

Below, Wilson W. Smith, Jr., my paternal grandfather.

My father, Jacob Smith, as I remember him in his prime.

My glamorous mother, Bettelou Bowers Smith.

Left, Jacob Abraham Smith in his WWII uniform. Dad rose to the rank of captain with the famed Buffalo Soldiers. He was a medical corpsman.

Below, Daddy barbecuing for his law partner, Lisle Carter, and a guest.

My parents lived an exciting life in an exciting time. This snapshot is a glimpse of some of their good times, at Birdland in New York, October 1955. From left, Count Basie, Dad, Mom, and Dad's sister-in-law and brother, Ozie and Wilson Smith.

Queens, 1955, the day the Dodgers won the World Series. My father Jacob with his brothers Wilson and Gene, who came to celebrate.

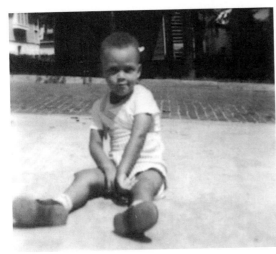

Left, summer in the city; I'm about two or three years old.

Below, kids from Queens, my sister Paula and me, when I was about six.

Above, Christmas was a big day at our house in Queens, and Daddy was the biggest kid of all. He took this snapshot of Paula and me with our mother just a few months before he was murdered. *Below,* Paula and me with our beloved Grandma Bowers.

At P.S. 15 in Queens, May 1959. That's me circled on the back row. I'm about eleven years old. Even in New York, the schools were segregated.

My high school graduation photo.

Above, a scholarship from the United Negro Democratic Club, presented by family friends Guy and Marie Brewer, helped me through Tuskegee University. *Left,* my grandmothers, Lula Smith and Rebecca Bowers, at my graduation from Notre Dame Law School.

As a member of the wedding party for my friend Chuck Tolbert.

As a striving young lawyer in Tuskegee in 1978, after I had left the Attorney General's office and set up in private practice.

Above, my life started over when I married Yvette in 1979.

Left, on our wedding day, with our daughter, Janay.

With my daughter, Janay, in front of my old law office in Tuskegee. The sign over the door says: The Jacob A. Smith, Esquire, Building. I was very proud of this tribute to my father.

Jury awards $1,875,000 to Midway man

According to Atty. Jock Smith, a Midway man has been awarded $1,875,000 by a Bullock County jury against Rental Village, Inc.

Atty. Smith, attorney for Willie Jordan, had sued Rental Village for $3,750,000—$3,000,000 in punitive damages and $750,000 in compensatory damages. After several hours of deliberation, the jury returned a verdict for about half that amount Wednesday afternoon.

According to testimony, Willie Jordan rented a washer/dryer from Rental Village in March, 1997. The contract was re-written in August, 1997. Jordan contended that he had an option to purchase the washer/dryer early if he so desired. He further claimed that he tried to exercise that option on several occasions but Rental Village would not honor that.

Rental Village contended there was no option for a cash buy-out, according to Smith.

Atty. Jock Smith argued the contract was full of contradictory language.

Rental Village was represented by Attorney Winston Sheehan of Montgomery. It is not known if the verdict will be appealed.

The case was heard in Circuit Judge Burt Smithart's court and the verdict was handed down late Wednesday afternoon.

Left to Right: Atty Jock Smith, Danielle Jordan and Mr. Willie Jordan

A newspaper article about one of my big cases.

Tuskegee is a historic place. It has Tuskegee Institute (now University), the Tuskegee VA Hospital, the airfield where the Tuskegee Airmen trained, and a lot of grand houses built by people who made money in the old plantation culture. One of those structures, known locally as "the old Allen house," was depicted on a postcard in 1906. I decided to buy the house and convert it into my new law office.

143

Above and *opposite*, the Allen house shown on the previous page, 306 North Main Street in Tuskegee, newly refurbished as my law offices, a monument to my father's memory.

The inside of the restored house. This is the first floor looking toward the front entrance.

Above, part of the "sports room" at my home in Montgomery. Over the years I've shared the collection with many visitors, including a few of the great athletes whose items I've collected. One such immortal was "The Killer," baseball great Harmon Killebrew, *below.* He's holding his 1969 MVP shirt from the Minnesota Twins; I'm holding one from his last year in baseball, 1975, with the Kansas City Royals.

My love of baseball—which was a way of keeping alive my memory of my father and the bond we shared through baseball in New York in the 1950s—led me to start collecting sports memorabilia. Today, I have a world-class collection, including what is now considered the world's largest collection of game-worn professional sports uniforms. Pictured *above*, in the "sports room" at our house in Montgomery, are a few of the prizes from my

collection of baseball and basketball uniforms. From left, bottom row, the full uniform of Tom Seaver, and the shirts of Ozzie Smith, Steve Sax, Luis Aparicio, Billy Williams, and, yes, Cool Papa Bell of the Homestead club in the old Negro Leagues. Top row, the basketball uniforms of Kareem Abdul-Jabbar, Julius Erving, Magic Johnson, and Earl Monroe. On the day that I first met Johnnie Cochran, I took him home and showed this to him. He couldn't believe it. *Left*, I get a kick out of showing people my own baseball card, from the week-long Mets fantasy camp Yvette treated me to in 1985.

Collecting sports stuff has enabled me to meet a lot of really outstanding athletes. *Above,* I'm with the great Joe Namath, holding his 1970 AFL All-Star jersey from my collection. His parting words to me were, "If I ever need a lawyer in Alabama, I'll know who to call." *Below,* the late incomparable Willie Stargell and I are holding different colors of his Pittsburgh Pirates game shirts from my collection.

Above, with "The Greatest," Muhammad Ali, when he came to Montgomery for a promotional event several years ago.

Opposite, top, I like to go into my sports room and touch the uniforms, as I'm doing with the training robe that Ali wore for the George Foreman fight in Zaire in 1974. Being close to these articles worn by sports heroes is an inspiration to me. Several years ago, I began sharing this inspiration with children through a special ministry, Scoring for Life. I go to schools and churches and take some of my collection and I talk to kids, telling them about overcoming adversity and working hard and becoming successful, just as all these great athletes did. *Opposite, bottom,* making the very first Scoring for Life! presentation, at Montgomery's Christian Life Church.

A few years ago, I met Y. A. Tittle at a sports memorabilia convention in Montgomery. He had been here as a college senior playing in the Blue-Gray Bowl many years ago. He asked me to drive him around and let him see how things had changed. We had a great time and I took him to my house, where he agreed to sign some of the items in my collection, including two Sports Illustrated covers of him. The one in his hands was the *second* issue of the magaazine.

Not all my heroes are sports figures. *Above,* with my shepherds, Pastors Steve and Denice Vickers of Christian Life Church of Montgomery. They have committed themselves to an integrated church. And *below,* with my surrogate parents, Sam and Willa Carpenter, also of Christian Life Church.

Local attorney Jock Smith joining sports agency with Johnnie Cochran

Johnnie L. Cochran Jr., the nationally recognized attorney who represented O.J. Simpson and Michael Jackson, has a talent for putting together a winning team and he has done it again.

Cochran along with C. Lamont Smith, a sports agent and attorney with 14 years of experience at the negotiation table for athletes such as Barry Sanders, prominent trial attorney Carl Douglas, seasoned sports and entertainment lawyers Barry Thomas and Donald Wilson, and one of Alabama's most successful negotiators and trial attorneys, Tuskegee's own Jock M. Smith, have announced the forming of

All-Pro Sports and Entertainment International.

The mission of the partnership is to provide the highest caliber of representation to athletes and entertainers in contract negotiations, marketing and promotional appearances. The company will also work in conjunction with prominent investment broker firms and financial planners to provide its clients with the best investment opportunities available.

It should be also specifically noted that All-Pro Sports and Entertainment International's president and co-founder C. Lamont Smith has

(See SMITH, P. 3)

Top and bottom, headlines in the *Tuskegee News* when I formed my sports agency partnership with Johnnie L. Cochran, Jr., and again a year later when we formed the national law practice. *Above,* with Johnnie at the opening of the Memphis office of the national firm in August 2001.

Local attorney Smith partner with Cochran in national firm

By GUY RHODES
Editor

A friendship that developed three years ago has evolved into a partnership for local attorney Jock Smith and Johnnie Cochran, perhaps the most prominent African-American lawyer in the country.

Smith and Cochran, who were already partners in a sports agency for professional athletes, are now partners in a national firm that has locations in New York City, Los Angeles, Columbus, Ga. and Dothan with another office to open soon in Atlanta and other sites.

While the sign hasn't been changed at his Tuskegee office in the old Allen home Smith restored several months ago, the Jock Smith office is now officially Cochran, Cherry, Givens and Smith.

The national firm had its incorporation papers filed in Macon County in July of 1998, a decision that was made because of the historical significance of Tuskegee and Macon County, according to Smith.

Smith, who serves as attorney for the Macon County Commission, first met Cochran during a book-signing tour by Cochran in Montgomery. That was after Cochran became a widely-known attorney for his role as a member of the "Dream Team" in the successful defense of hall of fame football player O.J. Simpson on two murder charges.

Cochran and Smith developed a friendship that led to the sports agency partnership and eventually partners in the national firm that will deal primarily with the practice of law in representation of injury victims in major tort cases. In fact,

154

The national law
firm senior
partners (l-r):
Keith Givens,
Johnnie Cochran,
Sam Cherry, Jock
Smith.

Jock Michael Smith,
Attorney at Law

Above, with my friend and law partner, Johnnie L. Cochran, Jr. *Right,* with some of the staff in Tuskegee: clockwise from top right, Tasha Scott, Tracy Adams, and Brenda Pinkard.

Ready to work on behalf of "the least of these."

With Brian Strength, attorney in our Tuskegee office.

An $80.8 Million Verdict

Jock Smith (above), an attorney in a firm headed by Johnnie Cochran, was the lead litigator in a lawsuit filed by Alabama resident Artie Mae Jeter against the Atlanta-based Orkin Exterminating Company. Smith alleges Orkin defrauded Jeter for two decades regarding severe termite damage to her home. "Jeter's legacy sends a message that large powerful corporations cannot prey on the poor, elderly, minorities or this country," Smith said. Orkin officials say they will appeal the verdict. (Photo By Philip McCollum)

An article from the *Atlanta World* about our winning a large verdict on behalf of Artie Mae Jeter, a poor woman who was defrauded by a big corporation.

THE *Atlanta* TRIBUNE

A magazine cover about our national law practice.

Jock, Yvette, and Janay.

been played. Yvette was gone to her church. Dark was falling on Montgomery. Ahead of me lay Monday, dreary Monday, the beginning of another week of what had become drudgery. I could sit there in the dark, nursing the blues and feeling sorry for myself, or I could go out and do something. Out of depression, or else from hearing my mother's voice, I found myself slipping on a suit and driving toward the church on the Bypass.

I was welcomed at the door by a man who said his name was Sam Carpenter. A sign inside the church announced "Jesus Is Lord," and that got me confused from the start. Being uninitiated, I thought God was the Lord. I took the last seat on the last row as a last resort and looked around. The pastor was white, and from the looks of it I had stumbled across a congregation that was thoroughly integrated in all respects: young and old, black and white, rich and poor. The one common denominator seemed to be that they were all, well, happy. There was no depression here, no sense that these were wretched souls grasping for some sign that life was worth living. I said to myself that these were either the greatest pretenders in the world or else they knew something I did not. Whatever it was, they had something that I surely needed. I might have material possessions and a good reputation in my line of work, but I wasn't at all happy in my spiritual life. Many of them, on the other hand, had little of this and yet they were living in victory. In short, something good happened to me on that night.

On the eighth day after that initial visit to Christian Life Church, before daybreak on a Monday morning, I had to attend a legal hearing in Mobile, Alabama. Over the years, my mother had been sending me inspirational tapes that by now must have totaled more than a hundred, none of which I had ever listened to, but as I was rushing out of the house I thought to go back to the armoire in our bedroom and pull out three of them: sermons, as it were, by Dr. Frederick K. C.

Price, entitled Faith I, Faith II, and Unforgiveness. It was going to be a long, monotonous drive, at least three hours on the interstate in our van. I played the first two tapes as I headed toward the Gulf Coast, thrilled by what I was hearing, and before I reached Mobile—at Atmore, in fact, where the state's death-row inmates were waiting to be electrocuted—I pulled onto the shoulder of the road and broke down in tears. I tended to my business in Mobile, then turned around for the drive back to Montgomery, this time playing the tape about Unforgiveness, the need to bury the past as preached by the Apostle Paul. Upon reaching home, I knew that I had heard the unadulterated truth and that I would never be the same again. My salvation was complete.

I became a member of Christian Life Church, where I've been ever since, and it didn't take long to discover who had made it one of the great churches in America: Stephen E. Vickers, "Pastor Steve," a white man who felt he had been called by God some years earlier to bring together an integrated church right there in the Cradle of the Confederacy. There had been many nay-sayers in the beginning and especially in the Eighties, when a building program collapsed because a bond company went under, causing church membership to shrink from 700 to 200. But Steve endured, turning down many opportunities over the years to jump to the Assemblies of God and other more established and lucrative denominational churches for the simple reason that he didn't believe that's what God had called for him to do. This was no easy matter, establishing an integrated church for the born-again in Montgomery, Alabama, few of them with the financial wherewithal to help smooth the way. He and his wife, Pastor Denice, had managed to pull it off out of sheer faith and an unconditional love for their congregation. When I mentioned my consternation over why anyone would even think about quitting Christian Life, as many did during the crisis over the failed building plan—"you've raised them in the Lord, given them victory, and now they're quitting over a building?"—he was firm. "You don't understand, Jock, because your daddy was a pioneer and he didn't raise a quitter. My daddy didn't raise a quitter, either. When people turn like that, we don't understand because we weren't raised that way. You and I aren't quitters."

Today, Christian Life Church is fruitful and vibrant, still fully integrated, boasting more than 2,000 members. With Pastors Steve and Denice leading the way, it is a place of love and strength, where the spirit is moving in the morning and in the evening. I have seen people sell out to the Lord. I have seen drug addicts brought in and healed. I have seen physical healings take place before my own eyes. I have seen prostitutes cleaned up. I have seen people who otherwise would never darken the doors of a church with their shadows welcomed and served the meal of Christ as though they were kings. A great many members of the church engage me as their lawyer whenever they have legal problems, be they black or white, just as it was with my father at Calvary Baptist in Queens. In fact, except for the fact that Calvary was all black, there are times when I am reminded of my childhood church when I am attending Christian Life; the fervor, the spirit, the brotherhood, they are all there.

Through my association with the good souls at Christian Life, I'm no longer confused by what I once might have called the "gobbledygook" of God's message. Once you have sat in the pews and listened to the message of Pastors Steve and Denice Vickers, and witnessed the wonders they have wrought, it becomes crystal clear what redemption is all about. It's right there on the first pages of the Bible, in Genesis, where we learn that God created the Garden of Eden so that man would live in peace and tranquility. But then Adam blew it and, because of his sins, we don't have it so good. Having fallen short of the glory of God, no thanks to Adam, we are all sinners who must be saved in order to cope with life. There is no good in man, only good in the Master, and thus we must be born again. Jesus is a healer, not a minister of death and disease. These insurance policies that refer to a hurricane or a fire or a tornado as an "act of God" are frauds. God doesn't act that way. He is a healer of such calamities, not a creator of them, and once I understand that I became, as Dr. Martin Luther King, Jr., said in another context, free at last. Free at last.

∾

There is no doubt that, once saved, I became a better man around the house and a better lawyer in the courtroom. In the old days, there had been a pattern to my Sundays that resembled the way Wade Nance and I used to carry on before his conversion: swigging beer, watching my beloved New York Giants or whoever on television, angrily snapping off the set if they lost, storming off to bed, dreading Monday. And in my lawyering I had also drifted away from the righteous course; had gotten so busy seeing how much money I could make for myself that I had forgotten "the least of these." I remember being deeply hurt when I called my mother with the great news that I had just won a $1.8 million judgment and all she said was, "That's good, son." It was only when I told her what the case was all about—a corporation had taken advantage of a couple over something as mundane as a faulty washer-and-dryer—that she got excited.

Yvette, of course, was always there to remind me that making money and advancing my career should be secondary to making decisions according to the oath I had taken as a lawyer: to be diligent and zealously represent my client, not myself. I remember a time in the early Eighties, not long after our marriage but years away from my salvation, when I was presented with a grand opportunity to make a pile of money. The case became known as *Estate of Willie Hayden, Jr., v. Parke-Davis Company, Tallassee Hospital, et al.*

Willie Hayden, Jr., was a beautiful teenaged boy, a model child and the pride and joy of his family, the only black player on his school baseball team. One day when bumps began breaking out all over his body, Willie's parents rushed him to the emergency room of the hospital in Tallassee, Alabama, where the doctor on call diagnosed hives or some other minor ailment. The boy had been having seizures, as well, so a week later his primary physician prescribed the drug Dilantin. The situation continued for the next couple of months: the bumps turning to sores, doctors continuing to insist that Willie had hives, more prescriptions for Dilantin, Willie's case worsening all the while. It got no better after stays for diagnosis in hospitals at Tallassee and Montgomery and, finally, the excellent children's facility in Birmingham. Once, in fact, when I went to see Willie for myself with an attorney named Howard Mandell—a medical malpractice expert I had engaged to assist with the case—we were ordered to wear white coats and gloves and masks, and we wee horrified to find that Willie looked as though he had leprosy.

Then Willie Hayden, Jr., died, and Howard and I went to work to find out why. As it turned out, the boy had contracted Steven Johnson Syndrome, a rare disease, a hypersensitive reaction to Dilantin, one that occurs only in African Americans. Now we had our case, so Howard Mandell and I brought a lawsuit for Willie's parents against the drug manufacturer Parke-Davis and all three of the physicians who had misdiagnosed their son's illness. But then the suit got hung up in the courts. Four or five years passed before it came to trial, and all during that time we were looking for a theory that we thought would stick. Then it hit me. A day came when I went before Judge Howard Bryan, Jr.

"We've got a theory, Judge," I told him. "Genocide."

"Genocide?"

"Failure to warn." I explained that the product manufacturer fails to warn African Americans that they can suffer from hypersensitivity to Dilantin, which can lead to Steven Johnson Syndrome, which always leads to death. "Genocide, Your Honor."

Judge Bryan turned and looked at the defense counsel. "Well, counsel, it looks like Jock's got himself a theory," he said. "He's sho' 'nuff got himself a theory, all right."

Visions of several million dollars danced in my head as I excitedly told Yvette the day's news; that Parke-Davis had caved in and was talking about settling with a significant offer.

"That's good to hear," she said.

"Well," I told her, "I'm not interested."

"Why not, for heaven's sake?"

"I want a trial, Yvette. I can win big-time, hands-down. I want to make the big bucks, get a lot of publicity, and show everybody how far I've come."

"Jock, Jock," she said, clucking and shaking her head at me, disappointment all over her face. "These people have lost their son. They're not interested in your career. They want justice now, not later."

"They'll get it in due time."

"Don't get greedy, Jock. God doesn't bless greed. Always put your client first."

❧

I went ahead and settled with Parke-Davis, as I would in several other similar situations, saving the Hayden family the considerable time and money and agony that would have come from dragging out a long and painful trial. The Hayden family couldn't get their boy back, in spite of the several million dollars we got for them on the failure-to-warn theory, but they did get some feeling of justice as a result of the settlement. I suppose I was the big winner in the case, if there was one. God was yet to enter my life, but until that happened I had Yvette to serve as my conscience.

12

The Sports Collector

WITH THREE OF major league baseball's sixteen teams located in New York City when I was growing up in Queens, there is no surprise that I would become a huge fan of the game. Baseball was everywhere during the Fifties—at Ebbets Field and the Polo Grounds and Yankee Stadium, on radio and television, in the playgrounds and in the streets—and if I wasn't being escorted to a game in person by my father and, after his death, by my uncles or even my pastor, I was either watching it on television or listening to my favorite broadcaster as I lay curled up in bed or else playing baseball or stickball until nightfall. My heroes were many, from the Dodgers' "boys of summer" to the lordly Yankees of DiMaggio and Mantle to the Giants' Bobby Thomson, and early on, like many kids all across America, I was into collecting baseball cards. It was a way of personalizing the players, like bringing them home so you could clasp them to your chest while you listened to their exploits being described over the air.

The cards were such an integral part of our lives that my two very best buddies and I concocted games around them. Irvin Culpepper and Chuck Tolbert and I created a league of our own, becoming "owners" of certain teams. It seems like I always had the Yankees, Irvin the Cincinnati Redlegs (with the Cold War going on, nobody dared call them the Reds), and poor Chuck the woeful Cubs. The games were complicated, as only three kids could make them, but suffice it to say that we laid out a diamond on a table using checkers to denote the three bases and home plate. Each of us had a "dugout," where we lined up real trading cards, representing our respective teams, and then the dice came out. Roll a two and you got a double; a three was a triple; four was a homer; five was a groundout; and so forth, down to twelve, which stood for hitting into a double play. We would keep statistics throughout an entire 154-game season, have a playoff, and follow up with a World Series of our own. We were just a bunch of pals in love with baseball, whiling away rainy days and off-seasons as best we could, waiting for the real thing to resume.

Needless to say, having to keep our teams intact as the seasons wore on, each of us amassed quite a collection of baseball cards during our childhoods. The cards were in our blood and stayed that way even into adulthood. I have no idea how many cards I had in my collection at its peak—several hundred, for sure, stuffed in cardboard boxes stowed beneath my bed—but if I were to find out, knowing what I now know after practically a lifetime of collecting sports memorabilia, I would break down and cry. One summer in the late Sixties, returning home from Tuskegee, I found that my dear grandmother, in a determined fit of housecleaning, had thrown out all of my baseball cards. I was destroyed. I had just qualified to wear one of those T-shirts that later became popular among sports collectors: "I was a millionaire until my mother threw away all of my baseball cards."

∽

I had never thought of those cards as investments, only as a reminder of my childhood days, and many was the time that my new bride, Yvette, heard me moaning about my loss and how much those cards had meant to me. One day in 1982, when we had been married for three years, she came home bursting with excitement. "Jock, you won't believe it," she said, "but there's a baseball card shop right here in Montgomery." I jumped into the car and Yvette drove us to the store in the Normandale Shopping Center, where I met the owner, an interesting gentleman named Thomas Tankersley, and before I knew it I was paying $45 for a card right out of my boyhood: a mint-condition Topps Mickey Mantle from 1957, the year of my father's death. Soon, Tankersley was introducing me to a pair of local white customers who were earnest collectors, Darryl O'Mary and Chuck Smith, and I was hooked. I've been collecting sports memorabilia ever since.

Ultimately, I went on to collect just about every baseball card from my childhood and had them preserved in these neat little plastic cases by card number and date. I was as proud of my collection as I could be, eager to show it to my house guests, but I seemed to be the only person excited about the cards. I was crushed. Surely, I figured, it's because Montgomery, Alabama, is a long way from the major leagues. I knew that, after all, people in Alabama save their passions for Alabama and Auburn football, not baseball. They knew nothing of the history behind those cards, of the memories they stirred in the heart of one who had been a kid in New York during baseball's golden years.

One day I was flipping through *Baseball Hobby News*, a collectors' magazine, when I came across an advertisement for uniforms. I called the gentleman whose name was listed, Ken Slater, at a place called California Numismatics, in Redondo Beach, California. We talked for a while about the fascinating underworld of collecting authentic game-worn baseball uniforms and the like; and, lo and behold, I found myself agreeing to pay $1,600 for a 1972 New York Mets Willie Mays in home white. When it arrived in the mail, I couldn't believe it; I was holding in my hands a piece of the history of baseball: a No. 24 jersey actually worn in a game by Willie Mays, whom I had seen with my dad at the Polo Grounds years before Willie's declining years as a Met at Shea Stadium. It was a thrill just to touch it, to close my eyes and imagine seeing the "Say-Hey Kid" stroll to the plate.

After that, I put together a list of the uniforms I wanted to collect: all of the baseball heroes that my dad and I had seen together, father and son, in those glorious days: the Dodgers' Jackie Robinson, Roy Campanella, Duke Snider, and Pee Wee Reese; the Yankees' Mickey Mantle and Roger Maris and Elston Howard (the first black Bronx Bomber). As soon as I finished one list, I would start on another. I had my heart set on collecting uniforms worn by the members of the 500 Homerun Club (which I accomplished just a year ago), the 3,000-hit men, the 300-game winners, and the Hall-of-Famers. Looking for the more distinct pieces, I finally got hold of a 1929 Philadelphia Athletics Jimmy Foxx jacket, the one with the white elephant logo. On and on it went. I was visiting baseball card shows in Atlanta and other neighboring cities on a regular basis, learning about the business, getting to know all of the dealers, driving and buying, about to fill our little house to overflowing with authentic sports memorabilia. I was putting together my own hall of fame.

One thing that jumped out at me from the very beginning of my uniform-collecting career in the early Eighties was that all of the dealers were white, whereas at least half of the uniforms they were selling were of African-American players, which is to say the greats of the game. Much the same had happened in the musical careers of many great black performers in the fields of jazz, soul, rock, and rhythm-and-blues, and I found that tragically interesting. Here was another predominantly white corporate industry where whites were making huge sums of money from selling the memorabilia of African Americans who had left the scene and, for the most part, had no money at all for themselves. It seemed, at once, both paradoxical but as American as apple pie. I hasten to point out, however, that most of these individual dealers were kind and honest gentlemen who loved the purity of the game, had private collections of their own to prove it, and used their earnings from sales not only to pay bills but also to buy pieces they had coveted since childhood.

From the very beginning, my goal was to collect sports memorabilia that had great personal meaning to me. For example, I remember making my first trip to a national sports collectors' convention, at Arlington, Texas, in 1986. There, I met the great Ken Slater of California, from whom I had bought many of my early pieces. I went up to Ken's room one day and he laid out two famous uniform shirts for me, saying I could take my pick; I could buy one of them, and he would sell the other to someone else. On one bed he placed a Ty Cobb, The Georgia Peach, arguably the greatest who ever played the game, whose career batting average was an astonishing .367. On the other bed he laid out a Jackie Robinson, home white, Brooklyn Dodgers 1956.

"What'll it be?" Slater asked.

"Jackie," I said.

"What?" He was shocked. "Robinson over Cobb?"

"You don't understand. You're not African-American. Jackie Robinson was the greatest player in terms of what he did for baseball *and* America." I bought Jackie's home white number 42 jersey that day, and it remains one of my proudest possessions. I was a pretty good prognosticator, I suppose, because on the golden anniversary of Robinson's breaking of the color line, in 1997, Major League Baseball ordained that the number 42 be retired so that no player would ever be allowed to wear it again. Consequently, the value of that jersey has risen out of sight in the fifteen years I have owned it. It is not for sale, at any price.

∾

As is true with many endeavors, getting there has been at least half the fun. The journey from deciding exactly which item I wanted to pursue to the actual procurement of it has put me square in the company, face to face, of a number of sports figures I have greatly admired over the years. That happens when the word spreads among the athletes that you're a serious collector, someone who not only is laying out good money for memorabilia but knows the game as well, and so you become a good bit more than a casual fan.

Joe Namath had always held a special place in my heart for a number of reasons, not the least of them being that he had quarterbacked the New York Jets. He may not have been the greatest quarterback the National Football League had ever seen, but "Broadway Joe" brought flash and style to the table, especially when he backed up his boast that the Jets would upset the Baltimore Colts in the 1969 Super Bowl, forcing the merger of the NFL and the fledgling American Football League. I had a pile of Namath items—footballs, helmets, cards, game-worn jerseys, statues, figurines, *Sports Illustrated* covers, you name it—and when I heard he was signing at the Castlegate Hotel in Atlanta I requested a private session with him. His eyes widened when he saw me dragging my collection into the room. We shook hands, chatted for a moment, and he bent over the table and began signing. He was a good-looking man, congenial and kind, and when he heard I was a lawyer he looked up and said, "I tell you one thing, Jock, if I ever get into trouble in Alabama I'll know who to call. Anybody who's got this much stuff of mine has got to be one hell of a lawyer."

Y. A. Tittle was another legendary New York quarterback from the Sixties, he with Big Blue, my Giants, and I was able to get even closer to him when a promoter named Steve Hart brought him to Montgomery. Tittle had learned about my sports collection, and after the public signing he agreed to go by my house to see it and to sign my

Tittle artifacts, bringing along a reporter from *Giants Magazine* who was interviewing "The Bald Eagle." Seeing that I was a civil lawyer and he was in the insurance business, he stayed on my case about the need for tort reform, and when he took a look at the big new house we had moved into he said, "See there? Every one of you characters that argue against tort reform lives in a mansion." He stayed, signed, posed for snapshots, and when I dropped him off at his hotel I thought that would be the last of it. But at 9:15 the next morning, a Sunday, just as I was dressing for church, he called; his wife was traveling with him and he wondered if I would drive them around Montgomery to show her two places from early in his career: Cramton Bowl, site of the Blue-Gray Game where he had played as a graduating senior out of Louisiana State University, and the Whitley Hotel, where the players had been housed. "I know this is an imposition, Jock," Monique Tittle said as we rode around in my white Lexus, she in the back seat, he at my side. "But you don't understand," I told her. "How can it be an inconvenience when one of your all-time heroes is riding shotgun in your car?" I still don't favor tort reform, but I'll never forget squiring Y. A. Tittle around my adopted hometown.

Sometimes you just get plain lucky, running into an admired athlete when there's no business on the table. I had driven over to Atlanta one day in the middle of the 1985 season so I could watch my Mets play the Braves, checking into the hotel where I knew the Mets stayed, but when the game was rained out I headed for the bar of the Hilton. Sitting at a barstool, all alone, was none other than Dwight "Doc" Gooden, the Mets' superstar pitcher. You never know what you're going to get when you run into a superstar in an unguarded moment, but we hit it off famously: Doc asking me about the law business, I talking enough baseball to let him know I understand the game. At one point I felt I had to ask him a question: "A couple of weeks ago, against the Cardinals at Busch Stadium, you had Jack

Clark set up. Two men on, a three-two pitch, you threw him a fast ball and he hit it out, game over." He said, "How can I forget?" I said, "The way you had him set up, you should have thrown him the curve ball." He didn't get mad at me, just said, "You're absolutely right. Gary Carter called for a curve, but I shook him off. Can you imagine? Shaking off a veteran catcher like that? If I'd thrown the hook, I would've gotten him. Boy, you know the game, don't you?" I said, "Doc, I know the game and I know you." Another of my New York heroes just grinned.

A few years later I had an encounter of a different nature with Muhammad Ali, arguably the greatest fighter who ever lived. A story in the newspapers had announced that he was going to be at a mall in Montgomery to promote the release of Muhammad Ali Cologne. He would greet his fans, sign autographs, and presumably sell a few bottles of men's cologne. I grabbed my copy of his book, *The Greatest*, and rushed down to Eastdale Mall to see how close I might be able to get to him. I was astonished by what I saw when I got there. The mall was swarming with people of all ilk—kids and adults, rich and poor, evenly divided racially—pushing and shoving, holding all manner of items to be signed, impatient for the man to appear. I had never seen that many people in one place in Montgomery since I had moved there. Then I began hearing a chant—*Ah-lee! Ah-lee! Ah-lee!*—signaling that the champ had arrived. He was in the early stages of Parkinson's Disease, his hands shaky and his voice nearly a whisper, but when I glimpsed him through the crowd I saw the same man we will always remember: kissing babies, shaking hands, hugging women, grinning, signing anything put in front of him. I got my book autographed and had a few words with him, but the thing I will remember the most is that chilling chant that followed him as he left: *Ah-lee! Ah-lee! Ah-lee!* In a way, it prepared me for the day I would go into business with Johnnie Cochran, whose appearances before crowds of African Americans took on the feel of the coming of Elvis.

∾

Now and then a casual meeting with a superstar at a card show might turn into an enduring friendship, which is what happened when I met Willie Stargell in Montgomery during the mid-Nineties. "Pops," as he was known when he led the "We-Are-Family" Pirates to victory in the '79 World Series, was in the Hall of Fame and was a minor-league scout for the Atlanta Braves when we met. He signed some cards and uniforms for me, we got to talking, and when he was left with some time on his hands, he proposed that we get something to eat: "Take me to some place on the black side of town. I need some soul food." We went to Dem Bones, a black barbecue joint owned by a group of doctors, and after we had ordered he spotted a beautiful black woman in the room. "Introduce me," he said, and soon we were joined by Kim Davis, a former news anchor for a local television station and a sister of my banker and friend, Robert Davis, president of the Alabama Exchange Bank.

During the meal, having been informed that Willie had been a baseball player, Kim asked, in all innocence, "Were you any good?"

Willie looked at her, hard. "Good?" he said. "Let me put it this way. I used a model K44 bat. I swung it like a war club. When I finished playing, I had hit four hundred and seventy-five homeruns with that bat and I was inducted into the Hall of Fame in my first year of eligibility. I trust that answers your question, madam."

"It sure does, *Mister* Stargell. It sure does."

Willie was single at the time, so he and Kim kept in touch while I tried to monitor the situation from a discreet distance. Whenever he called me, the first thing he always asked was, "How's our friend?" The romance never led to anything serious—Willie wound up marrying a lady from his hometown of Wilmington, North Carolina—

and I even managed to capitalize on that, many years later, the last time I saw him. He had sent me an invitation to that wedding, which I saved, like any collector worth his salt would do. I knew this would be a one-of-a-kind artifact, so I asked if he would sign it. "I would do this only for you, Jock," he said, and he signed it. *Wilbur Donnell Stargell.* That was almost as big a thrill for me as the memorable line he had delivered that day to Kim Davis: "I trust that answers your question, madam."

We maintained contact over the years, and I especially recall a day when both of us were in Atlanta for a show. Willie was wearing a big straw hat and dark shades that day as we were having lunch at a downtown hotel restaurant. (When a waitress asked if he was Willie Stargell, he told her, matter-of-factly, "The last time I checked.") I had brought along a bat I had purchased some years earlier, a Roberto Clemente model that I wanted to have checked for its authenticity, and I asked Willie what he thought. "Let's go up to your room and check it out," he said. He lay on the bed, got comfortable, then said, "Okay, pass me the bat." Eyes closed, feeling the grain and the weight and the balance, he waggled the bat, his mind light-years away. "Yep, that's the Great One's bat," he said, passing it back to me. "People don't understand, but Clemente was like a mentor to me. An idol. I'd check out his bats every chance I got when we were teammates, just to see what kind of magic was in 'em. That's his, all right."

I got more than I had bargained for that day. We rode out to the house he was renting in Atlanta, chatting for a while about the scouting and polishing of young ballplayers, Willie telling me war stories about such prospects as Ronnie Gant and David Justice as they had risen through the farm system, and then he allowed me to listen while he phoned in his latest progress report on the Braves' Double-A team at Greenville, South Carolina. Finally, he began laying goodies on me as though he was Santa Claus and this was Christmas:

an autographed LeRoy Neiman painting of himself, a limited-edition black bat that he signed in gold ink, his Hall of Fame license plate (888, his uniform number and the year he was inducted), and a lot of other stuff including a signed Willie Stargell Hall of Fame cap. "I want you to have these, Jock," he told me. "You've become a dear friend."

The last time I saw Willie was at the National Sports Collector Convention in Atlanta three years ago. He had been busy as ever, signing autographs, and when he was done he took me backstage, as it were, to the area where private signings were being conducted for certain big collectors. Among those in the room were Wilt Chamberlain, Magic Johnson, and Lenny Dawson. Soon a friendly debate broke out about which pitch you can hit farther: a curve or a fastball. Wilt said it had to be a fastball, what with the extra power the pitch itself would provide. Willie said he was out of his mind: "It's the hanging curve. The action on the ball stops by the time it gets to the plate. It's just sitting out there, saying, 'Hit me!'" Ron Reed, a former Braves pitcher, jumped in and settled the argument. "Believe me," he said, "I've tried 'em both. No matter what I threw, Pops hit it a mile."

The weirdest and most entertaining run-in with a notable sports personality took place on a plane, headed from Atlanta to Las Vegas, in April of 1994. I was buckling into my seat, looking forward to the world's heavyweight championship fight between Evander Holyfield and Michael Moorer, when a stewardess came over and advised me that a "Mister King" would be sitting next to me in first class. I thought nothing of it until I saw this black man strut into the cabin, his salt-and-pepper hair sticking out as though he had stuck his finger in an electrical socket, and knew that it was Don King, the flamboyant boxing promoter. Before we'd had a chance to introduce ourselves, he had flipped down his tray and begun shuffling cancelled checks—two million dollars here, three million there—as though they were playing cards.

We were barely off the ground when the stewardess came around and said, "Mister King, what'll you be having for breakfast?"

"Nothing," he said.

"But Mister King, you've got to eat *something*."

He glowered at her. "Ma'am," he said, "I'm going to be staying in the biggest suite they've got at Caesar's Palace, a place where I can have anything I want. And you're trying to interest me in *airplane* food?" End of conversation.

As the flight continued across America, we got to know each other a bit. He'd learned that I was a lawyer from Alabama, and I think I won him over when I talked about the case in which Mike Tyson, the heavyweight, had done time for raping a Black Miss America contestant. "If you'd hired me," I said, "the verdict would have been Not Guilty." He said, "I like your confidence, Jock Smith. One thing's for sure, you couldn't have done worse than that dumb sonofabitch I *did* hire."

We began swapping stories like bosom buddies. At some point, he said he fancied himself as something of a scholar of black history. "I will now chronicle for you every major event that has taken place in African-American history from the year 1619 to the present." I said, "Have at it, Mister King," and he confidently launched into a florid twenty-minute rendition of the key events in black history.

"Well, how'd I do?" he said when he had finished.

"All right," I said.

"What do you mean, 'all right'?"

"You left out a couple of things."

"Nobody's ever told me I left *anything* out." He was outraged. "What?"

"For starters," I said, "how about the Dred Scott Decision in

1857, where Dred Scott escaped a slave state and wound up in a free state, the issue being whether that legally made him a free man. Chief Justice Roger Taney, writing the majority opinion for the Supreme Court, ruled that Scott was still a slave since blacks had no rights that whites were bound to respect. And then you had the Hayes-Tilden Compromise of 1877, effectively ending the era of Reconstruction, when our nineteenth President, Rutherford B. Hayes, sold us out to the House of Representatives in order to get the one more vote that would get him elected."

Maybe nobody had ever corrected Don King like this. He stared back at me and said, "You're one smart-ass nigger, aren't you?"

∿

During the twenty years since I began my collecting, with the purchase of that 1957 Mickey Mantle card from the shop in Montgomery, prices have fluctuated wildly in the sports collectors' business. Weak economic times would soften the market, making it possible to pick up valuable artifacts at ridiculously low prices, and the opposite would be true when the economy picked up. There has been a strong resurgence in the last four or five years, with the disappearance of what I can only call carpetbaggers: people and companies who saw an opportunity to make huge sums of money by controlling the marketplace. They were into collecting not for the love of the game, the sheer joy of holding a Joe DiMaggio jersey in their hands, but for their love of the almighty dollar. They would buy low, fraudulently inflate prices, then sell high, often to auction houses, before disappearing.

Being a Certified Public Accountant and understanding numbers much better than I, Yvette predicted that the bottom would fall out for these carpetbaggers, and she was right. When prices were at an all-time low in the early Nineties, I was able to pick up many quality uniforms and other pieces at extremely low cost. This was particularly true of African-American artifacts, and I was able to capitalize on the fact that the market for memorabilia was controlled almost exclusively by white dealers. The prices for items once worn by white players were significantly higher than those of black players, whether superstars or not. The dealers assumed that this was the natural order of things, that there was a larger market for white memorabilia than black. I, on the other hand, knew better: not only were these my childhood heroes, but I was sure that over the passage of time the disparity would even out. In a way, I represented an almost solitary core demand for black players' memorabilia, and I was able to negotiate many pieces for a song compared to what they are really worth. I'm sure they could see me coming and see a win-win situation for themselves—*This black guy really wants this thing, and I'm gonna have a heck of a time getting rid of it, so why not unload it for whatever I can get?*—but the joke was on them.

Consequently, after two decades of buying and trading, it's quite possible that I have assembled the greatest collection of game-worn uniforms in the world. This unofficial authentication comes from some of the greats in the business, all of them white men. As I get it, the title once belonged to Barry Halper, a part-owner of the New York Yankees who owned more than a thousand baseball uniforms until he sold them to a famous auction house for a herculean sum of nearly forty *million* dollars. No less authorities than Andy Imperado and Ritchie Russek of Gray Flannel, the most famous uniform authenticators in the world, have said that my collection is tops, and I get the same reading from two other great collectors, Lou Lampson and Nick Capollo, the leaders in game-worn football and basketball equipment, respectively. When Lou came by the house last year to have a look at my collection, he said, "Sir, with regard to baseball, you are the king and I salute you."

The stuff, if I may call it that, is all over the place. One of the main reasons we bought the big old house where we now live in Montgomery was what Yvette and I call the Sports Room: a sort of mini-warehouse where I store the uniforms and other artifacts that I don't keep in the building housing my offices in Tuskegee. (I must say that I envy my friend Duke Hott, of Atlanta, an avid collector of anything Baltimore Colts, whose uniforms and other collectibles consume his entire house. I sort of admire a married man who can get away with that, if you know what I mean. And Barry Halper, before he sold off his collection to an auction house, had organized his jerseys alphabetically on one of those thingamajigs you see at dry-cleaning establishments, so if he wanted to show off a DiMaggio jersey, he pushed the "D" button and there it came.) Although my stuff is mostly baseball, especially that of African-American heroes and the New York teams, I branch out into the other major sports. Being a huge Muhammad Ali fan, I have many items of his that I'm particularly proud of: three robes, fight-worn trunks, shoes with red tassels, and so forth.

It's good to know that my collection has reached such value, might even have reached world-class status, but there's more to it than that. The collecting began as a way of reconnecting with the memories I shared with my father as a child and blossomed along similar lines: all of the New York teams, all of the great African-American sports legends, just about any athlete through whom I might have lived vicariously. It is Fandom Writ Large. Fandom on a large, personal scale. The problem became, as the immense collection threatened to drive us out of the house, what I might do with it rather than sit around fondling famous jerseys and losing myself in my fond memories. What had I actually learned from those thousands of hours as a sports fan? Was sports really a metaphor for life? Could this lead to something that might help others? I began to ponder how I might put the collection to a positive use, one that could help kids in a way that attending games with my father had helped me when I was a boy trying to fathom the mysteries of life.

13

'Scoring for Life!'

T HAT HOME WHERE we still live in Montgomery has been jokingly referred to as "more of a museum than a house," due to my collection of sports memorabilia, but it represents a great deal more than that to us. By moving into the huge old house on Lansdowne Drive, in the spring of 1990, Yvette and Janay and I continued the pioneering that had occurred during my childhood when my family moved into a formerly all-white neighborhood in Springfield Gardens, Queens, New York, some thirty-five years earlier. We had integrated a neighborhood right there in the Cradle of the Confederacy, in the same city where Yvette, as a child in a family with close ties to Martin Luther King, Jr., had participated in the bus boycott during the Fifties and the civil rights marches of the Sixties.

The fact is, by the late Eighties we simply needed more space. With my law practice expanding and Yvette having left the Public Service Commission to go into business for herself as a financial expert witness and litigation consultant, we certainly could afford a move into larger digs. For help in finding the right place, Yvette contacted Randy Allen, a white woman who had been her secretary and a great friend at the PSC and now was in business as a Realtor.

We looked at real estate all over Montgomery, finally setting our hearts on a house with fifteen acres in a nice community, but we were heartbroken when we saw a previous contract go through on that one. We were in the doldrums, wondering what to do next, when we remembered a house that Randy had shown us some time earlier. It was owned by a powerful white businessman named Bobby Lowder, a multimillionaire from his dealings in banking and real estate, and had sat vacant for a year and a half. Although the house was in one of the grand old lily-white neighborhoods in Montgomery, a really good address, it was dark and dingy on the day we first saw it, needing an estimated $50,000 in repairs due to water damage and general neglect. Lowder was asking $400,000 and, we heard, had just turned down an offer of $325,000 in cash.

About two weeks after the house on fifteen acres had been sold out from under us, Yvette was still pining for it. "I'm really disappointed we didn't get that place," she said late one Sunday evening.

"Why don't we make an offer on the Lowder home?"

"We can't afford it, Jock. We don't have that kind of money."

"But baby, we're not going to offer what he's asking. We'll offer two-twenty-five."

"You've got to be kidding. We'll be laughed out of Montgomery as 'ignorant Negroes.'"

"You're probably right, but I think I've heard from the Lord on this one."

We phoned Randy Allen that moment, at eleven o'clock, and she was at our house within half an hour. Randy seemed shocked when we told her how much we intended to offer Lowder, but out of deference to her friend Yvette she said nothing; just had us sign the contract. As she was leaving the house that night, Randy said she would tender the offer to Lowder's agent first thing in the morning. She would get back to us.

The entire next day passed without a word of any kind. I was at my office in Tuskegee, taking care of business. Finally, at four-thirty in the afternoon, my secretary buzzed me and said Randy Allen was on hold. I looked at that blinking light and thought *It's you and me, God.*

I stand on my faith. I stand on your promise. I picked up and heard Randy, beside herself, saying we had just bought ourselves a house: "I can't believe it. I need to go to church wherever you're going."

Randy filled me in on the day's events. She had dropped off the contract at Lowder Realty, as promised, at nine o'clock that morning. Bobby Lowder, who usually makes quick judgments on deal of this nature, paced the floor for a couple of hours before saying to his agent, "I don't know why I'm doing this, but give me that paper." He crossed out our figure of $225,000, wrote in $238,000, and said "not a dime less" before walking out the door. The agent had told Randy that he couldn't believe it, either; that everyone in the office was shocked to hear that Lowder had sold the house for such a deal to a *black* family; that they would have bought it for themselves if they had known they could get such a price. I would later find out that Lowder had made some discreet calls—most notably to a Jewish lawyer friend of mine, Eddie Raymond, who lived in the same community—and had heard enough about Yvette and me to decide that the time had come to integrate Lansdowne Drive and we were the right people to do it. I felt a little like Jackie Robinson, who had been selected by Branch Rickey as the man to break the color line in major league baseball.

After making the necessary repairs, we moved into the house in March of 1990. Given our separate histories, it's ironic that Yvette felt no qualms whatsoever about integrating the neighborhood while I was full of trepidations. She certainly knew what racial hatred was all about, having seen cross-burnings as a child of the South, but she had managed to put that behind her. I, on the other hand, the one who had experienced no such difficulties up East, worried that perhaps we were making a mistake to move into a neighborhood where we might not be wanted. My concerns were allayed right off the bat. A day or so after we had settled in, the doorbell rang and we saw that Bobby Lowder's sister-in-law and some of the other neighbors had brought cakes to welcome us to the neighborhood. And a few days later, as I was about to get into my car for the drive to Tuskegee, I heard a voice say, "It's about time." I looked up and saw an old white fellow, out for his morning stroll. "It's long overdue, long overdue." Before I could return his greeting, he said, "Carry on. Carry on." And then he was on his way.

∾

But then a sort of curtain fell, effectively isolating us from the rest of the world. We were there, the only black family on the block, but we weren't. When somebody asked how it felt to integrate a community, I said it "allows me an awful lot of peace and quiet. Black folks are afraid to come visit, and white folks aren't interested. I can watch all of my ball games without anybody ringing the doorbell." I hadn't exactly expected a daily outpouring of hospitality when we moved in, any more than I feared seeing a cross burning on the front lawn, but I certainly hadn't counted on utter silence. The only semblance of life I had, outside the walls of the house on Lansdowne Drive, was my law practice an hour away in Tuskegee.

This wasn't lost on Clark Arrington, my old buddy from the days at Notre Dame Law School. "What are you *doing*, Jock?" he asked me one day when he had come by the house to see my sports collection. He reminded me of how I had founded the Black American Law School Association at Notre Dame, was doing very well as a lawyer, had integrated an elite white Southern community, had assembled this prime collection of sports memorabilia, but had wound up behind locked doors. It was just me, my family, my uniforms, and my satellite dish. "Why don't you do something with this stuff," he said, "instead of just sitting around, looking at it?"

It was Clark, I'm sure, who made the phone call that brought Rose Sanders into my life. A well-known African-American attorney in

Alabama, Rose was the founder of Twenty-First Century Youth, a group of gifted black children from around the nation that she had brought together to take in cultural experiences and develop racial pride in order to help ease their way into adulthood. She called me one day in the mid-Nineties, not long after Clark's visit, to ask if I would consider speaking to her group in Tuskegee. Of course, I said— anything to get out of the house and help somebody—and I tossed some of the uniforms in the car as I headed for Tuskegee. I spoke to a bunch of kids that evening, using the uniforms as stage props while I talked about the lives of Doc Gooden and other sports legends as they apply to "the real world," and to my surprise I got a standing ovation. "You have a gift, Jock," Rose told me afterwards, "and you ought to be doing this on a regular basis."

When I got home that night, pumped up and pleased with myself about how things had gone, Yvette insisted that I re-create what I had done. I did the best I could for her, showing how I had talked about how baseball is a metaphor for life, tossing in sports stories as I showed off the uniforms. When I had finished my little private demonstration, I saw that Yvette had begun to tear up. "Rose is right," she said. "You've found a ministry. You've got something special. This is something you need to be doing." Things took off after that. Before I knew it, Yvette and Janay had come up with the idea of a nonprofit company that would incorporate the use of my sports collection with lessons on life. They even settled on an apt name for the endeavor— Scoring for Life!—that seemed to say it all. As Jim Brown honed his skills as a great running back, capable of scoring touchdowns on the football field, so can you hone your skills in the game of life through diligence and fortitude and plain hard work.

Toward the end of that year, 1995, the time came to test Scoring for Life! on a larger audience. With the help of Yvette and Janay, who had helped me fine-tune my presentation and produced a brochure that would serve as a press kit, we prepared for a debut performance, as it were, on a Wednesday night at Christian Life Church. I wanted to find out, once and for all, whether I did, indeed, have a valid Christian ministry worth sharing with young adults across the country. In attendance that night were many lawyers, judges, and other community leaders, as well as many of my friends and fellow church members. My presentation that night turned out to be much too long, but from the reaction it received I was giddy about its future. "We've got to work on this," said Pastor Steve Vickers, "but you've got something, Jock. Let me know what I can do to help."

Lord knows, I had stories to tell. I've never been what they call a "casual" fan, not even at the beginning when I was going with my father to watch the Dodgers at Ebbets Field and the Giants at the Polo Grounds. I've always felt that baseball, for instance, is much more than a game. If you look at it close enough, you will see that the show unfolding on the field is a drama, a morality play, good guys versus bad buys, life in microcosm, the joy of victory and the agony of defeat. The lessons learned while observing a sports event, whether it be a baseball or football game or a heavyweight championship match, can be directly applied to one's daily life. Afraid that you don't have the God-given natural talent to succeed? Study the little guys like Eddie Stanky and Nellie Fox, bite-sized second basemen who made it through sheer hustle. Think you're outmanned? Study the pitchers like Ted Williams did. Worried that you might not be able to handle success? Hear the sad story of how drugs got the best of Doc Gooden and Darryl Strawberry.

Since Scoring for Life! was primarily aimed at young African Americans, designed to prepare them for what is still, sadly, a white world, there was no doubt in my mind that the most instructive story

I had to share was that of Jackie Robinson. Many of these kids were too young to understand that what he did in the middle of the twentieth century, breaking the color line in major league baseball, was making all things possible for them today. What courage it had taken for this young black man, lifted from the poverty and racism of rural Georgia as a child, to endure the unspeakable pressures laid on him as he joined the Brooklyn Dodgers in 1947: racial taunts from the stands and the opposing dugouts, beanballs fired at his head, spikes slashing at his legs, having to sleep and eat separate from his teammates, all simply because he was black. As I recounted Jackie's story, in my early presentations for Scoring for Life!, the crowds of young blacks would grow deathly silent as though they were hearing a story out of the Old Testament. Then, to cap it off, I might close with the quote from my father as he came home at the end of a day: "The white folks are still ahead, but we're gaining."

Jackie Robinson was only the first black athlete to change attitudes toward African Americans and thus bring about social change in the nation. I love to tell the story of the 1966 NCAA basketball finals pitting little Texas Western (now UTEP, the University of Texas at El Paso) against the mighty Kentucky Wildcats. Texas Western, with a starting lineup of five black players, had surprised the country by going 25-1 during the regular season. In the finals they would go up against a coach, Adolph Rupp, who had always sworn that he would never use a black player. The Southeastern Conference had never had a black basketball player, in fact, and in his pregame interviews Rupp mercilessly berated black players in general, saying that they could run and jump, but not much else, and there was no way an all-black team could beat an all-white team. Texas Western's coach, a white man named Don Haskins, used the remarks to fire up his team, and instructed them to rip the rim from the basket on a slam dunk at their first opportunity in order to intimidate the Wildcats. They did that, and much more, in front a racially hostile crowd. ("I want you to guard that *coon*," Rupp was heard to shout in the locker room at halftime, down by seven points.) Down to the wire in the last nine minutes, the game on the line, those black players who were said to "choke" in such situations hit twenty-eight of thirty-four free throw attempts to win the game, 72-65. Beginning the next season, black players began to slowly dominate rosters in the Southeastern Conference.

A black quarterback out of Grambling, Doug Williams, had much the same effect on the National Football League some two decades later. He had already destroyed the myth that blacks didn't have the stuff to play quarterback in the NFL; that they couldn't think and play at the same time, couldn't throw under pressure, were too docile and timid to withstand blitzing defenders, were intellectually deficient to handle the job. But he had led the Washington Redskins into Super Bowl XXII, in January 1988, against the Denver Broncos, in San Diego. *No way,* said the oddsmakers of Williams's chances against John Elway, Denver's quarterback from Stanford, and that's how it looked in the first quarter when Denver went up, 10-0, and Williams went down with a leg injury. But then he came limping back into the game and had the greatest single quarter a quarterback has ever had in a Super Bowl. When the game was over, Williams had completed eighteen of twenty-nine passes for 340 yards and four touchdowns (all in that second quarter), and was named Most Valuable Player for leading the Redskins to victory, 42-10. As it was with Jackie Robinson in 1947 and Texas Western in 1966, Doug Williams had proved his critics wrong and, more importantly, society wrong. Never again has a black quarterback been viewed as a novelty in pro football.

I must say that I have patterned much of my life, as a father and a husband and an attorney, from lessons I've learned from closely following the lives of various sports heroes over the years. I suppose that much of my flair and flamboyant dress in the courtroom traces to Joe Namath, the first pro football player to wear white shoes; how many other lawyers in Alabama show up in court wearing royal blue suits, or red jackets and matching ties, Italian suits, or yellow coats with black ties? A lot of my confidence and colorful speech in front of juries is stolen from Muhammad Ali. (Often, out for a walk in the neighborhood with Yvette on the eve of an important case, I'll start dancing and jabbing, saying, "I'm gonna float like a butterfly and sting like a bee.") When all seems lost—three-two count, bases loaded, bottom of the ninth—I see visions of Bobby Thomson or Bill Mazeroski saving the day with a dramatic homerun in the gloaming.

Using the uniforms and various artifacts from my collection tends to bring the message home. I'll hear the kids whisper and gush— *gaahh!*—as I hold up Jackie Robinson's home white No. 42 Brooklyn jersey, the actual uniform he wore at Ebbets Field in 1956, and launch into the dramatic story of his life. The same happens when I produce a silky white robe with ALI on the back, along with a pair of shoes and boxing gloves worn by The Greatest, then tell how Ali lost his title for refusing military service in Vietnam ("I ain't got nothing against no Viet Congs, just the white men that want to send me there"). Similarly, it's easier for a kid to imagine Jim Brown tearing through the Green Bay defense when he sees a real No. 32 jersey worn by the real Jim Brown that very day.

∾

By the end of 1996, we were ready to introduce Scoring for Life! to the world. We had appointed a board of directors, including Pastor Vickers and Johnnie Cochran. Thanks to the legal work of Tom Kotouc, a Christian lawyer in Montgomery, we had achieved tax-exempt status. A handsome press kit had been designed by Ceeon

Quiett, a college friend of Janay's who had done public-relations work for Black Entertainment Television and the Olympics in Atlanta, and we used that as part of a presentation to the National Football League, requesting a block of time during the upcoming Super Bowl in New Orleans.

Permission granted, I hauled a goodly chunk of my collection down to New Orleans and set up for what seemed to be a golden opportunity. During the week leading up the Super Bowl XXXI, to be played between the Green Bay Packers and the New England Patriots on January 26, 1997, there would be a series of interactive events intended to attract fans to pro football. The one I was interested in was Super Bowl Kids Day, sort of an all-day carnival of games and rides and demonstrations and autograph signings: good food, good music, good speakers. Nearly 2,000 gifted fifth- and sixth-graders from the Deep South had been selected to appear, on the basis of their school achievements. Perfect. This was exactly what I had in mind when we began putting together Scoring for Life!.

Yvette and Janay and I prepared the stage with an array of uniforms, and I was anxious, naturally, before it came my turn to speak. I was preceded by two former pro football greats, Roosevelt Taylor of the Bears and Lionel Taylor of the Broncos, and although they were warmly received there didn't seem to be a great deal of excitement. When I took center stage, surrounded by all of those authentic uniforms, I pointed out the one that had been worn by Doug Williams and then told these 2,000 kids the Doug Williams story, of the doubters, of the pressure on him to break yet another color line, of his triumphs and his tragedies. I couldn't believe what happened when I finished. I got a standing ovation, was mobbed by the kids, and wound up signing three or four hundred autographs that day. And I wasn't the star, just the messenger. "See there, I told you so," Yvette said as we were packing up and moving to another location. "God sent you. You're on a mission."

✌

We were on our way. About a year later, thanks to the recommendation of Mac Gober, a Scoring for Life! board member who operated a project in Alabama called Canaan Land Boys' Home, I appeared on the Christian Broadcast Network's "700 Club." I was interviewed that day by a former Miss America, and the host, Pat Robertson, kept gushing over the uniforms I had brought to the studio. It was a chance to reach out to the entire nation, to spread the gospel of Scoring for Life!, and that kind of exposure led to so many invitations that I could hardly keep up with them.

Back home, in Montgomery, I was invited to appear at the Kiwanis Club and the Rotary Club. Since both of those organizations are nearly ninety-nine per cent white, composed of the white downtown power structure, I chose to play it safe by talking about Mickey Mantle. The Mick had been a hero to most of these men in their childhoods—a poor white kid from rural Oklahoma who had finished his career with 536 homeruns—and I made the point that he had actually hit one more homer in his life. That was at the very end when, more or less speaking from his death bed, dying from the ravages of alcohol, he warned the kids of America not to abuse their bodies as he had. "I'll never forget you, son," I was told by an older white gentleman after the Kiwanis appearance. "You've given me back my hero." More to the point, a conservative Christian lawyer by the name of Tom Parker came up to me after the Rotary Club appearance and said I was only the second speaker in the history of the club to receive a standing ovation. "That's significant, Jock. An African American, speaking to us, getting this kind of reaction, that means something."

Even more gratifying was a return appearance at the Rotary Club.

Talking about Mickey Mantle had been the cautious approach at both the Kiwanis and the Rotary clubs in Montgomery, but on this second time around I decided to bite the bullet by telling the full story of Jackie Robinson. I had my concerns about how this might be accepted at such a place, over lunch on a steamy day in Montgomery, Alabama, but I felt the Lord was telling me to go for it, give it a shot, try to make a difference. The Rotary got the full treatment from me about Jackie—the risks he took, the abuse he suffered, the victory over racism, what it meant to African Americans in particular—and, what do you know, I got another standing ovation.

Think about it: the whimsical purchase of my first baseball card at a Montgomery mall in 1982, a '57 Topps Mickey Mantle, had led to a full-blown ministry a dozen years later. There are times when I'll be sitting in the Sports Room on Lansdowne Drive—feeling the flannels, remembering my youth, thinking of my dad and those great times—fantasizing about a day when perhaps I could create my own museum, a Sports Hall of Fame all in one building, saving people the separate trips to Cooperstown and Canton and Springfield. There have been offers and vague plans to do so, and maybe it will happen one day. The collection has grown to be worth quite a lot of money by now, in the high seven figures at the least, but that's not the real point. The greatest value of the collection is found in its power to teach kids the lessons I have learned from a lifetime of understanding that baseball is much more than a game. It is life.

14

Enter, Johnnie Cochran

LIFE WAS GOOD as the Nineties progressed. We were firmly ensconced in our dream house in Montgomery. Yvette was turning heads as a highly successful independent business-woman, supplying expert-witness testimony to plaintiffs and defendants alike, a woman to be reckoned with. Janay, who liked me a lot more now that I had found the Lord, was on the first leg of her trek through Howard University. My law practice, following the $5 million verdict in the *Lucy Turner v. Southern Life* case, was picking up steam. I continued to take on major civil cases, most of them involving arrogance and the misuse of power by big corporations in their dealings with what they assumed to be powerless ordinary citizens. It was these cases that raised my dander, made the practice of law worthwhile, and often I could feel the presence of my father, looking over my shoulder with a smile.

One of my favorite cases during that time was *Mary Washington v. Goodyear Tire & Rubber Company*. It started very simply. There was a Goodyear outlet in Tuskegee called Tire Pro, Inc., which is where Mrs. Washington took the $400 automobile she had bought for her daughter. All she wanted was a couple of used tires for the car, nothing more, but after the managers kept insisting that she would need a Goodyear credit card she finally relented before going off to work. When her daughter showed up at Tire Pro later in the day to pick up her car, expecting the bill to come to $63, she found that she had been charged more than $500 in unauthorized "mechanical fees." Robert "Bobby" Segall and I were hired, and we filed a lawsuit not against little Tire Pro but against mighty Goodyear, for fraud and misrepresentation.

Goodyear failed to come to the table and negotiate, so the case went to a trial by jury. It was Goodyear's contention that Tire Pro wasn't really a Goodyear store at all, just a private local outfit. We, on the other hand, were traveling under the theory of "apparent authority," noting that everyone in Tuskegee was led to believe otherwise by a giant Goodyear sign overlooking the premises and the fact that Tire Pro carried only Goodyear products. I assumed that the jurors had seen what was being called the Trial of the Century on television—Johnnie Cochran's defense of O. J. Simpson against charges of allegedly murdering his wife and her boyfriend—in which Cochran, to make a point of possible misidentification by the Los Angeles Police Department, slapped a hat on his head and asked the jury, "Who am I?" The jury got the message, answering, "Johnnie Cochran," thereby destroying the prosecution's case.

With that in mind, I commissioned a huge enlargement of the Tire Pro shop, dominated by a Goodyear sign. In my closing arguments I told the jury, "They tell me, ladies and gentlemen, that a picture is worth a thousand words. I have a picture here that's talking to you, that wants to speak to you. The defendants have taken the position that the store here in town, in Tuskegee, though wearing the Goodyear emblem and carrying only Goodyear products, is not technically a Goodyear store but an independent outlet. I wanted to see what you all think." I reached back, picked up the enlargement, held it up, and thrust it in front of the jury. "Ladies and gentlemen," I said, "who am I?" When a female juror blurted out, "Goodyear," and the others began to laugh, I knew we had it made. Because they weren't satisfied to accept Mary Washington's sixty-three dollars for two used tires, Goodyear had to cough up $250,000.

～

There were many other cases like that during the Nineties. One that I particularly savored, for obvious reasons, involved the arrogance of a major league baseball star. Before he became a true superstar, the first player in the history of the game to become a Forty-Forty man (forty homers and forty stolen bases in one season), Jose Canseco had agreed to visit a baseball card shop in Montgomery. The original contract said that he would receive $13,000 for appearing at the store and signing 1,500 autographs. But now Canseco's agent, Dennis Gilbert of Beverly Hills Sports Council, noting his client's rise in prominence, was making special demands like arranging a private jet for Canseco. The owner of the store, Jim Pitts, was forced to accede to the demand, at an additional up-front cost of $3,500, because he had already sold many tickets and promised autographs to dealers who were planning to set up booths at the store.

Things got ugly on the day of the card show. For starters, it had been discovered that Canseco had cashed in the commercial airline ticket he had been sent by Pitts and put the money in his pocket. Then, when Canseco arrived at the show, four hours late, he signed only about a thousand autographs and abruptly left. Many of the baseballs he *did* sign, in fact, he treated with disdain; flipping them onto the table, letting them roll and bounce onto the floor, leaving Pitts's wife to pick them up, caring less that they had become smudged. Throughout his time at the show he had been arrogant and caustic, clearly sharing his agent's opinion that he, the great Jose Canseco, was above this, that he was living by a different standard now and didn't have to oblige much of anything anymore.

The trial took two weeks and turned out to be a show of celebrities. Among them were Dennis Gilbert and some of his clients, including

Bobby Bonilla and Danny Tartabull. I was infuriated by this lack of responsibility shown by a man who was fortunate enough to be admired by fans, many of them young boys, for his simple God-given ability to hit baseballs farther and to run faster than most mortals. During the closing arguments, I decided to imitate the great baseball announcer Vin Scully as he might describe Jose Canseco in action. Here was "Scully" on Canseco, in a game: "Canseco at bat, Nolan Ryan pitching. There's a high fly ball to centerfield. Going back, back, back! To the track, to the wall . . . *gone!*" My version of Scully on Canseco, the arrogant star: "To the limo, to the airport, to the private jet . . . *gone!*" The jury burst into laughter and promptly returned a verdict of $207,000 against Dennis Gilbert and Beverly Hills Sports Council. *Serves 'em right,* I thought, shaking my head and clucking to consider how Duke Snider and Bobby Thomson and Jackie Robinson would have comported themselves in a similar situation.

∾

Then came November of 1996, one of the most memorable months in my life. I was sitting in my office in Tuskegee one morning when I had a call from Delores Boyd, a prominent black attorney in Montgomery. Delores and I had been good friends for many years— she had served as my co-counsel in the Lucy Turner case against Southern Life—and I had been a faithful customer at Roots and Wings, a bookstore in Montgomery that she co-owned with another black female attorney friend, Vanzetta Penn McPherson, with whom I had worked in Bill Baxley's office back in the Seventies and who was by now a United States magistrate judge. Roots and Wings had become one of the most prominent African-American bookstores in the country, regularly hosting book-signings by such celebrities as Alex Haley, John Hope Franklin, John Lewis, and Nikki Giovanni.

"Brother Jock," Delores began, "Johnnie Cochran is coming to town and we need your help."

"Cochran? The one and only?"

"The man himself. He'll be signing his book at our place."

"What can *I* do, for goodness' sake?"

"Be his escort. How about it?"

Following his stunning victory in court, freeing O. J. Simpson from charges that he had murdered his ex-wife and her presumed boyfriend, Johnnie Cochran had become a virtual god in the African-American community. One of his lines during the trial—"If it doesn't fit, you must acquit," he said of a bloody glove allegedly used in the killings—had become a byword even on the late-night television talk shows. An articulate champion for justice, a Christian man who had risen from modest beginnings in Shreveport, Louisiana, Johnnie was riding a crest of great popularity. Now he was out on the hustings with a bestselling memoir, *Journey to Justice*, and he was booked for a busy visit to Montgomery. Delores and Vanzetta had been deluged by African-American lawyers, practically begging to squire Cochran around town, but they wanted me to do the honors because they felt I was the right man. "You'll treat him like a regular person," Delores said, "and he'll appreciate that."

Of course, I agreed, and from the moment I picked him up at the Montgomery airport we hit it off immensely well. We were two successful black trial lawyers, Christian brothers with Southern roots (his by birth, mine by choice), both of us big sports fans, both of us interested in helping "the least of these," and we became instant friends. Accompanied by Johnnie's longtime bodyguard, a gentleman by the name of Henry Grayson, we embarked on his rounds: book-signings, television and radio appearances, speaking engagements, various interviews. Everywhere Johnnie went, it was like the second coming of Elvis. He was a superstar.

On the second night, Yvette and her mother and sister prepared a dinner at our home on Lansdowne Drive. We had a small number of family members as guests—Yvette's parents, her sister and brother-in-law and their two children—and as we gathered around the dinner table, holding hands, Yvette asked if I would give a blessing. I must have prayed for a good five minutes, asking for a hedge of protection to be placed around "this great and noble icon, Johnnie L. Cochran, Jr.," that "prosperity and leadership and blessings visit his doorstep."

Later in the evening, I led Johnnie upstairs to my Sports Room and flipped a switch to turn on the lights. He stood there in amazement. There, before him, lay what was at the time the second-largest collection of game-worn uniforms in the world. All he could say was, "I can't believe it." He began examining the uniforms that were on display, and then I flung open two doors to a closet, revealing hundreds more. He seemed flabbergasted.

"Okay, Johnnie," I said, "who do you think are the greatest running backs in the history of pro football?"

"That's easy. Number one, it's Jim Brown."

I reached in and handed him my game-worn Jim Brown jersey.

"Number two would be Gail Sayers."

I produced a Chicago Bears jersey once worn by Gail Sayers.

"How about Franco?"

Here came Franco Harris's Pittsburgh Steelers jersey.

"Amazing. Just amazing."

"What the heck," I said, reaching into the closet for more, tossing them out in a scene reminiscent of Jay Gatsby's flinging his collection of brightly-colored shirts into the air for the benefit of his love, Daisy Buchanan, in the film version of *The Great Gatsby*. "Here's John Riggins, Washington Redskins. Here's Walter Payton, Chicago Bears. Oh, and here's a couple of Eric Dickerson's, from the Rams. How many more do you want?" Then, finally, as my *piece de resistance*, I took out a Buffalo Bills jersey and a helmet once worn by Orenthal James Simpson and placed them in Johnnie Cochran's hands.

I had found that Johnnie Cochran is dignity personified, but now he was acting like a kid on Christmas morning. "You *know* it's O. J.'s helmet when you check out the size," he said, laughing. "His head's so big, they had to have them special-made. Just look how much room is in this helmet, would you!?" I got out a camera and started taking pictures of Johnnie posing with O. J.'s jersey and helmet, for himself and for O. J. the next time he saw him, and he was still going on. "You're a visionary, Jock. You're a visionary, and you've got to be connected to accumulate this kind of collection." There was more of the same as he was leaving that night, noting the authentic autographed pieces throughout the house—historical documents bearing the signatures of Booker T. Washington, Frederick Douglass, Malcolm X, Marcus Garvey, W. E. B. Du Bois, and other great black leaders—not to mention the life-sized enlargement of Douglass displayed at the front door, as though you're entering a museum of African-American history.

The next morning, when I picked up Johnnie for an early appearance, with Henry Grayson riding shotgun as per protocol for bodyguards, Johnnie leaned over from the back seat. "Good morning, Brother Jock," he said, then expressing appreciation for the night before at our house. "I was so impressed with that prayer you gave. It really moved me. You know the Master." I was thinking that's how I normally pray to Jesus. Then he said, "You're a special man, Jock Smith. We're going to do some business together. Just you wait and see."

I had mixed feelings when Johnnie Cochran left that day. It had been a remarkable visit, on the one hand, and I was especially pleased that he had enjoyed my sports collection. But on the other hand, as I told Yvette afterwards, I felt an emptiness in my heart when he left, as though I had lost a lifelong friend. "Oh, no, Jock," she said. "I think you'll be seeing him again. I don't think this is the end of your relationship with Johnnie. I feel it in my heart."

∾

It didn't take long for me to discover that Yvette was right, Johnnie and I really had bonded during his visit to Montgomery. He called a few months later to say that he was scheduled to be the grand marshal at a parade in Selma, locus of the bloody police riot at the Pettus Bridge in 1965, and asked if I would be his escort. Although many police officers and state troopers were available to pick him up at the Montgomery airport and drive him to Selma, he thanked them but rejected their gesture: "I'm riding with Brother Smith here." As we rode in my car to Selma, escorted by a noisy convoy of police and state troopers, I felt we were floating on a cloud to heaven itself. Not long after that, I was invited by Johnnie to hang out for a couple of days at the annual jazz festival in New Orleans with what turned out to be a tight inner circle of his closest friends and advisers. He made it clear to them—the group included the famous black lawyer and Harvard professor Charles Ogletree and John Burroughs, the attorney who represented Rodney King, the black man whose beating at the hands of the LAPD had been caught on amateur video—that I was being welcomed into the circle.

Later that year, hardly twelve months following that first meeting in Montgomery, Johnnie and I became associates in a joint endeavor for the first time. Not surprisingly, it had to do with sports. During the many conversations we'd had since becoming friends, we had agreed that there was a need in the area of the management of African-American athletes and entertainers. A handful of individual black agents and lawyers had been able to penetrate the business, but there existed no minority-owned organization that provided world-class representation for blacks. Even though we had privately agreed that neither of us was the type to have partners, both of us being hard-headed cowboys who preferred working alone, we did agree that there might be an exception to the rule in this respect. Something should be done to ensure that black athletes and entertainers got a bigger piece of the pie in what had become a multi-billion-dollar industry. With my consuming interest in sports and Johnnie's name, maybe one day we might enter that world as agents.

I was on my way to Atlanta to see the Atlanta Hawks play basketball when the car phone rang. It was Johnnie, saying he thought the time had come. Would I care to join him in a venture we would call All-Pro Sports and Entertainment International? What could I say but "yes"? "Good," he said. "Now go and get your certification with the NBA and the NFL, and let's get to work." Hardly before I could catch my breath, I was attending a gala at the Beverly Hills home of Jim Brown, the great running back, to announce our partnership. Hundreds were there, many of them prominent African Americans from the fields of sports and entertainment, and we were up and running. After decades of worshipping my sports heroes, now I would be working to make sure they got what was coming to them in the way of contracts, endorsements, and the other benefits they so richly deserved. One of the first cases to come our way was that of Latrell Sprewell, a star player with the Golden State Warriors of the NBA, who was threatened with having his $32 million contract voided for choking his overbearing coach in a fit of frustration. "We're not condoning what he did," Johnnie said, "we just want to make sure the punishment is fair." The courts determined that it wasn't, and thus was saved Sprewell's career.

My new friendship with Cochran was not lost on Keith Givens, a white trial lawyer out of Dothan, Alabama, who was about to become president of the Alabama Trial Lawyers Association. Yvette reminded me that Keith had been asking me for quite a while if I could arrange a meeting with Johnnie and me, and when I managed to get my desk cleared I called him back one day. It seemed that he just wanted to chat, at first, just to check out the news that Johnnie and I had, indeed, become partners in a sports management firm. Then he told me that he and his partner in Dothan, Sam Cherry, were opening an office in Georgia and were wondering if I'd be interested in trying some cases there with them. I said yes, by all means, thinking that was all he wanted. But then I found there was more, much more. "Jock," he said, "I don't know about Johnnie's availability, but do you think he'd be interested in putting together an arrangement with us, all three of us, and trying some cases?"

There it was, an idea that went off like a light bulb, the biggest idea I'd heard in my life: a national law firm with Johnnie's name on it, one specifically designed to protect the rights of black people. In spite of improvements in race relations, especially since the landmark rulings and promises of Lyndon Johnson's Great Society, African-American citizens all over the country were still getting the short end of the stick when it came to legal justice and reparations, particularly in the Deep South, and it seemed time to do something about it. Here was a plan for three well-connected and successful Alabama trial lawyers, two white and one black, to join forces with the great Johnnie Cochran to form one powerful firm that would blanket the nation. I was spellbound over the possibility.

The next day I was on the phone with Johnnie, briefly outlining Keith Givens's proposal, and I could hear the wheels spinning in his head. "Well, brother," he said, intrigued but still cautious, "let's see what they have to offer." Keith had a chance to present the idea to Johnnie in person when he flew into New Orleans for another jazz festival that Johnnie and I were attending. After a three-hour session at the Windsor Court Hotel, Johnnie told me, "I like this guy. Let's keep talking." Discussions continued back and forth over the next two months, the phone lines crackling with the energy of fresh ideas and high hopes and grand strategy, and finally it all came together, as it happened, on my fiftieth birthday. On June 10, 1998, in the offices of Johnnie Cochran in downtown Los Angeles, the four of us—Sam Cherry, Keith Givens, Johnnie and I—met and shook hands, agreeing in principal to start a national law firm called Cochran, Cherry, Givens & Smith. It was some birthday present.

15

Cochran, Cherry, Givens & Smith

I T WAS CLEAR from the beginning that Cochran, Cherry, Givens & Smith had the makings of a genuine legal powerhouse, national in scope, one that would put fear in the heart of any large organization—whether a public utility, giant corporation, insurance firm, governmental branch, or whatever—still holding the belief that they could willfully take advantage of what the Bible calls "the least of these" without paying a huge price. We officially opened for business in July of 1998, barely a month after the handshakes in Johnnie Cochran's Los Angeles office on Wilshire Boulevard, so we could introduce ourselves by hosting a reception at that year's National Bar Association convention in Memphis. Thus, the word went out. We would be concentrating on catastrophic injuries, wrongful death, products liability, toxic torts, class actions based on fraud, and other high-ticket civil litigation matters. We opened two toll-free telephone lines so the aggrieved from all over the country could contact us with their complaints.

Immediately, we began to open offices in key cities from coast to coast. The official name of the firm was Cochran, Cherry, Givens & Smith, often followed by the name of the major local partner in that city. We referred to that person as our "rainmaker," a heavyweight well-known for his track record of winning major civil cases. (In Atlanta, for example, the firm is known as Cochran, Cherry, Givens, Smith & Sistrunk. The rainmaker there is Hezekiah Sistrunk, a great trial lawyer specializing in medical malpractice cases, who happens to be the cousin of former Oakland Raiders tackle Otis Sistrunk.) Not surprisingly, because of Johnnie Cochran's celebrity status, people began to refer to us in shorthand as The Cochran Firm.

No matter what we were called, at the core of the business were four founding fathers, as it were: two black and two white, committed Christians all, successful lawyers in our own rights, each with deep roots in the African-American community. We felt this was a most propitious time in the nation's history for the creation of such a firm, to the point of marveling that someone hadn't thought of it before. While it's true that more than three decades had elapsed since the passage of statutes outlawing racial discrimination in America, in areas ranging from public accommodations to employment, it's also true that the dominant white society continued to practice discrimination toward African Americans. Quite simply, racial equality might be *de jure*, but not *de facto*. As attorneys, our way of helping bring true racial equality was to heap punishment on those who continued trying to skirt the law.

∾

There's little doubt that none of this would have happened without the name of Johnnie Cochran emblazoned at the top. Johnnie was already recognized as a highly successful attorney long before the O. J. Simpson case came along. His early career, following graduation from UCLA and Loyola Law School in Los Angeles, included valuable experience as the L.A. Assistant District Attorney, where he had administrative responsibility for 600 lawyers. After opening his own law firm in 1981, he began racking up a remarkable series of courtroom victories that soon established him as one of the most outstanding trial lawyers in America. He represented both the famous like Michael Jackson and the not-so-famous like "ordinary" citizens injured in automobile accidents ("I work for the MJ's, the OJ's, and the no-J's," he likes to say, in his inimitable rhyming style). Johnnie's highly-publicized defense of Simpson may have aggravated many in white America (costing him millions of dollars in potential business, in fact), but it nevertheless had elevated him to superstar status. In 1995 he became the only lawyer in California history to be named both Civil Trial Lawyer of the Year *and* Criminal Trial Lawyer of the Year. This was followed by his bestselling memoir *Journey to Justice*, and his hosting a talk show on Court TV. In '96 he was selected for the Inner Circle of Advocates, which is composed of the top 100 personal-injury lawyers in America.

By the time the national firm was up and rolling, its successes were astonishing. In aggregate, the nationwide team of more than 65 lawyers had put up staggering numbers during their careers: six verdicts in excess of $100 million, more than twenty in excess of $10 million, and hundreds of verdicts or settlements exceeding $1 million. The results had come from litigation in almost every area of malfeasance known to man: a $240 million verdict against the Walt Disney Corporation for breaching a confidential relationship, stealing trade secrets, and breaking an implied contract; a $40 million verdict for a worker paralyzed when he fell six floors through an open elevator shaft; an $80 million verdict against Orkin for a woman whose home was destroyed by termites due to the company's negligence (my case, about which there will be more later); a $43 million verdict for an infant brain-damaged by unnecessary premature delivery; a record $104 million verdict for brothers paralyzed when diving into shallow water off a city pier without adequate warning signs; more than $250 million in other verdicts and settlements against municipalities for negligence, police abuse, or other wrongful conduct; a $114 million verdict for double-arm amputation due to a defective aerial lift device; more than $27 million in verdicts and settlements for victims injured by defective utility bucket trucks; a $195 million verdict on behalf of plaintiffs in a vehicle which collided with a tractor-trailer rig; and a record $100 million verdict in a pedestrian knockdown case when a mother and child were struck by a car.

But those are mere figures, like batting averages and earned run averages, the sort of cold black-and-white statistics we use to measure one's achievements. Impressive as they are, they don't go very far in telling us of Johnnie Cochran, the man. I'm not sure that I have ever met anyone with such charisma. It's almost comic, what happens when people see him in the flesh for the first time. They've seen him on television, read of his accomplishments, fully expect to see a giant of a man with the Godlike physical attraction of a John Wayne or a Bear Bryant, but what they see is a trim man of relatively short stature and modest composure, a confident man wearing a warm smile on his lips and a pin on his lapel that reads "Expect a Miracle." And then he grins and speaks—"If he doesn't fit, you must acquit"—and with that utterance he owns them. The crowd, like his partners, will follow him anywhere. The word "charisma" is an overused catchall that only begins to describe him. We who know him best could go on *ad infinitum.* Johnnie Cochran is, at once, a man of tremendous grace, tranquility, perseverance, vision, humor, and eloquence; a man blessed by the Lord, one who will show unconditional love no matter the audience, whether they be followers or nay-sayers. Carrying grudges is not a part of his game.

A couple of little stories come to mind, to demonstrate his deep-seated belief that faith and hope will win out over despair and negativity any time; not unlike the long-suffering New York Mets fans with their cry, "*You gotta believe!*" During the grand opening of our office in Chicago, a bunch of us got stuck in an elevator. There was panic on the part of everyone except Johnnie. "Our faith is being tested," he said, calmly and matter-of-factly, like a commanding officer steadying his troops in the face of possible disaster. "Don't worry. If you *believe*, the Lord will be along shortly." Sure enough, moments later, someone was opening the door for us and the crisis was over. In another instance, at the Essex House hotel in New York, where we were having a private dinner with our partners there, Johnnie overheard one of them say that his wife was seriously ill. Before anyone knew it, Johnnie had gotten up from his chair, walked to the other end of the table, unfastening the tiny pin from his lapel as he went, and then stuck the pin on the man's own lapel. "What does it say?" the partner asked. "It's for you and your wife," Johnnie said. "Expect a miracle and you'll get it." It was an emotional moment for everyone in the room.

With a leader like that, the hundreds of people employed by the firm from coast to coast quickly became a well-oiled machine; a true team dedicated to what our ads refer to as "a new level of justice." If the Realtor's mantra is "location, location, location," then ours is "preparation, preparation, preparation." Whatever the case, there is a lawyer somewhere within the organization with expertise in that area—medical malpractice, product liability, municipal negligence, etc.—ready to answer the call. We handle cases and get paid on contingency fees, that fee based solely on a percentage of the money we recover for our clients. The initial consultation is free. If there is no financial recovery for the client, then we charge no fee. This allows us to represent individuals who might not otherwise have the money to hire a lawyer.

∾

We couldn't have found a better man than Keith Givens to become the firm's chief administrator. Keith was raised in a strong Christian environment in Dothan, Alabama, in the far southeastern corner of the state, and to this day he has never smoked or drank or been heard to utter a curse word. His family ran a service station catering to African Americans in Dothan, meaning that as a boy working in his father's shop he learned early on to interface with black people and thus had no racial hang-ups to overcome as he grew up. A great lawyer, Keith's greatest strengths are as an administrator and a visionary. He is persistent and thorough, a man who dots the i's and crosses the t's and looks to the future as well. It was his vision that caused the merger of our firm in New York City with New York's most prominent law firm, Schneider, Kleinick, Weitz, Damashek & Shoot. Both firms happened to be vying to represent the family of a man who had died in a tragic accident, and it was Keith who jumped into the dispute, calmed the waters, brought the two of us together in a high-level meeting, and ultimately brought about a merger that has been beneficial to all. He would later orchestrate similar coalitions, including a business relationship with the famous John Morgan of Morgan, Collins & Gilbert in Orlando, Florida.

Sam Cherry, the other national partner and Givens's law partner in Dothan, had a background similar to Keith's. Sam, too, was raised in a strong Christian environment and grew up doing business with blacks. His mother was a political figure in Alabama for many years, noted for her sensitivity to the needs of African Americans, and as a boy Sam worked in a family furniture store that catered to black people. Like Keith Givens, then, Sam Cherry had no racial barriers to cross as he grew into manhood in small-town Alabama. He became known as a great litigator, a products-liability genius with great writing skills, and today when you enter his office you see an array of model die-cast bucket trucks, also known as "cherry pickers"; a nod to the time when he took on the bucket-truck manufacturers and set a benchmark with several multi-million-dollar verdicts designed to make them clean up their act. (To this day, Sam can tell you everything there is to be known about every moving piece, every electrical site, on those trucks that still present dangers for America's citizens.) So there you have the two other principal partners in the national firm of Cochran, Cherry, Givens & Smith: two Southern white men who, prior to their coming aboard, had a clientele that was predominantly black and a soul that is Christian to the core. I believe that when God framed the world at the beginning of time He laid special plans for the creation of a law firm that would truly serve the least of these, one composed of Christian men who would represent the disenfranchised, the locked-out, the shut-ins, and the have-nots in His name.

Fortunately, this compatibility extends beyond the firm and reaches our personal lives. The four of us spend a lot of time together, either traveling or visiting in each other's homes, and it's a happy circumstance that our wives get along famously. Each of us married well, to Christian women able to stand on their own achievements. Johnnie's wife Dale—Dr. Dale Mason Cochran—is a native of New Orleans, a dignified, poised, and intellectually gifted woman, reared in private schools, who shows tremendous grace and presence when she enters a room. An owner of W. H. Smith concessions in several major airports in the United States, including New Orleans and Washington, D.C., Dale speaks softly but carries a big stick due to her managerial experience. Johnnie never makes a major decision involving anything administrative within the firm without first conferring with her. Dale and my wife Yvette Smiley-Smith are a lot alike, as strong and independent businesswomen, and they get along wonderfully. Carrie Givens also brings an awful lot to the table. She was once a Miss Alabama contestant and later a television news anchor, as evidenced by her physical beauty, poise, and perfect speech, and you can always count on her to bring an enthusiastic mood to any situation. Maria Cherry knows everything there is to know about etiquette, hospitality, cuisine, and good taste, and owns a winery in Dothan. Every time we all gather in Dothan, in fact, both Johnnie and Dale and Yvette and I stay at Sam and Maria's stately mansion, where Maria serves endless rounds of pastries and hors d'oeuvres and other delicacies. It's like visiting a classic Southern plantation. I still remember taking a tour of the place on our first visit—seeing a television set of unimaginable size, poking around upstairs and downstairs, nearly getting lost amid such finery in a trip that took fifteen minutes—and being asked afterwards by Carrie and Maria, these two white Southern ladies, what I thought. All I could think to say was, "Well, I'm still black." They fell over themselves laughing.

Maria Cherry also owns more books advising about the best accommodations available everywhere in the United States than any person I know, and that came in handy during one particular visit we all made to New York. Somehow, we found that we had been booked into what amounted to a fleabag hotel: beds on the floor, psychedelic lights in the hallway, noises everywhere, a vision of another time in America. I had arrived ahead of the others, and when I saw Maria and Sam arrive I was laughing. "Wait'll you see these rooms," I told them. I followed them along, just to see their reactions, and they were shocked. "This place is a *dive*," said Sam. "This," Maria announced, "is totally unacceptable." Maria was already digging through her book of New York hotels, looking for another place, and soon she was at the front desk, demanding a refund. We gave a special thanks for Maria and her guide to the best hotels in New York City for getting us out of there. Everyone went gladly except for Keith Givens, who may live in a mansion of his own in Dothan but doesn't much care where he stays when he's on the road, and we had to remind him that that's not the style of Johnnie Cochran and Sam Cherry and Jock Smith and their wives. It's not that we're snobs, I told him. It's just that we've worked very hard, and when we're away from the center of the storm it becomes a necessity to close off from the outer world and get some peace and quiet. The thick walls of a Ritz-Carlton can do wonders for one's sanity and peace of mind.

∾

In the early going, we began to open offices all across the country. Always at the forefront in our thinking was the absolute necessity to have a big-name heavyweight local attorney, our so-called "rainmakers," in charge of each branch office. But at the same time, under Johnnie's instructions, we also wanted to make sure that we practiced what we preached by offering opportunities to a diverse range of employees at the highest levels: black, white, Asian, young, old, and by all means female. Johnnie, in fact, had become concerned over questions being asked about why the firm had no females as national or regional partners, and he quickly responded right there in his own office in Los Angeles. A black female attorney named Cameron Stewart had worked off-and-on for several years at his law firm, giving Johnnie a high level of comfort about her legal skills and her ability to manage an office, and within six months of hiring her full-time she was voted in as our first female managing partner. Subsequently, the LA firm was officially designated as Cochran, Cherry, Givens, Smith & Stewart.

Typical of how methodically we approached the establishment of branches around the country was our work in Atlanta. Our offices in Tuskegee and Dothan were of utmost importance in the overall scheme, of course, but after all Atlanta was the capital of the New South. I was attending a Braves game there one night, with one of my daughter Janay's sorority sisters from Howard University as my guest, and when I asked her about promising lawyers in town who might be interested in interviewing for the firm she told me of a young African

American named Audrey Tolson. Audrey at the time was practicing with another young lawyer named Shawn Williams in a group of four lawyers in downtown Atlanta. After a series of meetings with the two, it was determined that they would be our best bets to open our Atlanta offices. Though they didn't come with a lot of experience, they had an awful lot of integrity in the community, good track records in court, as well as much enthusiasm and willingness to learn. Johnnie had made it clear that the training of African-American lawyers was essential, that every office would have so many of them so we could pass on quality representation for another generation within our race.

With Audrey and Shawn in charge of the Atlanta office, now up and running, we turned our attention to finding an experienced civil litigator who would bring it clout. We interviewed several candidates for the job, but ultimately settled on Hezekiah Sistrunk, like his cousin Otis of the Oakland Raiders an imposing physical figure (he had played college football under Lou Holtz at North Carolina State before finishing law school at Duke). "Hez," as he is known, had been a defense lawyer for nineteen years in the "med-mal" area, winning 99.9 percent of his cases. He is a great trial lawyer, a visionary with great knowhow in and out of the courtroom. He became a regional partner after we agreed to add his name to the letterhead—Cochran, Cherry, Givens, Smith & Sistrunk—and, to make things sweeter, he brought along Jane Sams, who had been with his firm for six years and brought experience and excellent courtroom demeanor to the merger. Jane is quite a lawyer and quite a young lady, a specialist in medical malpractice, one who soon would settle a number of cases in the seven-figure range. And Shawn Williams received a $2.2 million verdict in his first case for the firm.

The Atlanta office became a major player from the start. "They know where the bones are buried," Keith Givens said of the team as they plunged into a number of med-mal cases. Then they took on

MARTA (Metropolitan Atlanta Rapid Transit Authority) in a high-profile case involving the deaths of two men who had been working as independent contractors. Although MARTA had been warned about the dangerous nature of working on its rapid-transit rail system, and had experienced difficulties in that area, nothing was done to improve conditions. The case was settled in the millions of dollars and, although that didn't return the father back to the widow or the son back to the mother, it did mark the firm as a major player in Georgia's civil-litigation arena. And all along, this being the South, where gun ownership is too often regarded as a God-given right, we joined hands as counsel to the City of Atlanta in litigation designed to keep guns off the streets. Butting heads with the powerful National Rifle Association is not easy, of course, not with their lobbyists continuing to make emotional appeals about "the right to bear arms" (based on an inaccurate reading of the original Second Amendment to the U.S. Constitution). Guns have been the source of many deaths over the years in Atlanta, a city with a majority-black population, and we feel a moral obligation to get them off the streets.

After opening in Atlanta, we moved on to Chicago. I knew little about the city and even less about its inner workings and who the star players might be, but I got lucky when I ran into a fellow graduate of the Notre Dame Law School. Ann Williams had been a judge with the United States District Court there, and on each of the many trips I made to interview lawyers for the firm she was there to show me the lay of the land, tell me who's who, and advise me as to what it would take to succeed in Chicago. In due time we found our man: James Montgomery, an elder statesman in Chicago legal circles and the only African American to serve as corporate counsel to the City of Chicago, a man who had engaged in numerous civil rights cases for little or no money back during the Fifties and Sixties. Jim was well known for once representing the estates of two Black Panthers, Mark Clark and

Fred Hampton, who were gunned down by Chicago police in the middle of the night as they slept. A tall, dignified man with a deep voice, Jim Montgomery reminds you of a learned professor who has descended from an ivory tower into the nitty-gritty of the real world in order to make things right for the less fortunate. He brought to the table that noteworthy presence and a stellar career (like Johnnie, he is a member of the American Academy of Trial Lawyers) and also, to our great good fortune, a wife to serve as manager of the Chicago office: Pauline, a native of Jamaica with strong family values, a stylish and knowledgeable woman whose addition brought both class and backbone to the mix.

As for New York City, I can't overstate the importance of Keith Givens's dogged persistence in mediating the dispute between our firm and Schneider, Kleinick, Weitz, Damashek & Shoot—the most powerful civil trial firm in the entire state—resulting in a merger that created The Cochran Firm, allowing us to practice law in the state. Up until then, Cochran, Cherry, Givens & Smith was located in modest offices in Greenwich Village, sharing space with a couple of first-rate lawyers from Johnnie's famous "dream team" of the O. J. Simpson defense, Barry Scheck and Peter Neufeld. Schneider-Shoot, at the same time, was located in the Woolworth Building on 33rd Street. Once the dispute had been settled, we not only had peace in New York but we also had the services of Scheck and Neufeld, masters of DNA evidence, and two of Johnnie's most trusted and respected friends. At last count, Barry and Peter had freed more than forty people from jails all over the nation, often on serious charges up to and including capital murder, on the basis of their work with DNA. Where once we had barely been able to get inside the door in my hometown, the greatest metropolis in the United States, we now found ourselves seated at the head of the table. As often happened during such times, I couldn't help but think of my father and how proud he might have been.

∾

Whenever possible, we tried to make the opening of a new office in a new city an *event*—not only a formal ribbon-cutting ceremony but a gala celebration as well—and that certainly describes what happened on the first Sunday in August of 2001 in Memphis. Sitting on the banks of the Mississippi River in western Tennessee, abutting the states of Arkansas and Mississippi, the city of Memphis had long played an important role in African-American memory. It was the home not only of Elvis Presley but B. B. King and bluesy Beale Street, a great steamy port where cotton picked by black slaves once was loaded onto barges owned by white plantation barons, and the place where Dr. Martin Luther King, Jr., was assassinated. Now, with a teeming black population of seventy per cent (and juries of a like makeup), Memphis seemed ripe for us. In spite of continuing injustices perpetrated against African Americans in Memphis over the years, especially in the areas of medical malpractice and workmen's compensation, the city was without a genuine black rainmaker until we came along. Thus, we had every intention of bringing a new standard of justice.

Again, as in Chicago and Atlanta and some of the other cities where we were establishing beachheads, I had served as point man in the search for the right lawyer to head up the Memphis operation. It didn't take us long at all to find the man who would become our general partner there: Julian Bolton, an African-American attorney of great organizational skills and personality and zeal, someone who had developed an intricate feel for the city's workings after serving as a county commissioner for more than twenty years, and after eleven years as a practicing attorney had shown that he not only was an able trial lawyer but also knew how to put money in the bank. Then the search began to fill the offices of what would become Cochran, Cherry, Givens, Smith & Bolton, and we were again fortunate to put together a first-class team that was varied in ages, gender, and areas of expertise. There was the lyrically named Dixie Ishee, with many years of specializing in medical malpractice, a big ticket in the area. Another profitable area of practice in Memphis was workmen's compensation, and for that we engaged a competent and experienced lawyer named Stephen Libby. With the addition of Danese Banks, a beautiful young lawyer with a bright future ahead of her (and whose father owned several hotels in Memphis, making him a powerful man in the city), we were ready to roll.

In keeping with our desires to taste only the best (no more dives like the one in New York), we were booked into the famous Peabody Hotel in downtown Memphis for the weekend, catty-corner across the street from the towering National Bank of Commerce building where the offices of Cochran, Cherry, Givens, Smith & Bolton were housed. Johnnie Cochran and the rest of the partners and major players in the national firm arrived on Saturday afternoon, to preview the offices and the reception venue and to meet with the local staff. Socializing, networking, reminiscing, and talking hard business all at once, we had dinner at the elegant Plaza Club and then, for those who wanted to get a feel for the music that had made Memphis famous, we wandered the sidewalks and the clubs of Beale Street.

The big show came on Sunday. Although each of the principal partners in the firm had business to attend, we weren't kidding ourselves. This was Johnnie Cochran's star turn, and we might as well take advantage of the enormous popularity he had been enjoying in the African-American community since the O. J. Simpson trial. Without that, there likely would be no Cochran, Cherry, Givens & Smith to bring us to Memphis on this griddle-hot weekend on the banks of the lazy Mississippi, bringing promises of a new day in

American justice to the bowels of the Deep South. More than five hundred people had been issued special invitations to attend the day's events, replete with speeches and eats and music, with the implied opportunity to meet the captain of the O. J. Simpson "Dream Team" of lawyers. As we went about our business, Sam Cherry and Keith Givens and I could rest assured that few of them had come to get our autographs or listen to us speak on the finer subtleties of practicing law. They wanted Johnnie.

He wore a white suit that day. With a contingent of the partners and associates and various aides tagging along on a chartered bus, Johnnie hit three church services on that Sunday morning, at the traditional black New Salem Missionary Baptist Church and St. Augustine Catholic Church and the evangelical Bountiful Blessing Temple of Deliverance, and when we arrived at the National Bank of Commerce Building in the early afternoon we were astonished to see the crowd already milling about the lobby, even though the Open House ceremonies weren't supposed to begin until five o'clock. Dressed in their Sunday best, toting cameras and copies of Johnnie's book to be autographed, they were his people—educated, articulate, Christian, African-American (about ten per cent were white), success-ful in law, politics, the church, education, whatever their calling— and there was no escaping them even if he had wanted to.

No matter what security measures had been taken, everybody seemed to have found a way to the firm's offices on the 26th floor of the NBC building, where there was a corner office for Johnnie's use whenever he was in Memphis. The view from there, especially on this bright summer afternoon, was spectacular. The Mississippi River sparkled in the sun, snaking its way around the downtown area on its long journey to New Orleans and the Gulf of Mexico, and you felt you could see through the tinted picture windows all the way to Little Rock 150 miles across the lush green fields of the Arkansas countryside. The guests were respectful as Johnnie held forth during a press conference in his office, explaining the firm's long-range plans to a gathering of media, but when it was over and time for a meet-and-greet photo session they swarmed him as though he were a major-league baseball star or a god suddenly dropped in their midst like a gift from heaven.

For the next three hours, downstairs in the lobby, the scene took on the feel of a revival meeting, political convention, and family reunion, all rolled into one. Snacking from plates of hors d'ouevres, moving to the music emanating from a baby grand piano and a horn and a guitar, excitedly chattering among themselves, the crowd had to be shushed when a brief program began as the sun slinked toward the horizon. There was an invocation by the Rev. Stephen P. Walker, up from Pope, Mississippi; some words from Jeanne Richardson of the Memphis office; remarks by the master of ceremonies, Clifford Stockton; a welcome by Jim Rout, the mayor of Shelby County, Tennessee; and an introduction and a few words from Julian Bolton, our new partner in the Memphis office. For the introduction of Johnnie, we turned to one of the great icons of the civil rights movement: Dr. Benjamin Hooks, now 75 and still pastor of his own church in his hometown of Memphis, wildly met by the older ones in the crowd who would never forget the days when he headed up the NAACP and later worked with Dr. King at the Southern Christian Leadership Conference during the darkest hours of the struggle for racial equality in America.

Finally, when Johnnie Cochran took the stand, it was as though we had reached the bottom of the ninth inning, tie score, the home team about to score the winning run. He was his usual spectacular self, joking about his height, praising the Lord for the good fortune of assembling such a staff, outlining the general plan we would follow, introducing me and all of the other partners and aides and other notable in attendance. You expected a *Can anybody say amen?* at any moment. It was that sort of day, but it wasn't over yet. Even though Johnnie had two radio talk-show interviews scheduled for early the next morning, he stayed around until he had signed the last of the 500 copies of *Journey to Justice* that he had brought along, made sure he had spoken personally to every single person in the crowd, and it wasn't until 10:30 at night that we all were able to sit down to plates of Creole cooking laid out by Yvette's aunt at her house on the outskirts of town. We had been welcomed to Memphis in style and were ready to do some business.

∾

At Johnnie's insistence, each grand opening of the various offices around the country was stylish and opulent.

Atlanta was phenomenal. We met during the day at the home of homerun king Hank Aaron, and in the evening more than 5,000 of the city's finest gathered for a concert by Stevie Wonder. Joe Edwards, a very close friend of Dale Cochran, assisted in the planning and development of the affair, with most of the proceeds from ticket sales benefiting an African-American museum in Atlanta that needed assistance, and Hezekiah Sistrunk worked tirelessly to ensure that it all came together.

In Chicago, managing partner Jim Montgomery and his wife Pauline, with the help of attorney Tom Murzooski, pulled off quite a weekend that was covered by at least ten television stations. More than 1400 people attended at the downtown Hyatt, prompting some to say that they had never seen so many Chicago-area lawyers, most of them African Americans, in one room. Soon Jim Montgomery and Johnnie would bring about a landmark settlement of $18 million in the case of a black woman's death at the hands of Chicago police.

The Los Angeles opening was held at Johnnie's original location, at 4929 Wilshire Boulevard, and our managing partner there, a great attorney named Cameron Stewart, did an excellent job of coordinating the event. Many stars and celebrities attended, befitting Johnnie's penchant for dignity and presence.

∾

Needless to say, this was a heady atmosphere for me, a grown-up version of the fatherless boy whose mother had once been advised that I might one day turn out to be a quite serviceable sanitation worker. So much had happened for me, so fast, since my first meeting with Johnnie Cochran, that it had taken eternal vigilance to keep both feet on the ground. My mother had always been there, not necessarily to celebrate the size of the settlements I had gained for my clients but to make sure they had been for a righteous cause. The echoes of my grandmother Bowers's homilies continued to ring in my ears whenever I was in danger of "getting too big for [my] britches" or might be forgetting that "The bigger they come, the harder they fall." And Yvette's presence in my life has been a daily reminder of where I was before I accepted the Lord as my savior, and what I have become since then with His help.

In this regard, my membership at Christian Life Church has served as an anchor. Whenever I have a serious problem squaring Christianity with my life as a lawyer, the people I talk to most often are Pastor Steve Vickers and his wife Denice, my good and true friends Sam and Willa Carpenter, and Cedric Varner, a church member who is a media genius. On Sunday mornings and on Wednesday nights, when I'm in town, I always sit in the pews beside Sam and Willa, right behind Steve and Denice, not far from Cedric, praying that their goodness will rub off. I'm convinced that African Americans can't win the fight to overcome inequality in the nation without Jesus at our side. I'll always remember Pastor Steve's response when I first asked him how he felt about Johnnie and the possibility of my joining him in a national firm dedicated to serving the least of these: "God has called you, son, you and Johnnie and your partners, to take the black lawyer out of the kitchen and place him at the dining room table so he might have a meal with his white brother."

I have a dream. For quite some time, as my business thrived and the national firm came to fruition, I began to embrace a dream of my own. It was modest, compared to Dr. King's famous vision of seeing absolute equality among the races of the world, but it was nevertheless important to me on a deeply personal level. From the first time I laid my eyes on a big old two-story Victorian house on Main Street in Tuskegee, empty and in dire need of a complete refurbishing, I envisioned something else. I wanted to buy that place, the site of a Primitive Baptist Church built in 1891, the second oldest building in Tuskegee next to the red-brick President's home on the Tuskegee University campus, and turn it into my offices. More importantly, for me, I wanted to name the structure for my father: the Jacob A. Smith Building. It seemed the best way for me to show to the public, to the world at large, the incredible debt I felt I owed to the man whose memory had at first haunted me and then lifted me as I tried to fill his shoes. I could think of no more fitting tribute.

The timing was certainly right. I could afford to buy the place and cover the considerable cost of fixing it up, for one thing. But for another I needed the additional space. My practice had long outgrown the little building beside the Macon County Courthouse in downtown Tuskegee. Now I was adding staff members, left and right, and needed space for them to operate. Once again, it seemed, I had managed to surround myself with strong women to help me carry on. By the time we made the move into the big house, and shortly thereafter, I felt I had assembled a staff that would be the envy of any lawyer.

The cornerstone, the rock, the office manager since she came over from the county board of education twenty years ago, is Brenda Pinkard. She has a quiet way about her that spills over to the others in the office, creating the sort of atmosphere necessary to get things done in a setting that otherwise might be hectic. Brenda knows my personal schedule better than I and makes sure I stick to it and that I'm prepared for all meetings, consultations, and trials. Being married to a major on the Tuskegee police force, she like all the rest has deep roots in Tuskegee and the black community. I met Tasha Scott at Christian Life Church, where she and her husband are members (Morris Scott is in the choir), and was impressed by her drive. She's the youngest in the office, and it's great to have such a talented Christian around to help us get things done. The same goes for Kimeletta Harris, our receptionist. And I'm proud to say that one of the newest members of my staff was one of the most dedicated straight-A students I had during my years of teaching at Tuskegee during the Seventies. Janice Spears (now Turk) had finished Howard University Law School, practiced law in Mobile, served as a municipal judge in the city of Pritchard, Alabama, married, and moved to Las Vegas. When she called to say she was moving back home to Alabama, I couldn't hire her fast enough. With her knowledge, drive, and experience, she has been more than able; even serving me from second chair in trials. Finally, another new asset to the legal staff in Tuskegee is Brian Strength, a young graduate of the University of Alabama. Brian previously practiced with a top defense firm and he brings great skills in legal research and writing.

∾

Friday, December 12, 1997, marked one of the happiest days of my life. More than 800 people came for the dedication of our new offices at 306 North Main Street in Tuskegee. Locals couldn't believe the transformation of what they had always known as "the old Allen home." Now, thanks to Yvette's sublime taste, it was a stately white antebellum mansion with six columns, porches upstairs and down, fourteen-foot ceilings, fireplaces, sleek hardwood floors, a conference room, separate offices for the staff, a modern communications system, a small kitchen, and even a room for meditation and prayer.

Scattered throughout the house are mementos representing my passions: sports, African-American history, and my father's memory. One of the rooms, doubling as the Scoring for Life! headquarters and Tasha Scott's office, has a home plate at the threshold as a sort of welcome mat and is filled with some of my baseball memorabilia. In the upstairs foyer is a mannequin draped in my father's drab wool U.S. Army uniform, and an enlarged photograph of my father with me when he was in his prime of life. Throughout the place are miniature statues of great black leaders from the past—Douglass, McLeod Bethune, Carver, Truth, and Tubman—and portraits of Dr. King, Justice Marshall, Presidents Truman and Roosevelt, the Tuskegee Airmen. In a back hallway there is an enlarged photo of me in a Mets uniform, taken when I participated in the first Mets Dream Week Camp in Florida, a present from Yvette.

We gathered beneath a tent set up in the rear parking lot, where there was plenty of food, drinks, and a band to celebrate the occasion. My daughter Janay Johnson served as mistress of ceremony, my stepfather Wade Nance gave the opening prayer, and a number of notables, all good friends of mine, were there to say a word: Benjamin Payton, president of what is now called Tuskegee University; State Senator George Clay; former Tuskegee Mayor Johnny Ford; Macon County Commission Chairman Jesse Upshaw; Tuskegee Mayor Ronald Williams; and Don Gilbert, executive director of the Alabama Trial Lawyers Association. There were remarks from Pastor Steve Vickers, my guiding light and spiritual advisor, from Christian Life

Church.

To end the day, in what we playfully referred to in the program as The Jock & Johnnie Show, Johnnie Cochran and I introduced each other. We spoke of many things—of this old house, of the formation of the new sports agency, of the hopes and dreams of African Americans in what Johnnie referred to as "a new day of justice"—and I was particularly touched when Johnnie concluded by saying, "The journey Jock has taken takes great vision. Service is the price you pay for the space you occupy. God is not finished with the work of Jock Smith." When it came time for me to summarize what all of this meant to me personally, I was finally able to come full-circle, gain closure, on the premature death of my father forty years earlier, on the spring day in 1957. I had come a long way from that little house on Nashville Boulevard in Queens to this lovely mansion in the heart of the Deep South. I couldn't help but think *Daddy, this one's for you.*

16

Lawyers in Groups

TO THOSE WHO know me best, the only surprise about my helping create a giant national law firm with Johnnie Cochran was that I've never been one to join organizations. Frank Sinatra's "My Way" had practically been my theme song from the very beginning, mostly due to circumstances beyond my control. I had been a black kid growing up in an otherwise white neighborhood in Queens, a fatherless only son after my daddy's death, an outspoken New Yorker on a bucolic campus in Alabama, one of the few blacks at Notre Dame Law School, a civil rights worker in Binghamton when there were few blacks interested in the cause, and so forth. For many long years I had labored alone out of my offices in Tuskegee, a lone wolf with a mind of my own, unwilling to run with the pack. I could count on two fingers the groups where I held membership—Alpha Phi Alpha fraternity and Christian Life Church in Montgomery—and that was the size of it. Although in due time I learned to delegate work and was advised by Pastor Steve Vickers that God, not I, was Master of the Universe, I still preferred to be, as Reggie Jackson put it, "the straw that stirs the drink." I had my own opinions about how things should be done, and I didn't like the idea of having to run them past a committee or a focus group.

Besides, I felt that organizations in general, and black ones in particular, tend to be bourgeois in their decorum and upper-middle-class in their mindset. Though many of them proclaim noble principles toward the less-fortunate among us, "the least of these," they mostly pay lip-service to the needy. Too often, their notion of helping the poor is to sponsor a dance on New Year's Eve or pass out turkeys on Thanksgiving or give an egg basket to a disadvantaged child on Easter Sunday. *Out of sight, out of mind* is how they look at it. *Let them eat cake.* Such contributions are miniscule in comparison to the bountiful blessings the Lord has bestowed on most members of these organizations, whether they be doctors or lawyers or businessmen. They surely aren't operating with God's Biblical charge that to whom much is given much is required. Consequently, at the beginning of my career, I felt I had better things to do than hang out with groups like that.

There were three major groups for lawyers in Alabama when I hung out my shingle in Tuskegee in the late Seventies: the all-black Alabama Lawyers Association; the Alabama Bar Association, a conservative white group that was more or less off-limits to the few black lawyers who were members of the Alabama bar (when I passed the bar in 1976, remember, I was only the twenty-seventh African American to have done so, *ever*); and the more liberal Alabama Trial Lawyers Association, which fostered the upward movement of successful civil litigators no matter their race. Despite my innate suspicions about most civic and professional groups, I warily joined the Alabama Lawyers Association around 1980. I was still in my apprenticeship as a struggling young attorney, working court-appointed criminal cases for as little as $10 an hour, scrambling to make ends meet, so I felt it might help if I got to know others in my profession. It worked on that level. I made many new friends who helped me on a personal and professional level.

Before I knew it, though, I was being elected president of the ALA for a one-year term beginning in 1983. I succeeded J. L. Chestnut, Jr., one of my real mentors, a fire-and-brimstone trial lawyer from the civil rights days (recounted in his memoir *Black in Selma*). Now, having seen how these groups work from the inside and being granted an opportunity to accomplish something, I had a vision. I would spend my year as president of the ALA trying to forge relationships between our beloved little organization for black lawyers with the two other groups: the staunchly conservative (and white) ABA and the more lenient (and powerful) ATLA. One of the highlights of my year in office came when I got up to speak at our annual banquet. "White folks are still ahead, but we're gaining!" I fairly shouted, quoting my father's famous line from nearly thirty years before, and the members were on their feet, roaring approval.

Sadly, they didn't really mean it. I found that many of the black leadership within our organization, at least the veteran attorneys who had made it, wanted no part of either the ABA or the ATLA. I wanted inclusion rather than exclusion, but they would just as well remain segregated. They wanted all of the benefits the other groups offered, all of the goodies that go along with membership, but they didn't care to participate with their white brothers. I found this dichotomy to be a bit strange at first, but somewhat understandable when I looked deeper. Some of these black lawyers, no matter how successful, still felt extremely uncomfortable in the company of powerful white attorneys and didn't want to admit it. Others simply felt that whites in general were so racist that nothing good could come from such relations and that, accordingly, it would just be a waste of time. I didn't believe that then, and I don't believe it now. Martin Luther King, Jr., had fought for inclusion rather than exclusion, feeling that if we are truly to have an upward movement in this society then we need to force these institutions to open their doors to *all* Americans.

∾

Little had changed, it seemed, by the mid-Nineties when I got a letter from Don Gilbert, at that time the executive director of the ATLA, inviting me to a meeting. In essence, they were attempting to recruit successful black lawyers for membership and this would be an introductory gathering. About fifteen of us black lawyers decided to attend, all members of the ALA, huddling together at the same table. It seemed clear from the beginning that most of these men still felt the same about keeping themselves segregated; that they had no intention of joining the ATLA; that they had come to this meeting out of curiosity more than anything. When Don Gilbert gave his presentation that night, he more or less waved an olive branch. The ATLA had made a mistake earlier, he said, by not reaching out to black lawyers earlier, and we should treat this meeting as a formal invitation for each and every one of us to join. The African Americans at the corner table merely nodded their heads as though to say thanks but no thanks, they'd heard all of this before.

When Gilbert had finished giving his invitation, I raised my hand. "Look, I'll participate, but I believe in Jeffersonian democracy," I said to him and the trustees and other leaders of the ATLA who were present that night. I defined "inclusion" for them as meaning full participation; that my point of view would need to be given equal weight with regards to the consideration of all issues involving the association. "Once proving my worth, if I decide to apply for a leadership position, then I expect to be given the same opportunity as any other member, an opportunity to learn and to lead and then to instruct." Don Gilbert assured me that this would be the case. I looked around and saw at least two African-American lawyers I could turn to for advice on the matter: Earnestine Sapp, another believer in inclusion, a pioneer who had made significant contributions in her career with the National Bar Association; and Tyrone Means, the only truly active black member of the ATLA, who appeared to be on track toward a top leadership position with the group. Based on their counsel, and the assurances of Gilbert, I joined.

For the next four or five years I actively participated in all of the association's seminars and conventions. I became a regular CLE (Continuing Legal Education) speaker on the ATLA circuit, and for the Alabama Bar Institute at the University of Alabama, as well as for the still-black Alabama Lawyers Association. I even served as a keynote speaker in a seminar about "the art of civil practice" held by the conservative predominantly white Alabama Bar Association. Within the first year of my joining the ATLA, I was selected to serve on the board of directors. I was finding my upward movement to be swift and fair, as Don Gilbert had promised, and there was no reason to think otherwise when, a couple of years later, I was selected for the executive committee, which votes on most of the major policy decisions made by the association. That sounded great to me until I learned that the ATLA had a group known as the Trial Trustees, six or seven individuals who were in actuality the ones who set policy for the association; who made the decisions and then passed it on to the executive committee to be rubber-stamped for approval.

Now that I was on the inside, I began to look around and see other things of that nature. Not surprisingly, given my cautious feelings toward groups of any size, I found both the good and the bad. It pleased me on the one hand to discover that many members of the ATLA were very open to the inclusion of blacks within the association, several of those serving as forward-thinking presidents. On the other hand, I wasn't particularly surprised to find that there were others in the group who still clung to their old ways.

To illustrate my point, there was the case of Tyrone Means, who ultimately became the first African-American president of the ATLA. One day I got a phone call from Jimmy Knight, who was serving as president at that time. Jimmy is a white man from Cullman, about an hour's drive north of Birmingham, an area known for its conservatism on matters of civil rights, a place of few blacks. He opened the conversation with, "Jock, I want to ask your honest opinion about something. It's about Tyrone Means, an African-American member of the association…" He wanted to know if I agreed that Tyrone would make a good president. I said yes, that he had been very active, had made significant financial contributions, and showed great leadership skills and a commitment to the trial bar.

Jimmy agreed and then asked if I thought Tyrone would be accepted by the traditional black leadership, which included the Alabama Democratic Conference and the Alabama New South Coalition, and I said yes again. I felt that Tyrone would receive the support of Joe Reed, executive director of the ADC, and of Richard Arrington, the outgoing black mayor of Birmingham and the director and founder of the ANSC. The way the ATLA works, one first has to get elected as an officer and serve for a four-year period before moving into the presidency during a fifth year. The question was, would a black person ever get into that rotation, guaranteeing a trek toward the presidency. Subsequently, after getting the support of Reed and Arrington, Tyrone's name began to surface as a possible candidate for president. With Jimmy Knight clearly pushing Means in that direction, things appeared to be going smoothly for a while. But then some rumblings began.

Tyrone had a son in Atlanta whose illness required special attention. This had caused Tyrone to miss an occasional meeting of the executive committee and other meetings, one involving a policy committee headed up by William Utsey, who had succeeded Knight as president. The rumblings didn't come from Utsey, who I found to be a fair and courageous president, but from some members of the ATLA who shall remain nameless. In fact, some of those members came to me and asked if I would be willing to be nominated, rather than Tyrone, because they didn't think he had what it took and didn't have the proper leadership skills. I disagreed with them, of course, telling them that Tyrone would get my full support. "Besides," I told one of them, "I'd never knife another African-American male in the back in order to get ahead in life. I wasn't brought up that way. It's just not right."

I soon discovered what their *real* problem was with Tyrone Means. He was a man who walked softly but carried a big stick. He was laid-back, calculating, questioning their actions at every turn, and that worried them. In short, they questioned just what Tyrone might do if he became president while I, on the other hand, had a different relationship with whites due to my background and personality. They felt more comfortable around me than with Tyrone, and if an African-American presidency seemed inevitable then they probably considered me the lesser of two evils.

Tyrone and I had many midnight conversations about strategy designed to ensure that he stay in the rotation toward the presidency in spite of the whites' concerns. At one point he became so frustrated that he felt he had to call on Joe Reed and Richard Arrington for support, and although I disagreed he turned out to be right. Tyrone was nominated, then elected, and recently concluded his year as president of the ATLA, the first African American to serve as such. Then the talk turned to my chances to follow in his footsteps.

I had already made a significant contribution to the organization back in the mid-Nineties when we were facing a severe threat from conservatives in Alabama that might put us civil lawyers out of business. The issue was tort reform, designed to severely limit the size of settlements in civil cases, and the bad guys were the Business Council of Alabama. Conservative Republican Governor Fob James had called a special session, thirty days in length, to deal exclusively with the issue of tort reform, and things looked threatening for us. It was clear that the BCA was out to get us, and just as clear that the ATLA would have to gather forces to stop them if we were to survive. The BCA seemed to have locked up the votes they needed in the State House of Representatives, and we were barely holding on in the State Senate.

President Utsey called a special meeting of the ATLA membership to address the situation. What we needed, he said, was a committee to fight the issue of tort reform. During the meeting, Jere Beasley, the state's most prominent civil litigator, said it was imperative that we have an African American on the committee. The most obvious choice was Tyrone Means, but he was absent that day, tending to his son's illness in Atlanta, so President Utsey turned to me. "How about it, Jock," he said. "Will you serve?" I knew that here was a huge opportunity being handed to me, a noble chance to serve the law, but at first I was reluctant. I was a sole practitioner at the time, not the member of a large practice, and I didn't feel I could afford to spend a month away from my office trying to stop tort reform. The room grew silent as the others waited for my response. Finally I realized that I had no choice. I said yes.

We began a series of meetings to discuss strategy. I was one of four statewide negotiators representing the ATLA—the others were Tom Methvin, Jim Pratt, and Garve Ivey, Jr.—and during the special session at the state capitol I had a chance to strut my stuff. The mediator was attorney Rodney Max, the most prominent in the state. Our choices were slim and none: State Senator Roger Bedford and Governor Don Siegelman were pushing for a fair tort reform package while another group led by Senator Steve Windom was for massive tort reform that basically would make civil litigation unnecessary, a sham, a thing of the past. There was no in-between. Both of our opposition parties, even those who favored a "fair" tort reform, wanted at least *some* way of putting a cap on civil judgments.

During the mediations, we found that some of the bills proposed by the BCA were downright preposterous; basically, they would wind up in effect excluding blacks from jury banks. One bill, in particular, proposed that juries be selected from five counties—the one where it had been filed plus four surrounding counties as well—the intent being, of course, to disenfranchise blacks by cutting out all-black juries throughout Alabama. I rolled up my sleeves and fought this vehemently.

I asked one of the BCA lawyers, "Why are you even proposing such a bill and putting in on the floor?"

"Well, we have a problem only with a few counties in the state," he said.

"You wouldn't be talking about African-American counties, would you?"

"In fact, I am," he said. "It's because blacks don't decide cases based on merit. They decide cases based on past wrongs."

Bingo. "I'm surprised to hear"—I was addressing everyone in the room, not just the BCA lawyer—"repeat, surprised to hear that you would so much as *acknowledge* that there have been 'past wrongs.'"

"Well, you know, in certain cases…"

I took him to school, reminding him that of Alabama's sixty-seven counties only six or seven of them were majority black. I told him about *McClure v. Maryland,* where Chief Justice Marshall wrote that the case was, in effect, "much more than about a bank," and that "taxation without representation is tyranny." I told him that taxation without representation, with no blacks on the jury books, was terrible, that his bill was downright racist, and he ought to be ashamed of himself. The room was silent. "Look," I said, "if sixty of sixty-seven counties are white, then you're still sixty counties ahead of me. So what's your gripe?" I had a rapt, captive audience as I ticked off the names of certain counties that were mostly white. "Can a black man get a fair trial in the Wiregrass? Can he get a fair trial anywhere in north Alabama? Can a black man get a fair trial in Lee County?" He said nothing. "Let the record reflect the silence," I said.

As the session broke for lunch, one of the BCA lawyers came over to me and said, privately, "I'm ashamed of this bill, Jock. We're wrong and you're right. I can't say it publicly, of course, you know that, but I'm ashamed." Rodney Max, the mediator, stopped me in the hall and winked at me. "I'm so glad I was here today," he said. "I wouldn't have missed this for anything."

Ultimately we got to the final day of the special session of the state senate, when the judiciary committee would vote. It seemed clear to many that some of these preposterous bills might get out of committee, that we didn't have the votes to stop them. I'd been lobbying for the entire month, had gotten to know each and every black member of the senate, had become a friend and confidante to such black senators as Sundra Escott-Russell, Charles Steele, Vivian Figures, and many others. After showing each of these the fallacies of tort reform and how blacks would be totally disenfranchised, that the legal system would be a mockery, they sided with our ATLA position. We were also able to galvanize every black senator except one, and all of those serving on the judiciary committee, against tort reform. And when it came time for the final tally, by one vote we kept those bills off the floor. In fact, every black senator on the committee along with a white senator, Pat Lindsey, voted to keep the bills off the floor. That's the only thing that saved us: the black vote. Jere Beasley turned to me as we stood in the room that day and said, "Jock, we owe you a debt that we'll never be able to repay."

∾

By now, of course, I was thoroughly enjoying my membership in

ATLA. After serving with the committee dealing with the ominous threat of tort reform, I began to receive a lot of cases from white trial lawyers across the state that enabled me to participate in trials where I never could have dreamed of appearing. Opportunities were galore everywhere. Everyone seemed to appreciate the extra effort I had given in stopping tort reform in its tracks and in shooting down other nefarious efforts to hamstring practitioners of civil law. There had been several other bills introduced along the way, above and beyond massive tort reform, designed to accomplish the same thing. One of them proposed putting a cap of $250,000 in damages on fraud cases, which wouldn't even have amounted to a rap on the knuckles to a large corporation guilty of committing egregious wrongs. There were other attempts to introduce bills that would allow no punitive damages whatsoever, or bills that would require having to prove impossible theories in order to even get the most fundamental cases to trial. It was clear that I had played a key part in the salvation of the ATLA. Without me, there would have been tort reform and the practice of law in Alabama, as we know it, would have been dead.

During Tyrone Means's tenure as president of ATLA, he had repeatedly told me that he was going to nominate me, or at least push for my inclusion in the rotation, for the presidency. He knew that I had paid my dues, and he felt that having only one black president would amount to tokenism. So when it came time for the nominating committee to consider me, I expected no resistance. I knew my record and I thought I had a good relationship with everyone within the leadership. I anticipated no problem. Boy, was I wrong.

I got a call one day from Tyrone, who told me there was concern in some camps about whether I could get the votes. "What do you mean?" I said. "I already have the votes." Then he told me that there were "one or two people" who were saying that during the previous election "your law firm"—Cochran, Cherry, Givens & Smith was up and running—had made a pledge of $50,000 to help political candidates but the pledge hadn't been honored. This was hogwash; no such pledge had ever even come up in any meeting of the firm. Anyway, had they forgotten to take into account all of the time that Jock M. Smith, Attorney at Law, a sole practitioner, had invested toward the very salvation of our livelihood? And now "they" were bringing up a pledge that the firm had never approved in the first place?

We were living in a world that still asked *What have you done for me lately?* I knew that and understood it, unfair as it might seem, but this was out-and-out subterfuge. Was racism behind it? I really don't know. All I can say is, my nomination or at least my journey toward it, was stalemated. I got commitments from Means, African-American attorney Lebaron Boone, Jimmy Poole, and my law partner Keith Givens, who had just served as president, which would have given me the four votes to get me out of the nominating committee and put my nomination on the floor. But I was informed that the opposition would be insurmountable and that there would be a bloodletting if I chose to fight it. At bottom, this was all about a pledge that had never been made in the first place.

Several meetings were held about this, but nobody seemed willing to compromise. At one point early-on, given my fighting spirit, I was all for a bloodletting if it came to that. But then I began to pray over it and determined that a raw open fight like that wouldn't accomplish anything for my race; would tear down the future of other African Americans to become leaders. I did manage to secure a letter of support from all of the members of the Black Senate Caucus, including its chairman, Sundra Escott-Russell, based on my relationship with them during the fight against tort reform, but that seemed to anger certain of the trustees rather than help my situation. One of those trustees said during a meeting one night that he was "sick and tired that every time a black person wants something he goes to a black organization." I retorted by asking, "Who do you want me to go to, the White Citizens' Council?" I simply felt they owed me; I had paid my dues not because I was black but because I chose to be a participatory member interested in the common good of the ATLA.

We were trying to work things out, getting nowhere, and when a conference call deteriorated into a heated verbal exchange Jim Pratt jumped in. "I've been listening in, gentlemen," he said, "and let me say this about Jock. He *did* make a significant contribution during tort reform. Everything he said he did, he did. I was there." There was silence on the phone. Nobody offered any justification for my nomination not to go through, and yet many of the leaders obviously intended to fight that nomination. Then someone said he would rather nominate Ralph Cook, a prominent African American who had served with distinction on the Alabama Supreme Court and had recently lost an election. My problem with Ralph was that he hadn't served or spent any time with the organization. I thought he was more than capable of making a good president (he and his wife Chelsey were my dear friends), but I also felt it was my time and that Ralph was being used by some of the leaders in order to get me out of the way. In addition, Ralph was a member of one of the most powerful law firms in the association, Hare-Wynn, which had given us presidents in the past and was looking for more in the future. That about did it for me as a candidate for president.

One day not long after that, I was surprised by a call from Jim Pratt, asking how I would feel about becoming a trustee; the first black trustee not only of the ATLA but of any similar organization in the nation, as far as he knew. He told me that he had already secured the votes, even those of the detractors with whom I had exchanged heated words during my failed attempt at the presidency. This was an interesting turn of events. They didn't want me to be president, but they would take me in as a trustee. Still feeling dislodged, disenfranchised, and under-appreciated, I told him I'd have to take it home and think about it.

Yvette, some of my law partners, and other confidantes strongly urged that I not accept the offer, since I hadn't been elected as an officer. I really didn't want to do it, to be honest, but I took a closer look at the situation and I prayed over it. I knew that the trustees approve all budgetary matters and also determine how much each candidate running for office should receive from the ATLA. I was very much aware that no African American had ever been included in those discussions, which made my decision even more pivotal. I heard the Lord saying that I should forget the angers I had been harboring: *No, son, you've got to be bigger than that. Go and serve your race. Break the color barrier and serve with distinction.* I suppose I also heard my father's words, ". . . but we're gaining." I had to think about the greater good, not about myself, and so with great reluctance I accepted the position.

Knowing that He is a forgiving God, one who forgives us of our sins and is in a covenant relationship with all of us, I decided to serve accordingly. I feel that I have a covenant relationship with all of my brothers in the ATLA, both black and white, and that this covenant is greater than any disagreements that I might have with them. So I buried the hatchet, extending them the right hand of fellowship and unconditional love, but with an understanding of my position as a watchdog, a gadfly, put in place to make sure that the rights and privileges of all African Americans are protected, as lawyers and clients and as ordinary citizens.

It's important to note, I think, that President Tyrone Means was most instrumental in the Jock-for-Trustee deal. Now, the first African-American president in the history of the ATLA was able to orchestrate a plan that brought about the election of the first African American as a trustee. That kind of leadership is what I had expected from him when he was named president. He had his heart in the right place, knew how to get things done, and he was looking out for the rights of African Americans. What my white brothers need to understand is that looking out for African Americans, a minority, is not in any way an act of racism. As Frederick Douglass said when times were much tougher for black people—"Power concedes nothing without a struggle"—was as true now as before. No one gives up power voluntarily. No one relinquishes a presidency, a trusteeship, a CEO position, or even the manager's job with a major-league baseball club without a fight (and we are still under-represented in each of those areas today). Every gain made by African Americans has been accomplished through the blood, sweat, and tears of blacks with the help of reasonable and forward-thinking whites.

We're not as far along as we need to be, even today, and it's not always easy going for people of either race who want to help the African-American cause. A few years ago, for example, when Don Gilbert resigned as executive director of ATLA, the association selected as his successor Ginger Avery, a white woman who had served in Don's shadow for many years as his assistant. Ginger had been most effective in working with the state legislature, and I found it most disturbing to hear the same old rumblings among some of the association rumblings merely because she was a woman and seemed to be helpful toward blacks. It took a while for the rumblings to subside. Thankfully, there has never been any controversy about Kathy Givan, head of our CLE program, the association's only African-American employee. "Kat" has always made sure that blacks have gotten fair representation regarding presentations, and she's always been a supporter to me both as a member and as a person; a great shoulder to lean on during times of need, particularly when I was having to make a decision regarding my involvement with the association.

In spite of all that has happened in the ATLA, both the good and the bad, I believe my point has been proven about the need for inclusion. As someone who had always been wary of joining organized groups, I had to learn that you have to work within the system. I never preached that the word "inclusion" would have "perfection" attached to it, but I did take advantage of every opportunity and was in the right place at the right time as a fully participatory member. How else would I have become a member of the special negotiation team during the fight against tort reform, or serve on the executive committee, or finally become a trustee? I would still be on the outside, looking in, if I hadn't accepted the challenge to champion inclusion in what might still be today a closed all-white society. It's been slow going—few African-American lawyers have become partners in major law firms, participated in blockbuster lawsuits, or bridged the gap to become known as major civil litigators—but yes, Daddy, we're gaining.

17

Politics and Race in America

LOOKING BACK, I can see now what a sheltered life I lived as a child. Racism was an alien concept to me, something I knew little about. Jackie Robinson had already broken the color line in baseball the year before I was born. We lived in an integrated neighborhood in Queens, and although we continued to attend an all-black church some of my best friends were white kids on the block and in school. If there was a "Negro problem" it was news to me, since all of our black friends were successful, and that certainly included my father, a partner in the only black law firm in Manhattan that had not originated in Harlem. Sure, I would hear my father's comments to my mother at the end of most working days—"White folks are still ahead, but we're gaining"—and take his advice that we, as black people living in a white world, had to be perfect; but blatant racism wasn't in my vocabulary in the Fifties.

I suppose that the first time it even entered my mind was in 1960, when I was twelve, and the campaign for the Presidency pitted the Democrat John Kennedy against the Republican Richard Nixon. I suppose I had seen some of their debates on television, between watching baseball and football games, because I recall being impressed by Kennedy's good looks, youth, and charisma. I was surprised, then, to hear my beloved Grandma Bowers, a good Christian woman, tell me one day that she wasn't about to vote for Kennedy. When I asked her why, she said because on "Meet the Press" he had said he "didn't know there was a Negro problem" in America. She voted for Richard Nixon that year, as did Jackie Robinson.

Obviously, both of them had misread Kennedy's statement. What Kennedy really meant was that there wasn't a "Negro problem," but rather a white problem with the Negro; the white man's fear that blacks might survive, endure, and even flourish in America if they were given half a chance at equality. He knew plenty about that, and cared about it a great deal more than Nixon, as evidenced by his liberal performance in the White House before he was assassinated for those very views. My grandmother admitted to me years later that she had been wrong about Kennedy, and Jackie Robinson said the same in his autobiography. But that was my first notion of a "Negro problem" and how important a part politics could play in correcting racial injustices in America.

∾

By the time I enrolled at Tuskegee Institute, smack-dab in the "Heart of Dixie," in the summer of 1966, my ignorance regarding tensions between the races had been considerably enlightened. Not since the Civil War, a century earlier, had the United States experienced such domestic violence and upheaval. Anyone who was fully aware of what was going on either wasn't paying attention or simply didn't care. The front lines were mainly in the Deep South, my new home, where every day, it seemed, brought more violence: dogs and water cannons, dynamitings, murders, skirmishes pitting redneck Klansmen and political demagogues against well-meaning white students from the East and embattled local blacks. The death toll was horrendous—assassinations, "redneck justice" freeing murderers in Mississippi and Alabama courtrooms, fatal rioting in city streets all over the nation—and now we had a long list of martyrs and bad guys to add to the history books: Medgar Evers, Martin Luther King, Jr.,

Viola Liuzzo; George Wallace, Bull Connor, and on and on and on.

Clearly, the key to racial equality was to gain full participation in the political process, and the only way that would ever happen was for African Americans to register and vote. White America, especially in the old Confederate states, had set up all sorts of roadblocks to see that that didn't happen: bogus "literacy tests" that few white voters could have passed, gerrymandering and red-lining black neighborhoods to dilute the scant black votes that did go through, and committing any number of other egregious violations of the U.S. Constitution. The real heroes and martyrs during the civil rights days of the Sixties were those who risked their lives, and there were thousands of them, while working on the Voter Education Project in the Deep South. Without the vote, enabling African Americans to enter public office, blacks would get nowhere.

As an undergraduate at Tuskegee in the late Sixties, studying philosophy and observing racism firsthand on a daily basis, I became politicized for the first time. I found that W. E. B. Du Bois had been right, as far back as 1903, when he wrote in *The Soul of Black Folks* that the greatest problem in American during the twentieth century would be a problem of color. Taking up the gauntlet thrown down by Frederick Douglass many years before—that you can't have crops without plowing the ground, and you can't expect rain without thunder and lightning—I began doing my little part as vice-president of the student body by leading protests against the Vietnam war and against George Wallace's Alabama National Guard. Now the quiet kid from Queens was into dashikis, Afros, and the clenched fist angrily pronouncing Black Power. I continued my activism later, during my three years at the Notre Dame Law School, by founding a chapter of the Black American Law School Association on campus.

The only time I would actively run for public office came when I returned to the Tuskegee campus in the mid-Seventies and became known as "Doctor Jock." I was teaching, studying for the Alabama bar exam, and working in the office of Bill Baxley, the fiery liberal state Attorney General. While later helping Baxley in his Democratic gubernatorial campaign—the one that failed when Republicans cast illegal crossover votes in the primary—I got bitten by the political bug. Politics being such a temptress, offering wild promises of fame and power, it happens to the best of us. Sticking to the grassroots arena, I giddily ran for the Tuskegee city council and was certain I had won until Johnny Ford's unbidden "endorsement" turned the voters against me—nobody wants to be told who to vote for—and I lost the only political race I would ever run.

Despite Baxley's failed campaign for governor and my own defeat, I still had enough belief in the political process to get involved in two more statewide elections. Both occurred in the Eighties, when I had hung out my shingle in Tuskegee and was learning law the hard way, taking on low-paying criminal cases, building a practice, learning my way around the Macon County courtroom, peeking over the shoulders of the greats like Fred Gray to see how they did it. This time around, I rode the wrong horse again—two of them, in fact—and the experience was enough to warn me that there must be a better way for me to help the nation's second-class citizens, my fellow African Americans, than through politics.

In 1980 I decided to support Jim Folsom, Jr., son of the famous populist ex-governor "Kissin' Jim" Folsom, in his campaign for the United States Senate. Jim had served as an Alabama Public Service Commissioner, where my wife Yvette had been employed as director of the trial staff. She and I had gotten to know Folsom and had some confidence in his liberal views and felt that he would help Alabama become a progressive state. He was running against a very good man named Donald Stewart, a liberal U.S. Senator with a track record of excellence, and we felt either would have been a fine senator. But I knew Folsom and I didn't know Stewart.

I really got my feet wet in Alabama politics that year. My desk at the Folsom headquarters was right across from Cornelia Wallace, the former wife of our old adversary George Wallace. I remember that she was a lively woman, wearing what seemed like a hundred diamonds around her neck, entering the room with an incandescent smile and lots of animated conversation. I also remember John Guthrie, a coal miner and the father of Jim's beautiful and charismatic wife Marsha, who taught me some of the complexities of Alabama politics. One day three prominent black gentlemen came to visit the headquarters and promised to deliver sixteen Alabama counties in exchange for well over $50,000. Guthrie was cool. At the end of the meeting, he placed $200 on the table and said, "Gentlemen, this is yours, a gift from the Folsom campaign for your support. Sorry we don't have fifty thousand dollars." They took the money and left in a hurry, the episode reminding me of something my mother had told me years ago, that "you can buy a nigger with a glass of beer." I was disappointed to find that it was still true.

Jim Folsom thought he was going to win that election, and so did I. Among my contributions was the wording of handbills that we delivered to households throughout Alabama. Traditional black leaders working for Stewart were so alarmed by the contents of the mailing, knowing they went straight to the soul and heart of the black community, that they called me and asked for a cease-fire. I told them that I was committed to Jim Folsom and therefore had to continue doing what I felt was right. In the end, Folsom defeated Stewart in the Democratic primary and we shifted our focus to the general election. Our opponent was the Republican Jeremiah Denton, a Vietnam veteran, and we all felt he was a joke. "They're going to elect me because I stand for what's right," Folsom told me, "and I'm a loyal Democrat. Besides, my daddy paved every road in north Alabama when he was governor."

Jeremiah Denton looked like a loser until three weeks were left in the campaign, when he came out with a television commercial showing him stepping off a plane; the first returning prisoner-of-war from Vietnam. I seemed to be one of the few who knew how devastating this ad could be in a state as patriotic as Alabama. Others in Folsom's camp didn't share my fears. They said Denton was a flash-in-the-pan and reminded me that no Republican had been a senator in Alabama for more than a century, since Reconstruction, and that the idea of someone beating the son of Gov. Jim Folsom was laughable. Even the pollster we had hired was telling us, right up to election night, that Folsom would win by ten or fifteen percentage points. As the results began to roll in on election night and Folsom fell behind, the chief strategist refused to believe what was happening: "Don't worry, our votes are coming in from the big cities and in north Alabama." But Denton's lead began to widen and by ten o'clock that night we knew it was over. That one ad on television had done us in, teaching me yet another lesson about politics: he with the big bucks and the right message wins.

Subsequently, in 1986, I got a chance to serve on the advisory board for a man named George McMillan when he ran for governor. George was an Auburn graduate, a lawyer with great charisma, a great delivery, and great enthusiasm for life, a visionary. He had already served with distinction as Alabama's lieutenant governor. "Without vision, the people perish," he would say as he trekked all over the state during his campaign. "It's time for excellence in Alabama." About a year before the election, McMillan was clearly ahead of all of his potential rivals, which included my good friend and former attorney general Bill Baxley, Jere Beasley, and several other prominent candidates. I thought for sure that McMillan would be elected the next governor of Alabama. But then he made a big mistake.

The McMillan people got the idea that Bill Clinton had successfully campaigned for governor of Arkansas on the issue of teacher testing, and decided that George should do the same in Alabama. When I heard of the plan, I cringed. "George, please don't do this," I told him during a telephone conversation one night. "This is a terrible mistake. You'll turn African Americans against you, and you already have that vote. They'll think that the test will be applied discriminatorily, just like the old days, forcing black teachers from the system." As it turned out, I was the only person on the advisory board who felt that way, because George reluctantly called me a few days later to say that he was coming out in favor of teacher testing.

When the black-and-white television ads came out, they didn't show the usual giant, strong-willed, charismatic McMillan but a shadow of that man. I expected the worst for him, but I did what I could to counteract the negative reaction that was sure to come from the black voters in the state. George called me again one night and asked me if I would deliver an address before the Alabama Cattleman's Association at a private club in Birmingham. "Why don't you get one of your white workers to do that?" I asked him. "Because Alabama is ready for you, Jock," he said. "These men will be impressed by you. A black speaker, in front of an all-white audience of cattlemen, this is how we're going to change Alabama."

The only other black man in the audience that night was my brother-in-law, Sam Munnerlyn, who drove me up to Birmingham to deliver the speech. The first thing I told the crowd was, "It's time for excellence. If you elect George McMillan as governor of Alabama, he'll throw the football on first and ten, the way Joe Willie Namath did at the University of Alabama, and the defense won't be set, and all you'll hear is 'Touchdown, Alabama!'" The crowd roared, and I had them in my hand the rest of the night. George spoke briefly and came to me afterward, nearly in tears, repeating himself: "I told you we're going to change Alabama, and this is how we'll do it." I still had my doubts about his chances.

His last big opportunity to turn everything around came when we went to Mobile to seek the endorsement of the New South Coalition, a powerful black group headed by Richard Arrington, its founder and the first black mayor of Birmingham. George had worked diligently to build a biracial coalition in Bull Connor's old town that made Arrington's election a reality, and that made him confident that he would get an endorsement from the New South Coalition. Speaking to them that night, he was brilliant—quoting Langston Hughes and Countee Cullen, showing that he was familiar with black literary artists and the black mindset in general—but it wasn't enough. Arrington and some of the other leaders told him bluntly, afterwards, that he had killed himself in the black community with his teacher-testing message; that they didn't think he could win; that the New South Coalition planned to endorse Bill Baxley for governor. Later that night, in his hotel suite, I found George with tears in his eyes and his hands over his face; shocked and devastated. He lost to Baxley in the Democratic primary and dropped out of sight in Alabama politics, never to return. As it turned out, that would be my last go-around, too.

∾

Distraught over how bad things kept happening to good people in Alabama politics, for reasons sometimes out of their control, not long after George McMillan's defeat I had one last flirtation with running for public office myself. I would, believe it or not, take a shot at becoming the state's attorney general. *Why not?* went my thinking. I was a good lawyer and getting better. I was well-known within the black community and among judges and other lawyers. If nothing else, I felt, merely by running for a statewide office I could instill pride and give hope to black people by breaking that color barrier.

This was soon after I had been born again and found a spiritual home at Christian Life Church. There was no question that I had better have a chat with Pastor Steve Vickers on the matter. I did most of the talking that day, giving him all of the reasons why I thought I wanted to run, and after ten minutes he stepped in with a question.

"Have you asked God?"

"No, Pastor, as a matter of fact, I haven't."

"It seems essential to me."

"I suppose you're right."

The room was silent for a few moments. "Jock, if you run for attorney general, we'll all be for you. I'll do everything I can to help you get elected. I'll call pastors across the state. I'll pray and do everything. You know that." He took a deep breath and looked deep into my eyes. "But there's something else I want you to know. In the midnight hour when the phone rings and it's a Ku Klux Klansman or someone else on the telephone shouting racial epithets, the only thing that'll sustain you during that time, because I won't be there during that hour nor will any of your other supporters, it's God. If you don't know you've been ordained by God to run for this office, then you won't last through those phone calls. You'll be destroyed and you won't have the intestinal fortitude to continue the race that's been set for you."

"Now that you put it like that," I said, clearing my throat, "my campaign has ended before it got started."

∾

It was almost as though a great burden had been lifted from my shoulders, a burden I had placed there myself. I spent a great deal of time talking to myself, to Yvette, and to God over the next few days, and the upshot of it all was that I more or less rededicated myself to accomplishing what needed to be done for the poor people of Alabama not in political office but in the courtroom. There's an old saying, "Find your power and use it," and that's what I intended to do from now on. I had learned a great deal about the workings of politics and government in the state, but now, letting go of politics, I was going to take my God-given legal skills and become a gunslinger for the little people, the disenfranchised, those who needed it the most. Let others run for office, gambling on fickle voters and the whims of advertising. I would do my work in the courtroom, where I had more faith in juries and my ability to handle them.

A closer look at history convinced me that good and faithful lawyers had accomplished more than politicians, anyway, when it came to serving the common good. Too often, politicians find themselves locked into a system that requires them to negotiate, to mollify, to make deals, to soften their stands on the issues, if they intend to stay in office. Many a good one in our history hasn't lasted long (see Jimmy Carter) if he refused to fit in with a "system" teeming with lobbyists and party loyalties and other forms of powerful "traditions" and self-interest. I like the word "gunslinger" to describe the energetic lawyer who rolls up his sleeves and goes to work in the lonely and often unglamorous business of taking care of one injustice at a time.

Many of these men had been charismatic giants, well ahead of their time, winning important cases long before blacks were allowed to sit on juries. Talk about gunslingers, unafraid of anything and anybody, how about Fred Gray in 1960, when the civil rights movement was barely in its infancy? Tuskegee and Macon County had always been heavily black, going all the way back to the days of slavery in Alabama's Black Belt, but at that time gerrymandering had become another devious way of denying the vote to black citizens. The city of Tuskegee, in fact, had been cleverly cut up into a twenty-eight-sided figure that succeeded in placing most African Americans outside the city limits, to the extent that exactly four blacks—count 'em, *four*—were allowed to vote. But Gray found a way. This one lawyer, not long after representing Rosa Parks during the bus boycott in Montgomery, brilliantly argued *Gomillion v. Lightfoot* before the United States Supreme Court and almost single-handedly won the case that would end gerrymandering in the city and county. And then there was Johnnie Cochran, who had filed a lawsuit to stop police use of the brutal "choke-hold" that had resulted in the loss of many African-American lives.

Curiously, carrying the banner for racial justice in those days had been both easier and more difficult, at the same time. It had been easier simply because the injustices were so blatant: separate public accommodations, illegal voting laws, discriminatory practices in housing, education, hospitals, and jobs. America was living in a system that amounted to out-and-out apartheid, no less than in South Africa, and it was clear for anyone to see what needed to be done. What made overcoming it so difficult was the white man's unwillingness to give an inch in the war against racism. A black lawyer or a white sympathizer—an "outside agitator"—could get killed for trying to overthrow the system, and many did during the Fifties and Sixties all over the South.

As the twentieth century drew to a close, the face of racism in America had changed dramatically. Segregation, per se, seemed to be a thing of the past, except in housing patterns and in churches on Sunday mornings. All of the blood, sweat, and tears shed during the violent years of civil rights activism had brought about justice and equality of a sort. We had plowed the ground and sowed the seeds and summoned the rain, and now the crops were coming in. Yes, some blacks were voting, serving on juries, attending the schools of their choice, sleeping and eating where they liked, practicing their chosen careers, and running for public office. On the surface, at least, it appeared that the "Negro problem" had been solved. In the late Nineties, before I had joined with Johnnie Cochran in the national law firm, our daughter Janay shocked Yvette and me one day when she said, "Mom and Dad, y'all just don't realize how bad blacks have it. You're educated, you live in an affluent integrated neighborhood, and you're both black professionals." We took serious issue with her. How could she say this? We had been there from the beginning, hadn't we? We had brought the walls tumbling down, had desegregated America. But, you know what, she was right. Racism lives. Particularly in the great sprawling urban ghettos, places like Newark and Watts and Detroit, the majority of African Americans have been utterly disenfranchised.

∾

The new racism that we see in America today is more subjective and harder to put a handle on than before. Many black people in the country, if given a choice, would say they would rather be white than black. White people might begin to understand it if they could be black for thirty days. Black people know, because they practically have a seventh sense, a *racial* sense, and we can see through the fog better than whites. When a brother is screaming "racism," we know whether he is faking it or is simply lazy, but by and large we know the chances are good that he's hit the target on the nose. It's the little subtleties that get to you after a while. I remember having a conversation once with a black client, Varnell Weeks, accused of murder, and asking him what values he placed on life. He said he'd like to ask me a couple of questions first. "Do you think you'll ever get the chance to be the general counsel for First Alabama Bank?" I said no, of course not. "Do you believe Martin Luther King was a good man?" I said yes, of course. "Well, they killed him. Does that's answer your question?" Utter despair had brought him to that cell on Alabama's death row. He was one of those angry black men in America who have become part of an endangered species—raised in substandard conditions without heating, air-conditioning, enough food, a decent job, or any hope that things might get better—and this response might as well have served as Varnell Weeks's epitaph. *Well, they killed him.*

Much of the racism practiced today is institutional. There is a glass ceiling at the upper levels of most corporations, blocking even the most talented African Americans from ever reaching the top floor, the penthouse, the domain of the elite executives. Blacks are still the last to be hired and the first to be fired; the ones who are overlooked for promotion and receive less pay than whites even when they hold the same job. After participating in several major cases where I traveled the country to interview blacks in order to inspect the workplaces and sort out the issues, I was astonished to find hangman's nooses and Nigger-Go-Home signs in black men's lockers, and regular use of the "N" word by white superiors in major corporations. On a visit to a plant in Greenville, South Carolina, I was told by a black woman that her supervisor was still referring to the workers under him as "black bitches." When the woman complained to the supervisor's boss, he told her, "You've got to give him time. This is the South. He'll get over it one day and change."

The worst racism of all, and too often the deadliest, is police brutality. We didn't need Mark Fuhrman, the racist LAPD cop who zealously tried to nail O. J. Simpson on killing his wife and her friend, to remind us of this. Hardly a day goes by that our law firm doesn't receive a call on our national toll-free numbers about an unarmed black male who has been gunned down by a white police officer. Black males, that most endangered of species, are more likely to be shot and killed without a weapon, most likely to be stopped by the police for no good reason, and most likely to be disenfranchised and humiliated in front of their families and loved ones. The term "Driving While Black" long ago lost its ironic humor for those who have seen blue lights flashing in their rearview mirror while they happen to be passing through a white neighborhood.

∾

I once heard a black man say that the only good Republican he'd ever heard about was Abraham Lincoln, and he wasn't even sure whether Lincoln was really trying to do anything more than save the Union during the Civil War. I wouldn't go so far as to say that all Republicans are "bad." Good ones coming to mind are Jack Kemp and Lowell Weicker, both thoughtful conservative Republicans regarded as moderate-to-liberal on issues of race—but all-in-all, though far from perfect, the Democratic party seems to be the best choice for African Americans and for Christians. There's an irony here: Republicans appear to be right on the issues of God and wrong on the issues of people, while the Democrats seem to be right about people but wrong about God. I say "appear" to be, because sometimes you have to decide just how truthful a political candidate is when he begins swearing on the Bible to make us believe that he is truly driven by Christian causes. I don't believe for a minute that Senator Jesse Helms of North Carolina, for example, is sold out to Jesus; many, like Helms, have merely learned to mimic Christian buzz-words as a smoke-screen to make us *think* that they're on the side of the Lord. We should watch what they *do*, not listen to what they *say*. After all, Jesus wasn't a right-wing card-carrying Republican. His pockets are empty to such injustices. There was nothing *political* about the arrival on the scene of Martin Luther King, Jr., to lead African Americans toward the Promised Land; the King of Kings sent King.

Even those of us involved in the born-again Christian movement are often guilty of dropping our guard and being lulled to sleep by these conservative Republicans. Many Christians have been duped into believing that there are only three issues that are important in determining whether to vote for a candidate: abortion, prayer in the schools, and saluting the American flag. Although I truly believe that those are extremely important issues—I am anti-abortion, pro-school prayer, and as patriotic as the next person—I don't believe that those issues alone should determine how one should vote. I'm much more interested in determining what's in the heart of a candidate; whether he has genuine compassion for his fellow man, unconditional love for his brothers, a commitment to serving "the least of these" as the Bible commands. I think Christians are going to have to learn how to become more informed and more careful in order to understand that Satan "comes as a thief in the night to steal, kill, and destroy (John 10:10)"; that you can be killing and stealing from yourself if you continue to elect people who want an America segregated not only on Sunday morning but at every other hour of the week.

The United States of America is the greatest country in the world, bar none, but what prevents us from being an even greater nation is racism. Oh, it's better these days—my father had it right when he said "white folks are still ahead but we're gaining" way back in the Fifties—but how do you explain the continuing use of the "N" word, or the fact that only three per cent of the lawyers in Alabama today are black, or the blatant disenfranchisement of black voters in Florida during the Bush-Gore Presidential election, or the shocking fact that fifty-five per cent of the voters in one Alabama county voted to keep that state the only one in America banning interracial marriages? Despite the good works of many thousands, even millions, of people of both races to overturn antiquated and barbaric laws and mores designed to "keep the nigger in his place," we are still two nations: one black, the other white. Decades have passed since Malcolm X noted that the "most segregated hour in America is eleven o'clock Sunday morning," and brother Malcolm would spin in his grave to see that not much has changed in the years since his assassination. Politicians and lawyers can only do so much. There comes a time when Americans must look deep into their souls and finish the job of creating true racial equality themselves.

Sometimes, sitting in the pews at Christian Life Church in Montgomery on a Sunday morning, I feel as though I'm living a dream. I look around and what I see is a white man, Pastor Steve Vickers, one of the most committed soldiers for Christ that I have ever known, preaching the word to a thoroughly integrated congregation: rich and poor, black and white, male and female, united mainly by their desire to do right in service to the Lord. My mind wanders to the time when Billy Graham took his crusade to South Africa, agreeing to go only when the government allowed integrated seating, and during the service saying that it "warms my heart to see white ushers seating black Africans, because that's what Jesus would have wanted." We will finally be turning the corner in the fight against racism when we heed the words of Billy Graham and Martin Luther King, Jr., and Steve Vickers and all of those other great Christian men of our time; that there is only one race, a *holy* race, saints every one, all of them committed to the notion that a man should not be known by the color of his skin but by the strength of his character.

18

It Was All About Termites

ONE DAY IN March of 1999 I got a call from Patricia Diak, an attorney with the firm of Ritchie & Rediker in Birmingham, about a case involving Orkin Exterminating Company. Trish told me that in the process of delving into a massive pile of documents during pretrial discovery for a pending class-action suit against Orkin in Dothan—the company had failed to perform its annual inspections as required by contract—she had stumbled across a remarkable memo regarding an Orkin client in Tuskegee, an elderly and poor black widow by the name of Artie Mae Jeter. Ever since 1977, Trish explained, Mrs. Jeter had been paying premiums on a lifetime contract with Orkin to insure her house against termite damage; and now the house was being devoured by termites, chomp by chomp, but Orkin was doing nothing about it.

I could practically feel Trish Diak's rage over the phone as she read from the memo she had uncovered. It was from a district manager named Bill Maxwell, addressed to a regional manager, regarding Artie Mae Jeter's house on Martin Luther King Highway in Tuskegee. Maxwell's memo to his boss admitted that the house was full of termites, could not be repaired, and that if Mrs. Jeter ever found out about the problem and hired an attorney, Orkin would be in deep trouble. It went on to say that she was old, black, and in poor health and might soon die anyway, suggesting that if she did pass away, Orkin's problems would die with her. Then came the kicker. Maxwell had scribbled a note, dutifully quoting Mrs. Jeter's complaint that if she weren't a black woman she wouldn't have been treated this way, and he wrote in the memo that he couldn't honestly say that he disagreed with her statement.

When I heard the excerpts from the memo, I became as outraged as Trish. Never, in all my years of practice, had I heard such self-incriminating evidence. Trish immediately drove to Tuskegee, showed Artie Mae Jeter the memo, and Mrs. Jeter retained the services of Trish's firm and mine against Orkin. That same month, March of '99, *Artie Mae Jeter v. Orkin Exterminating Company* was filed at the Macon County Courthouse in Tuskegee. I had been waiting for a case like this for years. It was the most egregious example I had ever seen of a smug corporation taking advantage of "the least of these."

In August, Mrs. Jeter came by my offices to give her deposition. Even though she was feeble, her health in rapid decline, she did extremely well during the deposition: talking of her life (for thirty years she had worked at John A. Andrew Hospital, changing beds and caring for patients), and of her house, the termites, and her sad dealings with Orkin. In December, she died at the age of seventy-eight, leaving the damaged house to her three sons. We lawyers in the case hastened to substitute the sons as representatives for her estate, in her behalf, to continue the suit. This was challenged by Orkin's lawyers, of course, but their efforts failed. I was busy that spring and into the summer, dealing with other cases, but then in July, during a docket call of all cases pending in Macon County, I found that the case was going to trial in August of 2000.

∽

When I finally read the memo in full, I got charged up and enraged, ready to go. A mediation was assembled for all parties, but when we wound up talks seven million dollars apart, an indication that Orkin's arrogance continued unabated, it was clear that we would be going to trial. I felt so confident that I called my daughter Janay's college sorority sister and closest friend, Ceeon Quiett, who was employed by the Montgomery *Advertiser*, to see if she could convince the paper to cover the trial in Tuskegee from beginning to end. I couldn't guarantee how it might go, but I just had a feeling in my heart and soul that we were going to do well; the same feeling I had about the deal going through for the house on Lansdowne Drive, and the same feeling when I felt Jesus sitting next to me in Judge Bryan's chambers during the *Wellman v. Seaboard* case in LaFayette. If I hadn't felt so positive of the outcome, I certainly wouldn't have invited the media to see for themselves. I wanted the world to read of Orkin's misconduct.

Prior to the trial's beginning, the other co-counsels in the case decided that I could choose any witness I wanted and play any role I deemed necessary. (The other counsels were Andy Hollis of Pittman, Hooks, Dutton & Hollis in Birmingham; Patricia Diak and Mike Rediker of Ritchie & Rediker in Birmingham; and Rufus Smith and Steve Etheredge of Dothan.) They had already determined that I would make a presentation during the opening statement and that I would be the last person to speak to the jury, during closing arguments. But there was no decision about whether I would examine the most critical witness in the case: a corporate representative who had testified more than a hundred times over the years for Orkin. Hollis and Smith and Etheredge had deposed this man many times, knew his deposition history backwards and forwards, and felt I shouldn't bother with him. Only Trish Diak, one night after dinner when the trial was underway, told me that I should take him on head-to-head.

The morning after Trish's advice, as I met with the others to plan that day's strategy, I told them I had made up my mind. "Gentlemen, and lady," I said, "I've decided to take on the corporate rep." They were shocked. "But Jock," one of them said, "you don't know this man's history." I said it didn't bother me, that I'd read his depositions in *this* case and that was enough, I was ready to go. "Well, you'd better get busy studying as much as you can," somebody said. "You're going to need it. This guy's a hired gun, ready for bear. He's a prepared witness who'll cut you to shreds if you make one error in your questioning."

I felt in my spirit that I was ready to go. I knew what to do, and I wasn't afraid of this witness at all. I had the Lord on my side. I felt like David that day. I had brought my slingshot to court. I began by asking whether he was a good company man, and he said yes. I asked if he knew Bill Maxwell, and he said yes.

"You believe in Bill Maxwell, don't you?"

"Yes."

"Bill Maxwell was an able employee of Orkin, am I right?"

"Yes."

"Would you believe Bill Maxwell under oath?"

"Yes."

"Did Bill Maxwell ever say anything to you during the twenty-plus years that you worked together at Orkin where it turned out to be not true?"

"No, sir."

Then I showed him the memo, dated December 12, 1988, authored by Bill Maxwell, and asked him if he had ever seen it before. When he said he had, I then went through the memo, concept by concept. I married him to the fact that Maxwell had said the house was unfixable. I married him to the fact that Maxwell had quoted Jeter as saying she was being treated differently because she was black, and that Maxwell had said he agreed. I married him to Maxwell's statement that she was old, poor, black, and in poor health and was going to die soon, anyway; and yet Maxwell was still leading her on, still had her confidence. I just plain flat-out married the witness to the document.

Orkin was doomed the minute the cross-examination was completed. As I went back to the conference table I was hugged by Andy Hollis, who was so full of excitement that he stood and applauded me. He whispered into my ear: "I can't believe it. That's the best cross-examination I've ever seen in my life. Boy, we've hit a big lick here." Later in the day he asked me how I had done it with so little preparation. I said, "Andy, this was about psychology as much as about preparation. There's no right or wrong answer he could have given me. If he'd said Maxwell was a dishonest employee, he would've buried the company. If he'd said what I expected him to say, that Maxwell was an honest employee of great truth and veracity, then I would simply marry him to Maxwell's memo." The company's witness, in the words of Martha and the Vandellas, had "nowhere to run, nowhere to hide." He was mine. We chopped him up and cut him down to size and then tossed him into the trash can where he belonged.

Andy Hollis opened our closing arguments by giving the background information and then advising the jury how critical this case was, telling them that they needed to return a substantial verdict. Then came the closing argument in behalf of the defendant, Orkin, by a brilliant African-American lawyer named Robert Thompson. I had gotten the idea that Thompson was only reluctantly assisting in Orkin's defense. He had been in and out of the courtroom during the trial, not participating very strongly, and it was clear to me that he had mixed emotions, that he didn't approve of his client's conduct in the case. But he did prepare himself well for the closing, and came out firing bullets. He indicated that the Book of Leviticus ought to apply here (a debt plus a twenty per cent "punishment"), saying that the jury should award us $500,000 and no more, which was what he calculated the Jeter estate was owed under the contract plus twenty per cent interest. He was making a plea for Old Testament justice, indicating that he and Orkin were there for atonement while we were there "for a *crucifixion!*" I remember thinking how right he was; it was too late for atonement, and a crucifixion was exactly what we wanted. We were going to win because this was the greatest case of injustice I had ever been involved in. Orkin was just dead wrong for discriminating against Artie Mae Jeter for twenty-plus years, and this was going to be the day it stopped. I prayed during the entire time that I would tap into God's anointing. It wasn't a battle of Jock Smith against Robert Thompson, but rather a battle between right and wrong, although I thought Thompson did such a brilliant job that the judgment otherwise might have reached a staggering $200 million.

ॐ

Finally, the time had come for me to deliver the rebuttal closing in behalf of my client. In sports terms, this would be the bottom of the ninth, two outs, bases loaded, the game on the line; time to deliver the *coup de grace*, the sword through the heart; time for the knockout punch; time for the slam dunk to put the game away as the final buzzer sounds. The evidence is already in. By now, if the lawyers have done their job properly, the one presenting the closing statement has read his jury and knows where to go with his final statement. You go straight for the soul with an emotional plea, a spin on the facts that have been laid out, something like an evangelist's call to come to the altar.

I began my final summation that morning, August 18th, 2000, by thanking the people on the jury for their time and reminding them that their decision would finally bring justice, even though posthumously, to a woman who had kept the faith for eighty-seven years until she died, unfulfilled, back in December. "The Bible says that you should leave behind to your children's children your inheritance," I said. "And this case is about how these defendants stole that inheritance. It is about your being trailblazers for justice and doing the Lord's work..." Now was the time to pull out all of the stops and go full-speed ahead.

"Her name was Artie Mae Jeter and for twenty-plus years they continued to cheat her. But this is the day—*this is the day*—that the word will go forth to the nation. This is the day that the word will go forth to the State of Alabama. This is a day that the Lord has made. And when you render a proper verdict in this case, the county, the people, and the world will rejoice and be glad of it, because you will have been drum majors for justice. I ask each and every one of you to search your heart, to search your conscience, to search your soul, to search your inner being as a soul that came out of the earth from the Father. When He formed man and made him in the image of God, He took him out of the dust, and we ask you, ladies and gentlemen, to respect, revere, and to honor that man that the Father made...

"[This] is not about 2604 West Martin Luther King Highway in and of itself. It's about a lifetime guarantee that turned out to be a nightmare. After paying three hundred and thirty dollars up front to these defendants, and paying year after year the inspection fees, and year after year taking that hard-earned money that she made at John Andrew Hospital as a nursing aide, all she got from this defendant is a house that is now ninety-five per cent damaged by termites. You have heard [an Orkin inspector] who worked in the State of Florida for eight years, looking at termite problems, and he came here and testified that they had consumed ninety-five per cent of this structure. *Consumed*, he said, and I wrote that down. And there was a contractor who testified, saying, 'I was afraid to stay in there, it was so bad. It's not livable, it's so bad.'

"We've gone over this memo, over and over again. Nobody made

Maxwell write this memo. He wrote this himself. And let me ask y'all something else while we are sitting here swearing and affirming about this memo. Do you think Maxwell ever thought the Jeter family would ever see this? No. They never thought this thing would hit the light of day. Yeah, yeah, Attorney Thompson is right, once Trish Diak got hold of it, she sure did tell Mrs. Jeter about it. They can call this a 'lawyer's lawsuit' all they want, but so was *Brown versus Board of Education*, which desegregated the nation. That was a 'lawyer's lawsuit' as well, and nobody believed in it, but it was right.

'The Bible says that 'out of the abundance of the mouth the heart speaks. *Out of the abundance of the mouth the heart speaks.* 'That's what the Bible says. And let's see what came out of the abundance of Bill Maxwell's heart so we can see how his heart is speaking to us. He writes all this stuff in this memo. 'We never told her the truth. We took her money and never told her the truth.' That's true. They sure did that. They took her money for twenty-plus years and never told her the truth. He's right about that. And they didn't intend for her to find out about it, because they never expected this sucker to surface. Never. Do you know when Artie Mae Jeter found out about it? In March. Do you know when she died? In December. For the last eight or nine months of her life, she lived in that house with this memo.

"'Out of the abundance of the heart the mouth speaks,' says the Bible. 'She's seventy-eight years old, black, and in poor health, with no money, and we do not have a graph.' *Out of the abundance of the heart the mouth speaks.* This is the real Bill Maxwell down there. That's what he thought about her. He wrote it. Didn't nobody make it up. Didn't nobody say he said it. It wasn't hearsay. It wasn't, 'I told you,' or, 'I heard, child, I heard, honey.' What did he say? 'What did Mama say last week?' Oh, what did Bill say on December 12, 1988, when he was stroking his little pen? Out of the abundance the heart speaks. His heart was speaking as he wrote on the paper. His heart is still speaking today. He's speaking. He's speaking. He's speaking. And what do you think about how he speaks? You like it? 'Ha-ha-ha! Blow it away. Small case. Let it pass. Ha-ha-ha! Insignificant. It doesn't matter. *It doesn't matter*. Look, just disregard it. Chalk it up.'

"And let me tell you all something else. Attorney Thompson asked why we didn't bring in these hundred-and-fifty cases where these people hadn't been told they had termite damage. Well, there are three answers to that. First, Bowman told the truth himself. He told us what he was told to do, what he was instructed to do. And when Hardy was on the witness stand, y'all heard it. Y'all were watching real closely when I was cross-examining Mr. Hardy. I said, 'You're a good company man, aren't you? You've been with the company over forty years. You've testified in over a hundred trials.' And he admitted, 'Oh, you don't tell the customer about the damage. You turn that in to the manager.' *Turn that in to the manager.* He already told you what the company policy was. The corporate rep, the guy who has been with the company for forty years, just confirmed what they have been doing. It was simply a buffer zone to further give credibility to the shoddy way that Orkin does business and treats people. 'We don't tell the customer.' In other words, if you take out a hundred-thousand-dollar guarantee, they are supposed to treat and re-treat your house. 'At no extra cost we will re-treat and repair the structure and the contents to remedy any new damage.' And you pay your hard-earned money, ladies and gentlemen of the jury, and they don't even tell you about the damage. 'Oh, we can't tell the customer *that*. We go back to the manager.' And the manager, well, I guess he can do something if he wants. 'He was bad, but we fired him,' ladies and gentlemen, 'so don't hold it against us. We fired him.' Let's say they *did* fire him. Did they fix the house? No....

"You know what? A man's house, or a woman's house, is his or her castle. That's been a principle in American understanding or common practice for all of the years of our lives and we all know that. It is the one place you can go [where] you can rest your head at night on a pillow and say, 'Boy, I got through another day. At least I've got a roof over my head. I'm having to pay a little note on it. I got some children I brought into this world and my husband has passed. I'm going to have to leave something behind for my children, following the Biblical principle of leaving an inheritance for my children, so I'm going to take out a contract to do that, to protect my home against termites.' *To protect my home against termites.* And then came a witness [for Orkin] who said he had failed to tell at least a hundred and fifty customers, just on his route, that they had termite damage. He said, 'But I didn't do that because I *wanted* to. I did that because they *told* me to. I *had* to do it that way.'

"What did Ms. Crosson [another Orkin witness] say? Barbara Crosson said I have been with the company for twenty-plus years and anytime there is a claim, it comes off the profit-and-loss statement of the manager. They don't make as much money. That's the Orkin system. Secondly, she said I worked for Bill Maxwell for six months. One of the inspectors brought a report in showing damage and Bill Maxwell came to her and said—I wrote this down word-for-word—Bill Maxwell said to her, 'You are to instruct the technicians not to write a re-inspection report on the client's termite damage. You are to'—listen to this—'you are to instruct the technicians not to write on the re-inspection tickets to clients that there's termite damage.' What did Barbara Crosson get out of this? The blonde-headed lady who came and sat right here had worked for them for twenty years was speaking about people of all colors and races, people who worked for the company and people who didn't work for the company. She was speaking about customers. We didn't inject race into this case, ladies and gentlemen. People are always talking about trial lawyers, [saying] everything we do is wrong. Well, I ask, who started it? *Who started it?*

'Out of the abundance of the heart the mouth speaks.' [I ask you to] be way-makers for righteousness and truth. Be way-makers for righteousness and truth where there appears to be no way. Be way-makers for their failure to honor this contract.

"Any time you ask a jury for a sum of money as a lawyer in any case, I think the first thing you ought to do is believe it yourself and pray about it [and understand] that the jury is working just as hard or harder than we to get to the truth. There ain't no sense in getting up here and asking for some sum of money that we don't think is justified, just to waste time. It wouldn't make any sense. The second thing is, I think a lawyer ought to have a conscience. Lawyers have done an awful lot to shape the nation. Thurgood Marshall was a lawyer, and I think something like ninety per cent of the Presidents have been lawyers. Thomas Jefferson, Abe Lincoln, all those guys. When you think about leadership, you think about lawyers. But the lawyers I respect the most are not the ones that have the most money, ladies and gentlemen, but the ones who are trailblazers for justice, those who live by the eye in the sky, and those who know that the Master is the sole determiner of anybody's worth, because He sits on the right hand of the Father.

"There are two kinds of damages in Alabama. The first is compensatory. Those are damages to bring something back to where it was before all this mess happened. Let me explain it to you. Compensatory means 'to restore,' to go back to before the wrong occurred. Having said that, we are asking for $25 million because of the $100,000 house. The other money we are asking for in the compensatory damages is for mental anguish. You know what happened. Mrs. Jeter's son Robert got right on this witness stand and said, 'Mama was different. Mama started calling me at five and six o'clock in the morning, crying on the phone about what these people had done to her with this house.' She incurred a great deal of mental anguish during those eight months that she lived before she went home to be with Jesus, and that is why we have come up with that number. She was even ashamed to have people come by the house after she finally found out the truth....

"Then there are punitive damages. That's another whole category. You've got $25 million that you write into the little box for 'compensatory damages,' and then there's another line that says 'punitive damages.' Judge [Ray] Martin is going to tell you much better than I what punitive damages are, but I'm going to tell you what they are with respect to this case. Punitive damages are meant to punish. Punish wrongdoers. *P-U-N-I-S-H.* Punish Orkin to stop them from raining havoc upon the citizens of Alabama and the nation at large. In that category we are asking you to write $250 million. Why? To send a message to the nation, that's why. To stop Orkin from doing what they're doing, and let the people find out what's happening, to stop it so other corporations will wake up and see it and say, 'I'd better take my fraud somewhere else. Those are tough folks down there in rural Alabama. You can't mess with elderly poor folks in Macon County because those people [you, the jury] spoke, and they spoke loud, and we're reading about it in the newspaper today.' Tell it. Shout it. If you don't send that kind of message there'll be no deterrence and those wrongdoers will continue to prey on the elderly, to prey on the rural citizens of our nation, continue to make them sign these little contracts and then let their houses be consumed by termites, and say, 'Well, we're not responsible for that.'

"Artie was old. She didn't get around too well. She was black. She was seventy-eight years old. Orkin is trying to say, 'Poor, poor lady. That ain't worth nothing. Five hundred thousand dollars ought to do it. That's it. Forget the mental anguish. Forget the eight months with the memo. Forget the deterrence. Forget sending a message to anybody. Forget stopping Orkin. Forget stopping any corporation.

Don't send nothing. Award some little ol' small verdict. Let's every-body go home. Cut the lights out to the courthouse. Next case, Artie Mae, let's go on to the next case. You're with Jesus now. You're looking down here. Thank you, ma'am, thank you.' Don't you let this happen. Don't you go back in that jury room and come back with a figure that doesn't stop what happened here. I've been practicing law for twenty-four years in this great state. It's a privilege to practice law, the greatest profession I ever could have been involved in. And do you know why? Because God called me into it. We should all answer the call from our Caller. I want to say this to you. In all the cases that I've ever been involved in, and I've been involved with quite a few, a lot of them here and some recently across the nation with my law partner Johnnie Cochran..."

Perhaps the reference to Johnnie Cochran was really behind it, Johnnie being a national hero to most African Americans across the nation, but at this point the counsel for the defense, Christian King of Birmingham, objected to my remarks about this being "the worst case" I had ever seen and asked for a side-bar conference with the judge. When I said that my associate, Andy Hollis, had already made that statement, King complained that it was "piling on." All it led to was the judge's reminding the jury that an attorney's closing state-ment is just that: an argument of counsel.

I continued with the closing. "As I said, I've been involved with several cases with Mr. Cochran around the nation. One thing that we have pledged to do is be ambassadors for Christ, drum majors for justice, to be servants of the people, to be prayerful and righteous, and to tell juries the truth. The truth, as the voice of the Bible says, will set you free. It is an awesome responsibility to live a life that way. But as the Bible says, 'to those to whom much is given, much is required.' More is required of those of us, Mr. Cochran included, who have been abundantly blessed...

"I ask you today from the bottom of my heart, because the evidence justifies it, to send out [a message] that will not only alert but *shock* the conscience of the nation. From John 10: 'He comes as a thief in the night, to kill, steal, and destroy, but I have come to give you life.' You are God's channel today, based on the evidence, to restore through compensatory damages that which has been broken by evil and wrongdoing. You are God's channel today not to make the Jeters rich, but to send out a message to stop this kind of conduct so that other corporations will be prohibited from doing this in the future in Alabama or anyplace else. That is what this case is about. Do it in the name of Artie Mae Jeter. For twenty-plus years they continued to cheat her, but this is the day that the Lord has made, so let us rejoice and be glad of it. A verdict for less than $25 million in compensatory damages or $250 million in punitive damages to stop this kind of conduct and to send a message to the nation for a total of $275 million, a verdict of less than that, we honestly, prayerfully, and truthfully, from the bottom of our hearts, we feel would be insufficient. If you search your hearts, ladies and gentlemen, and render this verdict and decide that $275 million total is not enough, then you render a verdict for any amount you fit to set the record straight. What I want you to do when you go back there is to show tough love. I want you to be as heavy-handed with the pen as Bill Maxwell was. Don't you let up a bit...

"You made me a promise when I asked you, before the trial started, if you had a ceiling on what you would award if you felt the conduct was reprehensible and we had proven our case. If you felt there was an egregious fraud, would there be a ceiling? None of you raised your hand. We have proven our case. Now is the time for you to fulfill that promise in Jesus' name. Amen and amen."

∾

The jury went out to determine the case. The greatest moments of fear in a trial come not during the trial itself but during the jury's deliberation. During that waiting period, you don't know what's going on back there in that room. After a couple of hours I began to worry, thinking that maybe there was a problem; if they had reached a substantial verdict they would have come back immediately. Robert Thompson came over to me and said, "Well, they're probably discussing two or three million dollars, maybe four." I said, "You're probably right. I guess that's it." Any lawyer who tells you he or she knows what verdict a jury is going to return is being untruthful, but in my mind I was sure hoping Thompson was wrong.

Then came the decision, read aloud to the court by Judge Martin. "We the jury find for the plaintiff and assess damages against Orkin in the following categories: compensatory damages, $800,000 dollars; punitive damages, $80 million." *Eighty million, eight hundred thousand dollars!* As I heard the words, my whole life flashed in front of me. I blacked out for a moment, from emotional excitement. I froze up. It had taken me twelve years, from *Turner v. Southern Life* in 1988, to get another multi-million-dollar verdict, and this was a whopper: the third-largest verdict in the history of Alabama, the second-largest fraud verdict in the state's history. I looked up again to the heavens and asked Jesus and my father how I had done. I felt as though both were speaking in unison, in the words of the Apostle Paul: "a job well done, my good and faithful servant."

There were tears and excitement in the courtroom. The three sons of Artie Mae Jeter hugged me. Attorney Thompson came to our table and said, "Did they say *eight* million?" I told him, "No. *Eighty* million." He said, "I'm out of here, then. The press is going to be all over this one." Indeed, the Montgomery *Advertiser* played the story on its front page the next morning. My partners were extremely excited, as well. Johnnie Cochran called four or five times after he found out that one of his three national partners had gotten a big one. I would later learn that what especially pleased him was the fact that the partner was black—Jock M. Smith of Tuskegee, Alabama— erasing any notions that I had become a partner merely because of the color of my skin. Sam Cherry said, "Jock, that's your Super Bowl. They can never take this one away from you. You'll always be known as the eighty-million-dollar man. You'll be judged by a different standard now." Keith Givens seemed so happy that you would have thought *he* had gotten the verdict. But this was becoming more than a law-partner relationship. It was about seeking and receiving justice for "the least of these."

19

On Being a Trial Lawyer

I MUST ADMIT that some of my earliest conceptions of what it is like to be a trial lawyer, besides the fact that my father was one of New York City's finest, came from watching the memorable television series, "Perry Mason," starring Raymond Burr. Growing up with "Perry" on a regular basis gave me, first of all, a winning attitude. Although the prosecutor would come up with something that appeared insurmountable at every trial, Mason would always come up with something better to outmaneuver him and ultimately win the case; either by flushing out a surprise witness or getting the key witness to break down and confess. It doesn't always work like that in real life, of course, but the show did convey the idea that where there's a will to win there's a way. Needless to say, the show offered much peripheral knowledge that would be valuable to one who wanted to follow his father's footsteps as a trial lawyer: the drama of the courtroom, cross-examining witnesses, playing mind games with the jury, outfoxing the prosecutor, and so forth. I still love that series today when I catch it on reruns.

My own experience taught me that the real essence of being a trial lawyer is service; that is, that a lawyer's first duty is to serve his client to the fullest extent of his abilities. My role as the trial lawyer is to present my client's case in the most favorable light to a jury of twelve, to give that client the best opportunity to prevail at the end of the proceedings. We aren't there to be popular, though popularity helps, nor are we there to actually decide the case. We are presenters, people making presentations based on the evidence, so that the jury might better be aided in ascertaining the truth. Dean Wigmore, a great authority on evidence, once wrote that cross-examination is "the greatest legal advice relative to the ascertainment of the truth."

A civil plaintiff's trial lawyer is there in most instances representing a blue-collar worker, an average citizen who has been wronged by a corporation or some other large entity. I keep quoting the words of Jesus in the Bible—"As you have done to the least of these, you have done unto me"—and that must be the philosophy of a trial lawyer with regards to protecting his or her client. That client, in most cases, is part of "the least of these": of the wrong race, the wrong sex, the wrong nationality or, in many instances, one who was merely at the wrong place at the wrong time; as one victimized by someone with more power. We are the protectors of the rights of the disenfranchised, the downtrodden, those who might otherwise have been shut out from justice. They cling to the bit of hope that somehow, if they get a Lawyer Cochran or Lawyer Chestnut or Lawyer Gray or Lawyer Smith, they might actually have a chance to defeat Goliath. We, as trial lawyers, take that journey on a regular basis along with our clients; that journey of hope, that journey of faith, that never-give-up philosophy that somehow we shall prevail.

Once on a radio talk show I described trial lawyers as being "hired guns." The host of the show took issue with what I had said, knowing that many civil litigators were being criticized for pursuing "jackpot justice," and asked exactly what I meant by using the term "hired gun." That's what I said, I explained, except that "we're the good guys, just like Matt Dillon, Wyatt Earp, Paladin, Roy Rogers, and the Lone Ranger. We wear the white hat and don't pull our gun unless somebody pulls their gun first. Then we become mercenaries, shooting the bad buys out of the sky, the same way George Bush shot down

Saddam Hussein's Scud missiles during Operation Desert Storm." We have our own Scud missiles, I said, and we have to use them against all sorts of aggression: surprise witnesses, witnesses who've been coerced into not telling the truth, witnesses who don't want their company to lose power and therefore feel obliged to stretch the truth.

A law degree or a legal education is second to none in terms of versatility. With a legal background, one can go into several professions—education, politics, writing, any of a myriad number of fields requiring intellect and a fervent belief in the truth—but for those who enter law itself, whether in government or with a partnership or as a sole practitioner, there is an ethical standard that must be obliged. That standard requires, above all, that a lawyer must represent his clients, no matter who they are, with the greatest degree of zeal.

Zeal is composed of preparation—"preparation, preparation, preparation," to quote Johnnie Cochran—along with enthusiasm. If you are there to protect the rights of your client, you must protect them to the fullest extent, as you would protect your own family or loved ones. Protection means putting a blanket or a hedge of protection around the client, guarding against trauma or danger during a trial. I define trauma and danger as evidence that is stale, ill-fated, untrue, or bloated so as to become something that it's not. Witnesses being sworn in at trials have a responsibility to tell the truth; but, as I've always said, if everyone was telling the truth about each and every instance in this life that we live, there would, of course, be no need for lawyers.

During my twenty-five years of practicing law, I've noticed there is a great distance between lawyers who are highly successful and those who are moderately successful or not successful at all. What separates them is one word: "obsession." It is my belief that one must be obsessed—eternally driven—in order to be highly successful. I see a lot of young lawyers and other professionals who, to put it bluntly, don't have the fire in the belly to make it. You have to be thinking and working for twenty-four hours a day, seven days a week, all the while pondering how to advance your career, whatever your profession. The Bible says that God has dealt every man the measure of faith. It's what a man does with that measure of faith that the good Lord has bestowed upon him. Working the hours necessary to be successful, being at work consistently and on time and being prepared during times that ordinarily be expected or obliged by others is also part of this obsession. It's not a chore, it's a responsibility. Lawyers making excuses for being unable to report to work on any regular basis lack this obsession. You have to go after your goal with fanatical fanaticism, with fidelity, grace, responsibility, and perseverance.

I learned early in my career that the role of an African-American trial lawyer is a bit more complex than it is for his white peers. The black lawyer carries a special burden simply by being there. He has fought through inequality to graduate from college, make it through law school, pass the bar, open a practice, and survive in a predominantly white world. In the eyes of the public, which can be quick to judge, he represents hope and faith, and is a symbol and a role model for what African Americans can accomplish. With others constantly keeping a close watch over his conduct, both inside and out of the courtroom, he must be above reproach. For example, since my conversion I've realized that a good lawyer, especially if he's black, should be extremely careful about where he is seen socializing. The saloons, the bars, and the night clubs should be strictly off-limits for a lawyer, particularly an African American, because that can send the wrong message: that you are not likely to be of much help if someone needs assistance with a legal matter. When people see you in public, what they should take away is a feeling of confidence in you. They should be able to sense an aura of truth, knowingness, temperance, righteousness, faith, all of which lead to trust. Without the average citizen believing in you, your case load will be miniscule.

∽

A lawyer has to make a living, of course, like everybody else, but I firmly believe that we have a duty to take on certain cases that are cause-oriented rather than money-oriented. That is to say, sometimes cases arise that involve such blatant injustices that they cry out for quality representation. One of my most cherished memories from my years as an attorney is the time I spent defending the poor black homeowners in Tallapoosa County, Alabama, from illegal foreclosures on their property by powerful and unscrupulous white landowners. I am equally fond of my work in *Lucy Turner v. Southern Life*, when the insurance company was found guilty of not paying off on a life insurance policy held by a poor black woman. Both of them corrected gross injustices toward the helpless and the downtrodden. Sometimes the money might not be there, but if the cause is right and you can find the time to do the job properly, you have an obligation to take on so many cases each year in order to correct evils and wrongs in the society. I was a thorough idealist when I first entered the profession, one who believed in the philosophies of Socrates and Plato, and as time went on my idealism was softened somewhat by the hard realities of life. But whenever I see a rank injustice that should not be allowed to prevail, that old idealistic streak flares up again, and it is on those occasions that I am reminded that the practice of law is, indeed, a noble profession.

No doubt about it, I like a good fight. There's no better place to find one than in a majority-white community where the greatest injustices have been perpetrated against African Americans. I firmly believe that a black lawyer isn't really a lawyer unless he is prepared to go into one of these "foreign" communities and take on the white establishment that's responsible for committing wrongs. There, after all, is where the sinners are most likely to feel they can get away with it. It's one thing to play in front of a friendly home crowd, to use another sports metaphor, but quite another to go on the road where the environment is going to be hostile. There's something about overcoming an antagonistic crowd that propels the outstanding athletes to their greatest moments (think of Jesse Owens in the '36 Olympics in Berlin, just before the breakout of the Second World War, with Adolf Hitler in the stands). Talk about "playing on the road" (not to trivialize it), how about Martin Luther King, Jr., during his fight to bring racial equality across America? The fight wasn't with friends in his own backyard, at black churches and neighborhoods and schools, but in such violent foreign fields as Birmingham and Selma and Memphis. You go where the fight is.

It is those men and women possessing the single-minded will to win, often against the odds, who have made America great. We all have our heroes. At the top of my list would be Paul Revere, Harriet Tubman, Sojourner Truth, Patrick Henry, Abraham Lincoln, Thomas Jefferson, and James Madison, from the nation's earliest years; the literary lions Mark Twain and Henry David Thoreau; Booker T. Washington, W. E. B. Du Bois, Mary McLeod Bethune, and George Washington Carver; Frederick Douglass, Malcolm X, and Martin Luther King, Jr.; Franklin Delano Roosevelt, John and Robert Kennedy, and William Jefferson Clinton. All of these men and women had the courage to stand up for what was right, no matter the cost (sometimes paying with their own lives), to purify the society against all manner of injustice: classism, sexism, racism.

I carry in the top of my head great quotes from great people, often to be used when I need their words to help me make it through the day. Frederick Douglass: "Those who profess freedom and yet deprecate agitation want crops without plowing the ground, want rain without thunder and lightning. Power concedeth nothing without a struggle; never has, and never will." Martin Van Buren: "I tread in the footsteps of illustrious men." Johnnie L. Cochran: "Service is the price we pay for the space we occupy." Martin Luther King, Jr.: "I have a dream that one day I will live in a society where a man will not be judged by the color of his skin but by the content of his character." Vince Lombardi: "Winning isn't everything, it's the only thing." Malcolm X: "Of all studies, history is the most qualified to reward all research." Huey Newton: "The spirit of the people is greater than man's technology." Patrick Henry: "Give me liberty or give me death." Ulysses S. Grant: "I plan to fight on this land if it takes all summer." Evangelist Mike Murdock: "God is not so much concerned about your problems as he is about your possibilities." The Bible: "The just shall live by faith," and, "Faith is the substance of things hoped for and the evidence of things not seen." Branch Rickey: "Luck is the residue of design." Denise Vickers: "A child of God's most powerful weapon is choice." And Yogi Berra, who turns out to be about as dumb as a fox: "Fifty per cent of the game is ninety per cent mental."

∽

The mission statement of the Alabama Trial Lawyers Association calls for us to preserve the adversary trial system as it now exists and to fight for the preservation of the rights of individuals; to resist any efforts to curtail the rights of persons who have been injured to seek redress in a court of law; to continue the education of the plaintiff's bar in all phases of trial practice; and to safeguard and defend the adversary system so that the rights and remedies of all individuals are protected; to serve and protect the public. In other words, we must protect the rights of the individual and not let the clock be turned back with regards to affirmative action and the rights of all plaintiffs. "Red and yellow, black and white, they are precious in his sight" means *all* of the people, not just the wealthy and powerful.

In one of our firm's advertisements in Memphis, Johnnie Cochran speaks of "a new level of justice," and I firmly believe that to be one of our mandates. For some time now, corporate America has been attempting through the Congress and Federal and state courts to lower the level of justice; to curtail the rights of victims, to put caps on punitive damages, to not permit corporations who commit egregious wrongs to be punished anymore or at least to put severe limitations on their punishment through the jury system. A terrible thing that is creeping up in Alabama and other states is arbitration, whereby many car dealerships and other corporate businesses are putting mandatory arbitration clauses into their basic contracts, making it impossible for a citizen to buy a car without agreeing to arbitration. Arbitration, of course, waives your right to a jury trial in the event something goes wrong and in effect aborts your case and makes it not worth pursuing since arbitration rules require thousands of dollars up front and rarely do arbitrators ever award punitive damages. In essence, the Sixth Amendment to the United States Constitution has been completely eroded.

Yet, few in the essentially white power structure appears to be alarmed about this. They are, in fact, the authors of this rollback in justice. It's a shame to see what's going on in America today, in these regards. Trial lawyers are being forced to do everything they can to do away with these arbitration clauses and to inform the public what they *really* mean. Jere Beasley, a prominent trial lawyer, has led the fight in Alabama to eradicate arbitration, and regards the practice as one of the most deadly evils that has ever been visited upon the plaintiff's rights and privileges relating to the administration of true justice.

America is about the rights of individuals. It is about those red-blooded citizens who have fought the wars and provided the labor and paid the taxes that enabled Corporate America to reach the modern computer age it now enjoys. None of this would have come about without the hard work of the "average" American citizen: the laborer, the teacher, the nurse, the engineer, the truck driver, and on and on and on. But now, in a bitter irony, these people find themselves being victimized by the very corporate giants that they created. I say that the real "giants" are the average Joes, the working men and women who made America's wealth possible, and they deserve the best in legal representation: lawyers who are uncompromising, unafraid, unabashed, and fearless; lawyers who have an eminent responsibility to stand up for their rights and privileges.

What's so ironic about all of the talk these days of tort reform and the melee surrounding it is that the jury system was perfect, as far as Corporate America and the power structure were concerned, as long as whites dominated juries. It was only when black folks began to serve on juries, along with women and other minorities, that they began to change their tune. For years there had been open fraud in the sale of insurance policies, for example, wherein agents would pocket the premiums but then, at the death of the insured, the beneficiary would receive nothing; and they had no legal claim simply because blacks weren't plugged into the system (*i.e.*, serving on juries). And there was the debit insurance business, where it is now being discovered that those white agents who had been doing door-to-door to see "Ms. Annie" and "Ms. Mae" to collect their premiums for these major companies had been charging blacks much higher than whites. No matter the scam to cheat unsuspecting blacks out of their hard-earned money, the big companies always had an excuse as long as the courtrooms were white. It was always *Well, it happened, but the statute of limitations ran out,* or, *Let's take it to arbitration,* or, *These excessive damages are bad for business.* That all began to come to an end when blacks and other minorities entered the jury box.

But the fight isn't over, not by a long shot. In most state houses and in Washington, especially in the U.S. House of Representatives, bills intended to roll back consumers' rights have been proposed with regularity. Some have passed, while others have been killed when they couldn't get enough votes in the Senate. The major automobile manufacturers, in particular, seem to never give up. They know full well that they are making vehicles that are unsafe—Ralph Nader's seminal book, *Unsafe at Any Speed,* still rings true—but still they claim otherwise. What do you mean, that sports utility vehicles can roll over and kill someone? What do you mean, that sometimes the door latch opens? What do you mean, that gas lines on the side of the car might explode if somebody gets broadsided? They continue their vigorous lobbying in Congress even when their own internal documents show that they knew of the dangers all along. Their corporate thinking goes, *Yeah, but you know, it would cost billions to fix it and we'd be better off just paying a few claims here and there.* And then they have the gall to continue working toward a day when there might be no such thing as a products-liability lawsuit. Go figure this: Alabama automobile dealers have an arbitration clause in their standard contract with customers, but in their agreement with the automakers they are fighting *against* arbitration. Hypocrites, downright hypocrites.

The founding fathers of this country were crystal clear on the issue of the right to trial by jury. James Madison, a delegate to the Constitutional Convention and our fourth President, indicated that right to trial by jury was as essential to the liberty of the people as any of the pre-existing rights of nature. Thomas Jefferson said he considered trial by jury "the only anchor ever yet imagined by man by which a government can be held to the principles of this Constitution." The Constitution he was talking about is embraced within the Sixth Amendment, giving an absolute right to a trial by jury. How Corporate America can feel about these arbitration clauses and other ways intended to curtail the very rights that the Founding Fathers gave us is beyond the scope of my imagination. Alexander Hamilton, when speaking in 1788 about trial by jury, said of the friends and the enemies of the plan when it came up during the Constitutional Convention: "The former regard it as a valuable safeguard to liberty; the latter represent it as the very palpitation of free government."

Let there be no doubt. The time line is clear. Corporate America thought everything about the courts was just fine until African Americans began showing up on juries. When they began to see black faces in the jury box, and black trial lawyers at the plaintiff's table, they knew they would have to address their sins. That's when they began trying to roll back one of our most basic rights, guaranteed in the Constitution of the United States more than two centuries ago, and tack on some amendments of their own, all in the interest of profits. I daresay it's not much of a match, these profiteers against the men who heard the call of Paul Revere, who drove the British out, who wrote a remarkable document that is alive and well today, the envy of the rest of the world. We trial lawyers have to fight to our dying day to keep it that way or else we'll lose everything and so will our people.

20

Full Circle

A S I WRITE this, approaching my fifty-fourth birthday, I continue to climb Jacob's ladder, that pinnacle of excellence my father left behind for me to conquer. To put a spin on one of his favorite metaphors, he's still ahead, but I'm gaining. It is early in 2002, and soon will come the forty-fifth anniversary of the moment that has been the driving force throughout my life: the brutal murder that left me fatherless as a young boy. Much has happened during those years, the greatest of them being my religious conversion, and I feel that I am indeed a man who has been deeply blessed. I'm surrounded by the undying love of dear family and friends; have as a law partner the most visible trial attorney in the United States of America; am a proud member of a church that knows no racial boundaries; and am fortunate enough to be able to share with others a passionate belief that sports is a metaphor for life. It's been a long haul, fraught with challenges, but one that I wouldn't hesitate to tackle again.

All of this came down on me with a swoop during Christmas of 2001. Christmas is always a time for reflection, a time to look both ways and give thanks, and never was it more so than during the celebration of Jesus's birthday at the beginning of the new millennium. Although living in Alabama can seem to be a foreign experience, particularly for an African American who grew up a Yankee, my in-laws have ensured that there is more than enough love to go around for everyone during the holidays. Until I married Yvette I thought Christmas was for kids, not adults, but it turns out that I was wrong. Yvette's parents, Marion and Gloria Smiley, have always inspired a tradition of family togetherness, especially at Christmas, and this one was no exception. I couldn't help remembering the glee with which my father, in those long-ago years past, hustled everybody around the Christmas tree at daybreak, more excited than anyone in the house.

A typical Christmas Day at our house on Lansdowne Drive in Montgomery begins as Yvette and Janay and I exchange gifts while singing Motown carols (nothing better than hearing Nat King Cole crooning about "chestnuts roasting on an open fire" as you rip open a present). We have a jolly time together, but the real shindig soon begins in Mobile Heights, Yvette's childhood neighborhood. As soon as you enter the Smileys' house you are overwhelmed by stacks of gifts. There are certain rules to be followed. First, we must unload our gifts and place them under the tree; second, we must eat a Southern feast of down-home country and Creole delicacies. Then it's time to open gifts, the rules there being that the youngest go first, so we start by cheering for my nieces Samarria and Lloria Munnerlyn, both of whom, I'm proud to say, are preparing to become attorneys. They are followed by Janay; then my sister-in-law and brother-in-law, Sam and Marielle Munnerlyn; and Yvette and me. I might add that those who aren't opening gifts must stay and watch, creating a lot of *ooh*-ing and *ahh*-ing, laughing, and clapping. Finally, the time comes for Mr. And Mrs. Smiley, the beloved elders of the family, to open their gifts. In due time we find ourselves going back for second helpings of oyster dressing and collard greens before we start an all-night round of Monopoly or penny-ante poker.

I must admit that midway through the poker Sam and I usually find our way to the back of the house for football on television and a little nap. The women, meanwhile, laugh and play and cut up for hours. I'm lucky if I get Yvette and Janay out of there before sunrise. I don't verbalize it often, but the comfort and warmth of the Smiley family have given me great strength over the years, both personally and professionally. Well before I committed my life to Christ, Mrs. Smiley, a devout Catholic, always encouraged me to pray and find a church home. A real "people" person, Marielle often works on cases with me as an expert jury analyst, and Sam, a college dean of student affairs, is a well-respected educator all over the state. Little wonder, then, with a wife and daughter and in-laws like these, that Christmas would be just about the most joyous day of any year.

When you come right down to it, a man can't make it through this world if all isn't right inside the family circle. There, again, I'm fully blessed. I'm pleased to note that my mother is alive and well in her retirement, still residing in the old house on Nashville Boulevard in Queens, an eternal pillar of strength: always there, Christ-like and humble, a dedicated soldier of the kingdom, still cautioning me, like Grandma Bowers before her, about getting "too big for your britches." Likewise, my sister Paula, the original inspiration that led me to Jesus, is like a rock—steady, prayerful, as supportive of me now as the day in 1988 when she sat in the courtroom to watch as I won my first million-dollar verdict in the *Lucy Turner v. Southern Life* case—and my prayer for her is that she realizes her dreams as a singer and writer in Los Angeles.

Closest to home, of course, are my daughter Janay and my wife Yvette. Janay is thirty-one years old now, continually moving upward in the corporate hierarchy at Gillette in Boston as a product design engineer, and in my mind sure to get rich one day through the invention of something akin to the microwave. But she's already rich, if you ask me; rich in her soul. As for Yvette, I have written much about her—as a modern businesswoman, a soulmate, a caring fellow Christian, the engine that drives me as a trial lawyer—but I haven't said the most important thing of all. Quite simply, I love her from the bottom of my heart. Without her tender loving care, her constant prayers, her daily presence, her friendship and understanding and unfailing love, I would be nothing.

Beyond family, there are two special friends who are always with me: my boyhood pal from the days of growing up in Queens, Irvin Culpepper; and a major force in my sports-collecting career, Darryl O'Mary. I don't know many people who can say they remain fast friends with someone out of their childhood, as it is with Irvin and me, but we have virtually held hands with each other as we matured and moved upwards in our respective callings. I have celebrated Irvin, like I would a brother I never had, and I'm proud of the heights he has reached: the only African-American partner at Kelso, a major venture capital firm in New York City, the top of the mountain in corporate America, living in Stamford, Connecticut, with his dear wife Brenda. Darryl is much more than the man who got me into sports collecting in a big way, but also a born-again Christian—a blue-eyed, blond-haired white man, a native of Jasper, Alabama—who always calls Yvette and me on the birthday of Martin Luther King, Jr., to wish us a "Happy MLK Day" and to talk about Dr. King's contributions toward making this a better world for all of humanity, both black and white. He also happens to be one of the great experts about authenticating sports uniforms, autographs, and other artifacts from the world of sport.

Of my peers, no lawyer has had a bigger impact on my career than Robert D. "Bobby" Segall. Bobby and I have handled in excess of 150 cases together, among them the one involving Jose Canseco and his sports agent (a settlement of $207,000), the $250,000 verdict against Goodyear, and an automobile accident case where we received a

$200,000 verdict when the actual damages to a car was only $127. Whatever I have learned in taking a successful deposition I gleaned from Bobby Segall, a great American and a great servant of "the least of these," a man who bleeds for everyone who has been trampled by the system. He is always there for wise counsel, even serving as personal attorney for both me and my family.

From Christian Life Church in Montgomery, which has been an extension of my family since the day I first walked through its doors, I feel I have been practically adopted by Pastors Steve and Denice Vickers, and Sam and Willa Carpenter. I still remember with great clarity what Pastor Steve said to me that day in 1998 when I asked how he felt about my joining Johnnie Cochran in the national law firm: "The good Lord has called you and Johnnie to take the black lawyer out of the kitchen and to place him at the dining table so he can have a meal with his white brothers. He's called you to change nations, tear down racial barriers, to tear down strife and division based on race, color and creed. You're destined to do so, Jock." As for Sam and Willa Carpenter, they have served as surrogate parents to me, separated as I have been from my mother in New York City for all of these years. Never have I been in a home exuding such unconditional love. No matter the problem, no matter the time of day or night, they always greet me at the door of their home with a warm smile, tender loving care, and great patience. They have taught me, by their example, to show unconditional love to people rather than to condemn or judge them. There are times when I feel as though I'm their son.

∾

The time has come, it seems, for me to expand my horizons as a partner with Johnnie Cochran in an important national law firm. Along that line, I have added an accomplished young lawyer to my own office in Tuskegee: Brian Strength, a twenty-seven-year-old graduate of the University of Alabama with roots in what we call The Valley, a textile center just east of Tuskegee in Chambers County. A man of great integrity and qualifications, previously employed by one of the top defense firms in Alabama, Brian brings great skills in legal research and brief-writing and, what's more, he will be integrating my office. That's very important to me, sending such a message to the larger society, and with Brian at my side I should be freed to spend more time away from the office on broader matters.

Part of this expansion involves the firm's becoming partners in a major mass torts cartel with one of the nation's most prominent law firms—led by Fred Levin, Mike Papantonio, and Mark Proctor—along with John Morgan of Morgan, Colling & Gilbert. Mass torts, of course, are those committed against the general public in the form of harmful drugs pulled off the shelves by the Federal Drug Administration, and other mass wrongs such as environmental catastrophes, automobile defects, and unfair practices by insurance companies and other corporate bullies. The main focus of the mass torts cartel is to represent "the least of these," citizens who have been victimized by institutions and would otherwise have no voice to champion them, and we have begun a series of seminars called "Practice Made Perfect" to help our attorneys sharpen their abilities in the area of mass torts. The seminars were originated by John Morgan, who has become a major player for the firm.

It was John, in fact, who inspired me to take a leap in faith and begin advertising the firm through television ads. For many years, this was regarded as a no-no by established corporate law firms, a shadowy place occupied by questionable ambulance-chasers, but I changed my mind when I saw the quality spots being produced by Morgan and his people in Florida, Debbie Singleton and Sandra DeLucca. My ads are of substance, talking about what we can do for people who always thought they couldn't afford a lawyer, and they certainly get the job done. We focus on products liability such as automobile rollovers and shady nursing homes, promising a new level of justice in America, and we seem to be reaching the heartbeat of Alabama. Each of my ads closes with the words, "Just call Jock," and that's become a familiar cry wherever I go across the state.

I can't exaggerate the importance of John Morgan to me and to the Cochran firm. He is a great trial lawyer, first of all, and a great visionary as well. He had known all along that having great television ads was one way to level the playing field when up against the giant law firms; that no matter how good a lawyer one might be it means little if you don't somehow get the business, sign up the cases. He took the entire fee from a case back in the Eighties to finance his first television advertising campaign, and suddenly he began getting all of the business he could handle and becoming something of a celebrity at the same time. This created a sort of anti-Morgan clique among the big firms in Florida, which intensified as he began to take business away from them, always representing poor plaintiffs, "the least of these." But soon he began to convince other attorneys of the validity of television advertising—including Johnnie Cochran, from a generation that had frowned upon it—and now even Johnnie uses it in a big way. Johnnie's ads, promising "a new level of justice," have the firm's phones ringing off the hook these days.

Speaking of television, albeit in a more playful way, I've been having the time of my life in recent years as an announcer working Tuskegee Golden Tigers football games on tape-delay over a cable station based in Tuskegee. This all came about quite innocently one day while I was talking with Jimmy Johnson, the owner of TV 6 in Tuskegee, and he asked if I was so busy with my business that I couldn't announce the games. *Too busy? To go into the booth like the heroes of my youth like Mel Allen, Red Barber, Vin Scully, and Marty Glickman?* He had to be kidding, I thought, but he wasn't. And so it was that I began announcing Tuskegee home games alongside a college student named James Arrington.

It's been great sport, announcing the games, even if I did stumble a bit in the early going. My respect for those announcers from my days as a kid in Queens soared when I found out just how difficult the work can be. You have to be able to fill the dead space between plays, learn to be creative, keep your head in the game, know the players, the penalties, the offensive and defensive formations, and most of all understand that your duty is to be the eyes and ears of those who can't be at the game in person. By the end of my first few games in the booth, I would be sweating as though on a summer's day, my head throbbing with pain from the intense concentration it had taken. I got better in time, however, and I remember saying during one game this year something like, "I like the way those Golden Tigers are *matriculating* that ball down the field." Suddenly, the phrase caught on in Tuskegee. People would come up to me and say, "Jock, I like the way we matriculate the ball down the field." I think that's neat, a lot of fun, certainly a far cry from the courtroom and the speaking circuit. Jock-in-the-Booth has been quite an experience.

It has also brought me into a close relationship with the Tuskegee coach, Rick Comegy, and in a way strengthened my belief in sports as a metaphor for life and as a way to prepare young men for life after football. Coach Comegy once said to me, "More than football, I'm trying to make men out of these individuals. It's men that I'm trying to raise, not just football players, and I want them to know their Lord and Savior Jesus Christ. I want them to know the price that He paid and I want them to live their lives accordingly." We were in agreement, of course, and that's how I wound up as the keynote speaker at the Tuskegee athletic banquet last year. My message? The story of Doug Williams, the man who showed that an African American can play quarterback with the best of them.

Along those lines—the part that sports plays as a metaphor and a great teacher in American life—my collection of game-worn uniforms now ranks as the largest in the world. It has long outgrown the Sports Room upstairs at my house in Montgomery, and now I'm having to give serious thought about taking it to the nation. I have dreams these days of housing an all-pro sports or baseball-only or an African-American hall of fame in one location; maybe in Orlando, a great site for that sort of enterprise, or maybe in my hometown of Montgomery, where I was recently selected as co-chair of the sports and recreation committee of Envision, a metro-wide organization seeking to bring broad improvements to central Alabama. We are hoping to build a first-class ballpark in order to secure a minor-league baseball franchise, and my museum would fit nicely there. I also intend to take Scoring for Life! nationwide, through a television ministry, to further spread the gospel about the power of sports, and I'm delighted to say that I have something new to show the black kids of America: finally, thirty-two years after I got up and left in the middle of a game because of racist remarks in the stands, Notre Dame has hired an African-American head football coach by the name of Tyrone Willingham.

ॐ

Recently, while searching through the Bible for an explanation of my roots, I came upon some interesting facts. The original meanings of my father's given names, Jacob and Abraham, were "protector" and "father of many nations." It's not too much of a stretch, I think, to see how prescient it was when my paternal grandparents passed those names on to him during difficult times. In a contemporary sense, he too became the father of many nations: an integrated neighborhood in Queens, an African-American law firm in Manhattan, a world that fostered upward mobility for people of color. And he truly became a protector: of justice for "the least of these," of the rights of all Americans, and of his only son. The bloodline continues. In turn, as the son of Jacob Abraham, I have benefited from his teachings by endeavoring to become a protector of the many clients throughout this great nation and the world who seek our counsel. I think he would be proud to know that I have carried on the work that was abruptly halted by an assassin's bullet on that long-ago day in lower Manhattan.

Jesus says in the Bible, "There will be much tribulation, but I have overcome the world." With each step up Jacob's ladder, I have been attempting to do just that; to overcome the imperfect world that my father left behind. There have been tribulations, for sure—my dark years following his death, the racism I encountered at places along the way, the struggles to establish myself as a young attorney, overcoming the stigma attached to being a black man in the Cradle of the Confederacy—but I have managed to impact that world, step by step, to the point that now I'm a partner with the great Johnnie Cochran in a firm that promises "a new world of justice" in America.

There is no doubt in my mind that all of this was divinely inspired. No amount of planning or conspiring could have brought about this union. Some might call it pure happenstance that the two of us met and happened to like each other on that day he came to Montgomery on business, but I am certain that it was God's destiny. It was in the cards. It was part of a grand plan designed by the Father of us all. It was meant to be. As it was with Jacob Abraham, so shall it be with his only son.

Amen, and amen.

AFTERWORD

By Pastor Stephen Vickers

O ut of the tragedy of his dad's death has come the triumph of a dream fulfilled. What could have been a life of mediocrity at best has become a life of destiny and purpose with all the challenge, excitement, and joy that a man's heart can hold.

Many blame society, environment, life experiences, and other individuals for the quality and direction of their own lives. But the truth is, we are responsible for our own destinies. It's not too much what happens to a man as it is his attitude toward it, and his choices as a result. Jock Smith has proven that beyond question. His dad's death could have been a stumbling block that caused him to be a bitter, angry young man who defied authority and lived a life of lawlessness. Instead, he used it as a stepping-stone into the destiny his dad began and he is now fulfilling. Jock chose to rise above the prejudices of society. In spite of its resistance, he has forged a life built upon the principles taught him by his mother, his church, and the legacy left by his father.

Climbing Jacob's Ladder shows clearly what can happen when a person refuses to allow circumstances or people stop him in the pursuit of his dream. Because Jock has chosen the road less traveled, he has carved out a path for others to follow. His faith in God, and his compassion for the least of these, has created for him a notable place in society. He is loved and respected by all who know him.

Now that you have read this book, realize that you too can make the choices that will make you the man or woman of greatness you were destined to be.

ACKNOWLEDGMENTS

By Jock M. Smith

F irst of all, I want to give all glory and honor to Jesus, the author and finisher of my faith who, from everlasting to everlasting, I will lean upon in this continuing climb up Jacob's ladder.

There are many people who were not referenced in this book due to considerations of space, and I want to take this time to acknowledge them here for their significant contributions to my life, both personally and professionally.

I'd like to begin by expressing my deepest gratitude and appreciation to my collaborator Paul Hemphill, who faithfully captured the true Jock Smith; I'll be eternally grateful him for his significant contribution. I would also like to express my deepest appreciation to everyone at NewSouth Books, especially Randall Williams and Suzanne La Rosa, for giving me an opportunity to publish this work and thereby fulfill a dream, and for the technical assistance of Ben Beard and the design talents of Rhonda Reynolds.

There are many close family members I want to recognize. First, there is my Uncle Gene Smith, my father's youngest brother, who gave me much wisdom when I was growing up and was the one who explained the significance of my father's life and death and what I had to do to finish the dream; thank you, Uncle Gene, for your significant contribution to my life. And the late Elaine French, my aunt, who during those hot, sweltering summers in Kansas City helped raise me along with my grandmother Rebecca Bowers. To my late and great Uncle Marion Smith, "Kansas City Smitty," who took me to Yankee Stadium for years after my father's death and instilled in me what my father had begun: an appreciation for the greatness of the game, and the greatness of family. Also to my stepfather, Mr. Wade Nance, a true Christian gentleman.

Also to my lifetime friends Fred Banks, Betty Nance, the late Walter Brown, the late Irving Culpepper, Sr., Shirley Culpepper, Chuck Tolbert, and Irving Culpepper, Jr., and his wife Brenda.

Special thanks go to the extended family on my wife's side, the Smileys, all black pioneers in Montgomery's march toward freedom, including my supportive sister-in-law Marielle Munnerlyn and brother-in-law Samuel Munnerlyn. Also to my nieces, Godchild Samarria Yvette Munnerlyn, now in law school at the University of Alabama, and LLoria Munnerlyn, awaiting graduation at the university. Also, Dr. Emmett Smiley, for all the free dental care he has provided over the years, as well as his expert testimony in civil cases, and my brother-in-law Harold Smiley, a true friend and gentlemen and an encouragement in my life. And there are many others, including Mary Joe Smiley, Dr. Daniel Ward, Liletta Morris Ward, Riché Smiley Outlaw, Ray Smiley, the late Dabney Smiley, Sylvia Smiley, and the late Richmond Smiley.

I owe much gratitude to those sports collectors who assisted me in accumulating the world's largest authentic game-worn collection of professional sports uniforms, including the veteran and knowledgeable collectors Lou Lampson, Nick Capolla, Kevin Barnes, Duke Hott, Toni Cocchi, Josh Evans, Bob Presley, Steve Hart, Chuck Smith, Ken Slater (who got me started with the first uniforms I acquired), and Andy Imperato and Richie Russek of Grey Flannel Collectibles, who are the authenticators for the Professional Basketball Hall of Fame as well as my own collection. And, of course, my deepest thanks go to Darryl O'Mary, a friend and a great Christian gentleman, along with his wife Joanne, and daughter Candace.

Among the many lawyers who have assisted in my legal development and career and with whom I've enjoyed working on cases and have become personal friends with are William M. Russell, Jr., and his wife Sarah, Robert Thompson, Tyrone Means, Garve Ivey and his wife Helen, Jere Beasley, Greg Allen, LaBarron Boone, Dee Miles, Walter McGowan, Linda Henderson, Stella Owens, Tom Methvin, Larry Morris, Kenneth Ingram, Jr., J. L. Chesnutt, Hank Sanders, Rose Sanders, Julian McPhillips, William Gill, Tripp Walton, Thomas Fields, Montgomery District Attorney Ellen Brooks, Attorney General Bill Baxley, and Milton C. Davis.

Also, to my regional partners, as well, including Julian Bolton in Memphis, James Montgomery of Chicago, Cameron Stewart of Los Angeles, and Phil Damashek, Arnie Kleinick, Ivan Schneider, Harvey Weitz, and Barry Shoot of New York. In addition, Shean Williams, Stella Owens, Audrey Tolson, Jan Lamberti Sams, Tom Marszewski, Brian Dunn, Randy McMurray, Frank Hanson, Dixie Ishee, Steve Libby, Justice John England, Justice Ralph Cook, U.S. District Court Judge U. W. Clemon, U.S. Court of Appeal Judge Ann Williams, Macon County District Judge Aubrey Ford, Jr., Clark Arrington, Denese Banks, Earnestine Sapp, and Fred Gray, Jr. Also, to the new mass torts partners Fred Levin, Mike Papantonio, and Mark Proctor; and especially Hezekiah Sistrunk, the firm's first regional partner of Atlanta, Georgia, who has given so much wisdom and insight as a mentor, role model, and personal friend. And once again, last but not least, I thank Robert D. Segall, Robert Cheek, and John Morgan.

I would be remiss if I did not acknowledge—one more time—my esteemed national law partner, America's greatest lawyer, Johnnie L. Cochran, Jr., who along with my gifted partners, J. Keith Givens and Samuel Cherry, gave me an opportunity to become a senior partner in what I believe to be America's greatest civil litigation law firm: Cochran, Cherry, Givens & Smith.

Gracious thanks go out to my wonderful, devoted legal staff at the Tuskegee office of the national firm: the incomparable taskmaster Brenda Pinkard, our newest employee Kimeletta Harris, along with our dedicated attorneys, the disciplined Janice Spears-Turk and the rising superstar Brian Strength. And I'd like especially to thank Tasha Scott for transcribing the many hours of tapes that led to this book, as well as for her tireless efforts in chairing the committee to assist in the promotion of this book throughout the Christian community of the United States of America.

Also, I'd like to acknowledge the assistance of many of our support staff, paralegals in our various offices who have been so kind and generous to me, including from our Dothan office Bonnie Niver, the national firm's administrative assistant, Sheri Roberts, Dianne Brown, and Stephanie Curtis; from our Atlanta office Merlyn Coore, Adrienne Rushin, Vickie Amos, Faith Thompson, Karen Bailey, Millsy Hicks, Kenshanna Oree; from our Los Angeles office Eloise McGill, Sonia Davis, and Jan Bowers; from our Chicago office Pauline Montgomery; from our New York office Kyle Washington; and from our Memphis office Alex Bolton, Gail Starks, Janice Halley, Yolanda Marshall, Sonia Walker, Mira Hamilton, and Billie Hanson. Also, my dear court reporters who have given me stellar service over the years, especially Karen Regan, Kim Pruitt, Judy Shelton, and Tiffany Blevins.

I am appreciative to my friends at the Alabama Trial Lawyers Association, including former Executive Director Don Gilbert, Executive Director Ginger Avery, Continuing Legal Education Director Cathy Givan, and Joy Whatley.

I want to give special thanks to those individuals who have made a great spiritual contribution into my life, among them the late Rev. Walter Pinn of Calvary Baptist Church, Bishop George F. Austin of Tuskegee, Bishop Leo Lewis of Montgomery, the Rev. John Alford;

and many fellow church members of Christian Life Church, including Bruce Hudgins, Walter and Teresa Preston, Richard Businger, Pam and Dr. Tim Williams, Pastor Norris and Cindy Braswell, Youth Pastors Brian and Stacy Hebert, Gene and Misty Ballard, Little Denice Vickers, Stephen Vickers, Jr., Tom and Janice Willard, Nellie Burge, Margaret Ellison, Gil and Delores Melendez, Ardith Dorrough, Lou Enriquez, the Rev. Mac Gober of Canaan Land Boys' Home, Tané Miller, Nancy Kirchoff, Rex and Lisa Davis, Raul Glover, Rosie Brock, and Cedric Varner.

I'd also like to especially thank fellow church members Debbie Enriquez and Heather Buesinger, along with Amy Methvin, for their service on the Christian committee to promote this work.

Many thanks to those individuals from the financial world who assisted me in the development of both my law practice and my sports collection, including bank presidents Robert Davis of Alabama Exchange Bank of Tuskegee and Jim Wright of First Tuskegee Bank, as well as Roy Nutt, formerly of Merrill Lynch, now with First Union Securities.

I'm grateful to Jimmy Johnson of TV-6 in Tuskegee for giving me an opportunity to live part of a dream, doing the play-by-play of Tuskegee University football games.

Special thanks go to United States Magistrate Judges Vanzetta Penn McPherson and Delores R. Boyd for giving me an opportunity to meet Johnnie Cochran through a scheduled book signing at Roots and Wings that ultimately led to our partnership in the sports agency, and then in the national law firm. I'll forever be indebted to those two, for without their introduction to Johnnie there would be no national law firm or sports agency.

I'd also like to thank Circuit Judges Howard Bryan, Jr., and the late James Avery, who showed me the way in the trial court during my formative years of early development.

Also, I'd like to thank Daniel Mitchell of Mitchell Roofing, my roofer for life, and our dear housekeeper Linda Givan.

Lastly, and most significantly, I'm deeply grateful to Pastors Stephen E. and Denice Vickers, along with Sam and Willa Carpenter, who continue to serve as my shepherds and surrogate parents, respectively. Also, to the many individuals who have assisted me in maintaining good health and personal care, thanks to my spirit-filled physician Dr. Roger D. Glymph and his wife Joanne, along with their children, my Godchild Sydney Nicole Glymph and their son Austin Glymph, and Dr. Simon Mirelman, my surgeon, who literally saved my life. To all my dear friends at Kreatif Hair Design, Prattville, Alabama, especially my hairstylist Kelli Stephens, as well as all my friends who have assisted me at Baines European Spa of Montgomery, Alabama, including Delilah Ellis, manicurist Patty White, esthetician Gwen Berger, and masseuses Polly Zeigler and Shelly Kelly. And all my friends at Heavenly Body Spa, especially Donna Radford and Cynthia Berryhill.

Also, to all of the citizens of Tuskegee, Alabama, who took me in as an adoptive son, both as a college student and as a lawyer, especially Dr. Walter C. Bowie, who assisted in bringing me to Tuskegee and acted as a father to me during my college years, and Dr. Velma Blackwell of Tuskegee University. And many thanks to my dear friends in the Alabama Senate, Sundra Escott-Russell and Charles Steele, Jr., who were so helpful with the Alabama Trial Lawyers during my election as the first African-American trial trustee in history.

And most of all I give thanks to the greatest physician known to man, Jesus Christ, my healer, from Genesis to Revelation.